Introduction to
Health Economics

David Wonderling, Reinhold Gruen
and Nick Black

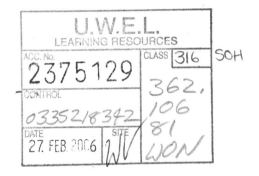

Open University Press

Open University Press
McGraw-Hill Education
McGraw-Hill House
Shoppenhangers Road
Maidenhead
Berkshire
England
SL6 2QL

email: enquiries@openup.co.uk
world wide web: www.openup.co.uk

and Two Penn Plaza, New York, NY 10121-2289, USA

First published 2005

Copyright © London School of Hygiene & Tropical Medicine 2005

A catalogue record of this book is available from the British Library

ISBN-10: 0 335 21834 2
ISBN-13: 978 0335 21834 9

Library of Congress Cataloging-in-Publication Data
CIP data applied for

Typeset by RefineCatch Ltd, Bungay, Suffolk
Printed in the UK by Bell & Bain Ltd, Glasgow

Contents

Acknowledgements

Open University Press and the London School of Hygiene and Tropical Medicine have made every effort to obtain permission from copyright holders to reproduce material in this book and to acknowledge these sources correctly. Any omissions brought to our attention will be remedied in future editions.

We would like to express our grateful thanks to the following copyright holders for granting permission to reproduce material in this book.

p. 90–94 'Are increase in cigarette taxation regressive?,' P Borren and M Sutton, *Health Economics*, 1:245–253, 1992, John Wiley & Sons Limited. Reproduced by permission of John Wiley & Sons Limited.

p. 250–51 'Evaluation of a hospital picture archiving and communication system,' S Bryan, G Weatherburn, J Buxton, J Keen and N Muris, *Journal of Health Services Research Policy*, 4:204, 1999, RSM Press, by permission of RSM Press.

p.98–99, 130–32, 172–73 & 180–81 C Donaldson and K Gerard, Economics of Health Care Financing: The Visible Hand 2nd edn, 2005, Palgrave Macmillan, reproduced with permission from Palgrave Macmillan.

p. 120–22 H Edwards and D Passman, 'All mixed up', *Health Service Journal*, 23 June 1997.

p. 191–92 P Eklund and K Stavem, 'Community health insurance through prepayment schemes in Ginea-Bissau' in *Financing Health Services Through User Fees and Insurance: Case Studies from Sub-Saharan Africa* by Shaw, Richard Paul. Copyright 1995 by WORLD BANK. Reproduced with permission of WORLD BANK in the format Textbook via Copyright Clearance Center.

p. 65–66, 134–35 & 153–56 Reproduced with the permission of the Office of Health Economics from M Green (1995) 'The Economics of Health Care'.

p. 251 'An economic evaluation of comparing two schedules of antenatal visits,' J Henderson, R Tracy, J Sikorski, J Wilson and S Clement, *Journal of Health Services Research Policy*, 5:69, 2000, RSM Press, by permission of RSM Press.

p. 188–90 C Normand and A Weber, 'The desirability of social health insurance' in *Social Health Insurance: A Guidebook for Planning*, 1994, World Health Organization, by permission of World Health Organization.

p. 48–49, 75–81 & 82–84 *Economics 5th edition*, M Parkin, M Powell and K Matthews, Pearson Education Limited. Copyright © 2000 Addison-Wesley, Inc.

p. 20 A Williams, *Health Economics*, 1987, Palgrave Macmillan, reproduced with permission of Palgrave Macmillan.

Overview of the book

Introduction

Cigarette consumption among the young, the increasing prevalence of obesity, rising health care costs and international shortages of key health care workers are just some of the challenges facing public health policy makers and practitioners at the start of the twenty-first century. And to help them resolve these problems, economics has a central role.

This book will introduce you to economic techniques that can be used in public health. It will help you understand the specific features that distinguish demand for health care from demand for other goods and services. It will provide insight into the economic methods that are being used to promote public health policies, analyse health care delivery and shape health sector reforms. You will be better able to make use of information on economic evaluation of health care interventions and you will better understand the strategic debates on use of market elements to improve health service performance and use of financial strategies to promote the health of the public.

Economists are usually accused of three sins: an inability to agree among themselves, stating the obvious and giving bad advice. Hopefully you will reject this statement once you have worked through this book. But you will find that there are areas of disagreement on particular economic policies. Important too, there is often a gap between theoretical concepts and political implementation. You will also find that economic policies that worked in one country don't work in a different cultural context. You will find an extensive discussion of these and other issues. Emphasis is placed on evoking a critical understanding of the issue and presenting different views held on the subject, rather than imposing a single view. Throughout this book effort has been put into presenting the empirical evidence that supports a particular theory and providing case studies and examples which show how economic advice works in practice.

If you don't have a background in economics you may find the language economists use and the way they explain their theories challenging. Don't panic. This book tackles economic issues from first principles and it has been designed for students who have no previous knowledge of economics. A certain amount of economic theory is indispensable to understanding the strength and limitations of economic concepts as applied to health and health care. We have tried to visualize complex economic concepts by using graphs rather than equations and we have made sure that lists of key terms help to clarify new concepts and terminology. If you don't understand something, don't worry. You may proceed and come back to the problem later. You will find plenty of examples and some self-assessment questions to help you better understand difficult issues and to let you compare and contrast what you have learned with your own experience.

Why study health economics?

You may ask yourself what economics has to do with health and health care. Should health and health care, as fundamental concerns, not have an absolute priority? You may, however, already know the answer. Resources are inevitably scarce and choices have to be made in the allocation of resources. And health economics, as you will see in this book, is about making choices to employ resources in a way that improves health status and service delivery. Though economics is a relatively old discipline, its systematic application to health systems is relatively new. It is only during the last 30 years that health economics has established itself as a subdiscipline of economics and gained influence in the health sector.

Managers and policy makers rely increasingly on economic analysis. Economic thinking has gained influence on decision making and economic ideas have fuelled health sector reforms. These changes are part of a larger process of public sector reform since the 1980s, which has been shaped by economic ideas. In pursuit of these reforms, multilateral agencies, such as the World Bank, have been aiming to redefine the relationship between the state and the private sector and to promote slimmer government services and an increased engagement of the private sector. A growing number of countries are using economic techniques to prioritize health services and to evaluate new health care technologies. The drugs industry has started to provide information on cost-effectiveness as this may provide a competitive advantage in promoting their products. But you should be aware that for most health care interventions, information on effectiveness and efficiency is not available. Health economics is still a developing discipline which is increasingly gaining acceptance of its methods.

Structure of the book

This book follows the conceptual outline of the 'Introduction to health economics' unit at the London School of Hygiene & Tropical Medicine. It is based on the materials presented in the lectures and seminars of the taught course, which have been adapted for distance learning.

The book is structured around a simple conceptual framework. It starts by introducing you to economics and goes on to consider the concepts of supply, demand and markets. You will then learn about how health systems can be financed. Finally we consider how health care interventions can be evaluated and how such economic information can be used in policy making.

The five sections, and the 20 chapters within them, are shown on the book's contents page. Each chapter includes:

- an overview;
- a list of learning objectives;
- a list of key terms;
- a range of activities;
- feedback on the activities;
- a summary.

The following description of the section and chapter contents will give you an idea of what you will be reading.

Economics and health economics

Chapter 1 gives a definition of economics, explains some basic concepts and introduces health economics. In Chapter 2 you will learn about the methods and tools used in economic analysis.

Supply and demand

This section explores how individual markets function, how market forces operate in health care and how they influence output and price for health services. It starts by considering the concepts of demand (Chapter 3) and of supply (Chapter 4). Chapters 5–7 analyse demand further and introduce the notion of elasticity of demand before attention turns to costs in Chapters 8 and 9.

Markets

Chapter 10 focuses on markets and the conditions under which free markets operate well. You go on to learn the reasons for market failure in health care (Chapter 11). One of the main problems is the failure to achieve equity, the subject of Chapter 12.

Health financing

Chapter 13 provides a framework for assessing health care financing systems. It looks at the different sources and uses of funds, in particular private health insurance (Chapter 14) and social insurance (Chapter 15).

Economic evaluation

The final section explores the key concepts and components of an economic evaluation (Chapter 16). Methods to determine the costs of health care interventions are discussed in Chapter 17 before the two principal ways of combining costs and consequences are considered: cost–benefit analysis (Chapter 18) and cost-effectiveness analysis (Chapter 19). The final chapter provides an overview of their major areas of application.

A variety of activities are employed to help your understanding and learning of the topics and ideas covered. These include:

* reflection on your own knowledge and experience;
* questions based on reading key articles or relevant research papers;
* analyses of quantitative and qualitative data.

Acknowledgements

The authors would like to acknowledge the contributions of Susie Foster, Li-wei Chao and Dan Fishbein who developed an earlier version of the section on economic evaluation, on which the present content is based, Anne Haworth for reviewing the entire book, and Deirdre Byrne (series manager) for help and support in preparing this book.

SECTION I

Economics and health economics

What are economics and health economics?

Overview

This chapter provides an introduction to the discipline of economics and to health economics. You will learn about the types of questions that economics is concerned with and some of the key concepts that it uses. If you have not studied economics before, this chapter will introduce many expressions and concepts that may be new to you. You will find that you come to understand them better as you progress through the book. You will also explore the applicability of economics to health and health care.

Learning objectives

After working through this chapter, you will be able to:

- **explain what economics is and the problems it seeks to solve**
- **describe what is meant by efficiency and opportunity cost**
- **define and use a number of fundamental economic concepts**
- **explain why economics is applicable to health**
- **define health economics and describe the scope of health economics**

Key terms

Allocative (Pareto, social) efficiency A situation in which it is not possible to improve the welfare of one person in an economy without making someone else worse off.

Commodities (or production outputs) The results of combining resources in the production process. They are either goods or services.

Demand The relationship between the price of a good and the quantity demanded (economic definition).

Market Any situation where people who demand a good or service can come into contact with the suppliers of that good.

Normative economics Economic statements that prescribe how things should be.

Opportunity (economic) cost The value of the next best alternative forgone as a result of the decision made.

Positive economics Economic statements that describe how things are.

Production possibilities frontier (PPF) A graph that illustrates the different combinations of outputs that are achievable with a limited set of resources.

Resources Every item within the economy that can be used to produce and distribute goods and services; classified as labour, capital and land.

Utility The happiness or satisfaction a person gains from consuming a commodity.

Welfare (or social welfare) The happiness or satisfaction a population gains from consuming a commodity.

Economic problems

Those responsible for determining and managing health systems are typically forced to consider questions such as:

- At what level should hospital user charges be set?
- Are taxes on cigarettes a useful way of promoting health through reducing the prevalence of smoking?
- Which is the more effective method of increasing the take-up of health services: price controls or subsidies?
- How should doctors be paid?

You would probably agree that all of the above can be seen as economic problems. But what is economics and how would you define it?

Economics is the systematic study of resource allocation mechanisms. It can be applied to any social behaviour or institution where scarcity exists and there is consequently a need for making choices. Fundamentally, economists believe that the behaviour of people and institutions in making choices about scarce resources is to some extent predictable. Underlying this predictability is the assumption that people on the whole act in a way that makes them and their families better off rather than worse off.

There are four questions that are the primary concern of economics:

1 What products are being produced and in what quantities? (For example: what types of malarial prevention measures are being provided and how much of each type?)
2 By what methods are these products produced? (What resources are required to produce these malarial prevention measures?)
3 How is society's output of goods and services divided among its members? (Who has access to these measures?)
4 How efficient is society's production and distribution? (Can we get the same amount of protection from malaria using fewer resources? Would an AIDS awareness campaign be a more effective use of resources than malarial prevention?)

Now that you have some ideas about the problems that economists seek to solve, you will learn about some of the most important concepts employed by economists.

The concepts of economics

'The economy' refers to all the economic activities and institutions (that is, anything involving scarcity and choice) within a geographically defined area. So you might refer to the performance of a specific national economy, or the global economy, or perhaps a regional economy.

'Resources' are every item within the economy that can be used to produce and distribute goods and services. Resources are classified as labour, capital and land:

1 Labour refers to human resources, both manual and non-manual, skilled and unskilled.
2 Capital refers to goods that are used to produce other goods or services, for example machinery, buildings and tools.
3 Land refers to all natural resources. It also refers to manufactured consumables (i.e. almost everything else that does not fall under labour or capital).

Most resources are not, in themselves, useful to us as individuals but they can be combined to make something that is useful. This process is called production. Commodities (or production outputs) are the result of combining resources in the production process. They are either final products, which are then used to satisfy people's wants, or else they are intermediate products, which are used to make other commodities. In economics the terms utility (for individuals) or welfare (for populations) are used to describe the satisfaction or happiness provided by commodities.

Commodities are either goods that you can hold or touch (for example a drug) or else they are services that happen to you (for example a consultation). There are three essential characteristics that distinguish different commodities:

1 *Physical attributes* – an ice cream and a cup of tea are clearly different commodities because they require different manufacturing techniques and because they satisfy different wants.
2 *The date* (and sometimes time of day) at which the commodity is available – an ice cream that is available on a hot summer's day is a different commodity from one available in the cold midwinter; furthermore an ice cream available this summer is a different commodity from one that will become available next summer.
3 *The place* where the commodity is available – a cup of tea available in a fashionable café is a different commodity from tea available in a local supermarket.

There are three things you can do with a commodity or resource. Consumption describes people using up a commodity in order to increase their utility (happiness or satisfaction gained). Taking an aspirin is an example of consumption because it increases utility by relieving the pain of a headache.

People invest because they expect the utility they gain from the final product to be greater than the utility they gain from directly consuming these resources. This involves an initial sacrifice followed by subsequent benefits (the return). Often, an investment entails a risk such that the end return may be smaller than was expected at the time of investment.

If you do not invest or consume a commodity then you can trade it (that is exchange it) for some other commodity or resource.

Figure 1.1 illustrates the different ways of using a resource (consumption, investment and exchange). Whichever route is taken, the result will be increased utility for the owner of the resource. The route chosen by the owner should depend on which one yields the largest increase in utility for them.

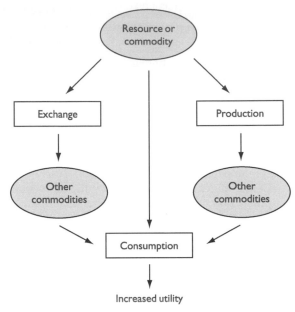

Figure 1.1 Alternative uses of a resource

Markets

In economics, the term 'market' is used to describe any situation where people who demand a good or service can come into contact with the suppliers of that good. For it to be a market the buyers and sellers do not have to physically meet.

The amount of money that is exchanged for a commodity is the price. You will find out in this book how the price is influenced by the number of suppliers in the market and the amount of money they are prepared to accept. The price is also influenced by the number of buyers in the market and the amount of money they are prepared to pay. These influences are described as the market forces of supply and demand. Individual consumers or households are usually thought of as being buyers while firms (or businesses) are associated with supply. However, this is not true in the cases of markets for resources and markets for intermediate goods. For example, in the labour market, households will supply and firms will demand labour.

Figure 1.2 shows a simple model of the flow of commodities, resources and money between households and firms. Households own resources (labour, land, shares in capital) and supply them to firms in return for money (wages, rent, interest and profit). Firms turn resources into commodities and supply them to the households,

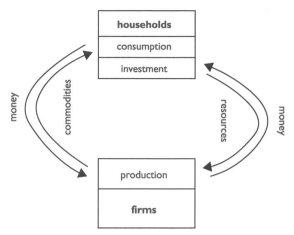

Figure 1.2 The flow of money, resources and commodities

again, in return for money. Households that supply more resources will receive more money and therefore will be able to consume more commodities.

This, essentially, describes free markets – that is to say, markets that involve only firms and individuals buying and selling commodities and resources. In reality, most markets have some kind of government intervention. Such intervention in the market might involve levying taxes, fixing prices, licensing suppliers or regulating quality. Alternatively, the government might decide to take control of demand for a commodity and prohibit private demand, or it might decide to take over supply entirely and prohibit private supply. On the other hand, a government might make laws that are intended to 'free up' market forces and make markets more easily accessible.

In some economies, the government plays such a large role that markets scarcely exist at all. Such systems are referred to as command or centrally planned economies. Because of the difficulties involved with planning a whole economy and the problem of trying to motivate workers and managers, command economies have rapidly diminished in number over the last couple of decades. Almost every country in the world today has a mixed economy, a system in which market forces and central planning both play a role.

✏ Activity 1.1

Try to answer the following questions without referring back to the text.

1 What were identified as the two defining concepts of economics?
2 In Table 1.1, match up the terms with their definitions.
3 What terms are used to describe the satisfaction or happiness gained from consuming a commodity?
4 What are the three ways of employing a resource?

Table 1.1 Some economic terms and their definitions

1 Subsistence economy	a	A system where exchange takes place without the use of money
2 Global economy	b	The economic activities and institutions around the world
3 Barter economy	c	An exchange economy with little government intervention
4 Exchange economy	d	An economy with an absence of exchange
5 Mixed economy	e	A market economy with substantial government intervention
6 Command economy	f	A system where trade takes place
7 Market economy	g	A system where few resource allocation decisions are left to market forces

↻ Feedback

1 The two defining concepts of economics were identified as:

a) the vast range of human wants

b) the relative scarcity of resources that can be employed to meet these wants.

The consequence is that we have to make choices about which wants are to be satisfied and which ones are not. We then have to allocate resources between these wants.

2 The terms can be matched up to the definitions as shown in Table 1.2.

Table 1.2 Some economic terms and their definitions (solution)

1 Subsistence economy	d	An economy with an absence of exchange
2 Global economy	b	The economic activities and institutions around the world
3 Barter economy	a	A system where exchange takes place without the use of money
4 Exchange economy	f	A system where trade takes place
5 Mixed economy	e	A market economy with substantial government intervention
6 Command economy	g	A system where few resource allocation decisions are left to market forces
7 Market economy	c	An exchange economy with little government intervention

3 'Utility' is the word most often used by economists to refer to the happiness or satisfaction gained from consuming a good or service. The terms 'welfare' and 'social welfare' are also used, especially when talking about the aggregate utility of a population. Quality of life and well-being are other commonly used words with roughly the same meaning. It is important to note that the core of economic theory is dependent only on the assumption that people can differentiate between states that have higher or lower utility. (It is not necessary to be able to measure utility.)

4 A resource can be employed in one of three ways: consumed, invested or exchanged.

Efficiency

It is worth looking at scarcity and choice in a little more depth. Consider a clinic that provides ambulatory care for patients with tuberculosis (TB) or angina. Let's suppose that:

- the only input is nurse time;
- TB and angina consultations are of the same duration;
- given current staffing the maximum number of consultations per day is 200.

Under these assumptions, we might represent the maximum output of the clinic with what economists call the production possibilities frontier (PPF) – a graph that illustrates the different combinations of outputs that are achievable with a limited set of resources.

Figure 1.3 shows what the PPF might look like for our clinic. In this example, a straight line represents the PPF – we can produce a maximum of 200 consultations per day regardless of how we prioritize the two conditions. The straight line relationship implies that transferring a nurse from one disease to another has no impact on overall output.

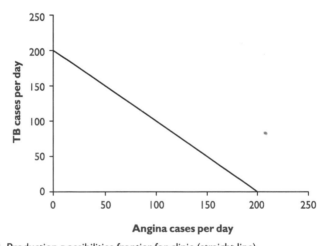

Figure 1.3 Production possibilities frontier for clinic (straight line)

Suppose instead that some nurses have skills that mean they are better at TB consultations (they can achieve more with a given amount of time) and others are better at treating angina. In these circumstances transferring from TB to angina a nurse who is specialist in angina treatment could actually increase output. The PPF in this case is illustrated in Figure 1.4. The frontier is now concave to the origin, rather than straight. It is the form that we typically expect PPFs to take, as long as it is the case that resources are not equally productive in all activities. As we gradually increase a particular output level, with each additional increment we have to use resources that are less and less suitable (less productive).

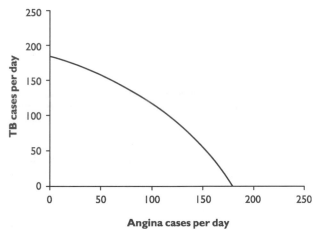

Figure 1.4 Production possibilities frontier for clinic (concave to the origin)

Figure 1.5 shows a PPF for an economy as a whole. Every point on the PPF represents an efficient level of production. Allocative efficiency requires that we are at a point where we cannot increase one output without reducing another – hence the PPF represents efficient points by definition. We could also say that we cannot increase an output level without incurring an opportunity cost. The opportunity cost of an action is the level of benefit one would have got from the best alternative action. So, in terms of Figure 1.5, the opportunity cost of increasing health care from 0 to 500 units is the benefit from the 600 units of other commodities (food, education, transport) that we have to go without in order to achieve it. Notice from Figure 1.5, that as we continue to increase the amount of health care, the opportunity cost of each 500-unit increase becomes greater and greater.

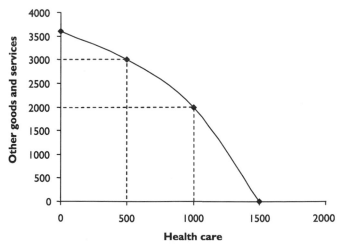

Figure 1.5 Production possibilities frontier for the economy

Activity 1.2

To extend your understanding of the concepts just described, try the following questions:

1 Which of the points in Figure 1.6 (A, B, C and D) are:

i) Efficient?
ii) Inefficient?
iii) Not feasible?

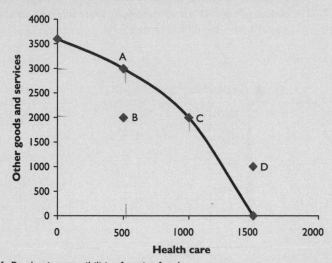

Figure 1.6 Production possibilities frontier for the economy

2 What is the opportunity cost of increasing health care from 500 to 1000 units?

a) Starting from point A?
b) Starting from point B? (This is not such an easy question!)

3 Show on Figure 1.6, other things remaining the same, what you think would happen to the PPF if:

a) there is a decrease in the size of the population or
b) there is an improvement in health technology.

 Feedback

1 If a combination is within the PPF then you know it is feasible (points A, B and C). It is only efficient, however, if it is exactly *on* the PPF (A and C) – there will be excess capacity (inefficiency) when combinations are within, but not on, the PPF (B). If a combination lies to the right of the PPF then it is not feasible, given current technology (D).

2 The opportunity cost of an increase in health care of 500 units from point A is the

benefit associated with the 1000 units of other commodities that have to be given up to achieve it. If there is a move from point B to point C the cost is effectively zero since the production of other commodities does not need to be reduced. However, the opportunity cost is in fact still 1000 units of other commodities. This is because, by moving from B to C, the society misses out on the benefits that they could have gained by moving from B to A instead (assuming that point A is the best alternative to point C).

3 Labour is a vital input in the production of all commodities, especially health. A fall in population will result in a reduction in the amount of production that is feasible. Hence the PPF shifts towards the origin (PPF2 in Figure 1.7). An improvement in technology, by definition means that more can be produced with a given set of resources. Hence this would shift the PPF outwards, although the maximum amount of non-health production remains the same (PPF3 in Figure 1.7).

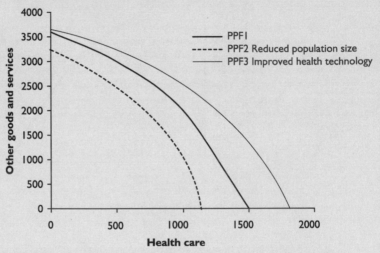

Figure 1.7 Production possibilities frontier for the economy – shifts of the PPF

The important implications of this analysis are:

- If a system is operating inefficiently then it is possible to produce more commodities and therefore more welfare with current resources.
- If a system is already operating efficiently, then to increase the quantity produced of one commodity you have to reduce the quantity produced of some other commodity. There is a trade-off, an opportunity cost.
- The only other way that more of every product can be produced is if there is technological improvement such that more output can be produced with the same amount of resources or if there is an increase in the amount of resource available (such as an increase in population).

The concepts of allocative efficiency and opportunity cost are fundamental to economics. If for no other reason, economic analysis should not be overlooked, because it attempts to consider the opportunity cost of particular actions as well as the benefits.

Categorizing economics

Like any academic field, economics has a number of subdisciplines, defined either by the types of questions that are examined or by the methods that are used – health economics being one of them. Two other important categorizations of economic thought are as follows.

Microeconomics and macroeconomics

Microeconomics is concerned with the decisions taken by individual consumers and firms and with the way these decisions contribute to the setting of prices and output in various kinds of market ('micro' implies small scale). This is the focus of this book.

Macroeconomics is concerned with the interaction of broad economic aggregates (such as general price inflation, unemployment of resources in the economy, the growth of national output). It is also concerned with the interaction between different sectors of the economy ('macro' implies large scale).

Positive and normative economics

Positive economics refers to economic statements that describe how things are. Such statements can be universally true, true in some circumstances or universally false. This can be established through empirical research.

Normative economics refers to economic statements that prescribe how things should be. Such statements can be informed by positive economics but can never be shown to be true or false since they depend on value judgements.

For example, the following statement is positive:

> *The presence of patents for drugs has led to greater expenditure on research and development in the pharmaceutical industry.*

In principle the presence of drug patents can be observed and so can the level of expenditure on research. With the appropriate statistical techniques we may or may not find that this is the case or it might be the case only in some countries or under certain circumstances. The following statement is normative:

> *Patenting should be implemented in the pharmaceutical industry.*

To be useful to policy makers, economists make use of both positive and normative economics. Positive statements can describe what will happen (or not happen) if a particular policy is carried out, but in order to make a recommendation we need to evaluate the policy according to one or more criteria. One such criterion that you've already encountered is efficiency. Other criteria often encountered in economics are equity, which you will read about in Chapter 12, economic growth and macroeconomic stability (both outside the scope of this book). Be aware that studies often contain both positive and normative statements; in everything you read you should try to spot statements that go beyond description (like this one!).

Economists have a reputation for disagreeing with each other. This is understandable when one considers that:

- economists are keen to influence policy;
- policy recommendations are normative and are underpinned by value judgements; and
- value judgements vary between individuals.

On this basis one should expect a great deal of disagreement among economists, reflecting disagreement in the wider world. Reassuringly, surveys, such as those reported by Alston *et al.* (1993) or Fuller and Geide-Stevenson (2003) seem to confirm that there is more agreement among economists on positive issues than there is on normative ones. Economists are slow at reaching a consensus on particular ideas because, due to the nature of the topics under study, it is either impossible or difficult to conduct experiments that can monitor changes in the variables of interest and at the same time hold all other potential influencing factors constant.

Can economics be applied to health?

Anyone who has worked in health care will be well aware of the scarcity of resources. Therefore choices are inevitably made about what treatments are provided and about who receives treatment; that is, there is some form of rationing. Economists advocate making such rationing decisions explicit. Most importantly in the context of limited resources, the provision of one service, X, necessarily means that a second service, Y, is displaced. The health gain that we would have got from service Y is the opportunity cost of our decision to provide service X. Economists try to ensure that the opportunity cost of providing X does not exceed the health gain from X.

There are various reasons why the demand for health care continues to exceed supply: an *ageing population* in which the elderly require more health care than younger adults; *new health technologies* which means more conditions have become treatable; and increased *expectations* from people.

Economics is the study of scarcity and choice; it follows that if economics is relevant anywhere then it should be relevant in health. However, health care has some interesting characteristics that mean the more basic economic models should be used cautiously (Arrow 1963). None of these characteristics is unique to health but the combination of characteristics together with their sheer number have contributed to health economics becoming a distinct subdiscipline of economics. Another characteristic of health economists that has moved them away somewhat from mainstream economics is their interest in measuring and optimizing an objectively defined 'population health', rather than 'social welfare', which is explicitly based on individuals' preferences. This approach is often referred to as 'extra-welfarism'.

The aim of health economists is often to inform decision makers so that the choices they make maximize health benefits to the population. Health economics is not concerned with 'saving money' but with improving the level and distribution of population health with the resources available. Over the course of this book you will be able to decide for yourself the extent to which the specific methods of health economics provide useful insights for health policy.

Schools of thought in health economics

The three broad paradigms of economics are: neoclassical economics, the Austrian school of economics and Marxist economics. Although it may be influenced at times by the other paradigms, the neoclassical paradigm very much represents the mainstream of thought in health economics. The main features of neoclassical economics are:

- the notion that the value of a good or service is defined by people's preferences;
- marginal analysis – the examination of small changes in particular variables;
- optimization – calculating at what point a particular variable (e.g. profit or utility) is maximized.

While there are no clearly demarcated schools of health economics, there are differences of emphasis between economists who support markets in health systems and those who do not (see Table 1.3).

Table 1.3 Comparison of pro- and anti-market health economists

Pro-market health economists place more emphasis on	Anti-market health economists place more emphasis on
Industrial economics (including examination of the size, power and strategies of health providers)	Welfare economics and extra-welfarism
Private insurance and direct payments for health	Social insurance and tax finance
Health care	Public health
Freedom of choice	Equality of access

More about the structure of this book

You already have some idea of the content of this book. At this stage, it is useful to refer to Williams' framework of health economics (see Figure 1.8) in order to gain a clearer understanding of the structure of the book. However, it does not follow the scheme precisely and does not cover every area in equal detail or in equal depth.

- Chapters 1 and 2 are an introduction to the scope and methods of health economics.
- Chapters 3–12 look at interactions within the health care market – Boxes C, D, F and G in Figure 1.8.
- Health planning and finance – Box H, will be covered in Chapters 13–15. These chapters also look at the material in boxes C, D and F at a more applied level than Chapters 3–12.
- Chapters 16–20 look at evaluating the cost-effectiveness of individual health programmes – Box E. This necessarily covers the valuation of health – Box B.

Now that you know how economics can be applied to health care, you are ready to learn about the methods used by economists to solve health economic problems. These are the subject of Chapter 2.

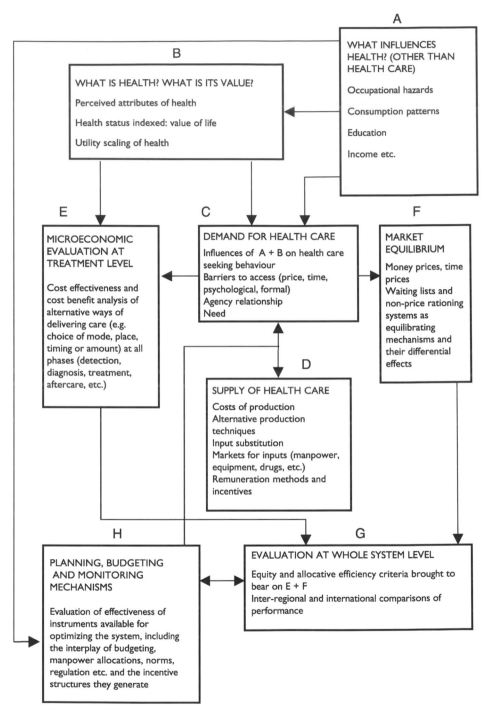

Figure 1.8 Schematic presentation of the main elements in health economics
Source: Williams (1987)

Summary

In this chapter you have read about some of the fundamental concepts of economics including resources and commodities, markets and efficiency. Economics may adopt a micro or macro perspective, and be positive or normative. Health economics is a subdiscipline of economics, which applies the theories and methods of economics to all aspects of health and health care.

References

Alston RM, Kearl JR and Vaughan MB (1993) Is there a consensus among economists in the 1990s? *American Economic Review* 82:203–9.

Arrow KJ (1963) Uncertainty and the welfare economics of medical care. *American Economic Review* 53:941–73.

Fuller D and Geide-Stevenson D (2003) Consensus among economists: revisited. *Journal of Economic Education* 34:369–87.

Williams A (1987) Health economics: the cheerful face of the dismal science, in Williams A (ed) *Health and economics*. London: Macmillan.

Further reading

Folland S, Goodman AC and Stano M (2000) *The economics of health and health care* (2nd edn). New Jersey: Prentice Hall.

McPake B, Kumaranayake L and Normand C (2002) *Health economics – an international perspective*. London: Routledge.

Witter S, Ensor T, Jowett M and Thompson R (2000) *Health economics for developing countries*. London: Macmillan Education.

2 | The methods of economics

Overview

Before learning about the principal concepts of economics and their application in health economics, you need to understand something about the methods used in economics. In this chapter you will learn about the use of graphical and mathematical ways of representing the relationship between inputs and outputs, including the essential concept of the margin.

Learning objectives

After working through this chapter, you will be able to:

- **describe the methods of economists**
- **describe how graphs and equations can be used to represent economic relationships**
- **explain marginal analysis**

Key terms

Ceteris paribus The assumption that all other variables remain unchanged.

Economic model Representations of the real world, which omit all variables that are not relevant to the specific issue the model was designed to address.

Marginal analysis The study of the consequences of small changes in a variable.

Marginal utility The change in total utility derived from a one unit increase in consumption.

Production function The functional relationship that indicates how inputs are transformed into outputs in the most efficient way.

Economic analysis

Economic models are representations of the real world, which omit all variables that are not relevant to the specific issue the model was designed to address. Models represent the relationships between different variables. They can be used to make predictions in the form of 'if . . . then . . .' statements. Models, by definition, are able to make predictions about the effect of a change in one particular variable, while all other variables remain unchanged. The assumption that all other variables remain unchanged is referred to as the *ceteris paribus* assumption.

However, in the real world it is difficult to find a situation where the 'other' economic variables are constant. Some economists carry out experiments to test theories about economic behaviour. In these situations the investigator has a large amount of control over the study environment. Most economic theories cannot be tested under experimental conditions and for these we have to rely on observations of economic transactions as they happen in the real world. The biggest problem with this type of investigation (that is, observational studies) is determining causality – just because two events are associated doesn't mean one caused the other. You will now look in more detail at how economists express their models.

Modelling economic relationships

Economic models are represented in three ways:

- verbally (in words);
- graphically (in graphs and diagrams);
- algebraically (in mathematical formulae).

In this book you will come across all three types but emphasis will be firmly on the first two. What you learn in this chapter will help you interpret the economic models you will be reading about over the course of the book. Much of the rest of this chapter takes the form of a worked example based on a scenario which is designed to illustrate the use of graphical and algebraic analysis in health economics.

The scenario

An acute hospital is just about to close. The nursing manager of a nearby acute hospital is deciding how many new staff members will be required to treat the patients who previously went to the other hospital.

The usual ratio between patients and nurses in acute hospitals in the region is four patients to every one nurse. Currently there are 50 nurses at the hospital treating 200 patients. If the ratio is maintained then 75 nurses will be required to treat 300 patients or 100 nurses to treat 400 patients.

The slope of a straight line

This relationship between the number of nurses and the number of patients treated can be represented as a formula as follows. First, you can say that the number of patients seen, your output, is a *function of* (is dependent on) the number of nurses you have:

$Q = f(N)$

where Q is the output level (in economics Q is conventionally used to refer to output) and N is the number of nurses. More specifically you can describe the relationship using the following equation:

$Q = 4N$

which simply states that for every nurse there will be four units of output. This relationship can also be plotted on a graph, as shown in Figure 2.1. The slope of the relationship is defined by $\dfrac{\Delta Q}{\Delta N}$ which is the change in output divided by the change in the number of nurses (the symbol Δ is used to designate the difference). This you already know to be 4 but Table 2.1 shows how it can be calculated directly from the graph.

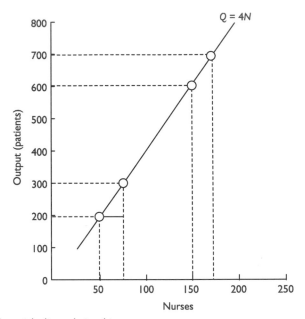

Figure 2.1 A straight-line relationship

Table 2.1 The slope of a straight line

Movement	Slope
50 nurses to 75 nurses	$\dfrac{\Delta Q}{\Delta N} = \dfrac{300-200}{75-50} = 4$
150 nurses to 175 nurses	$\dfrac{\Delta Q}{\Delta N} = \dfrac{700-600}{175-150} = 4$

For a straight-line graph the slope is always the same over the entire length of the line. In an equation of the type $Y = bX$ (in this case $Q = 4N$) or $Y = a + bX$, the constant b (in this case 4) is always equal to the slope of Y with respect to X (in this case Q with respect to N). These types of equation are always straight lines when plotted.

This is also true for relationships with multiple variables of the form $Y = a + bX + cZ + dW$. The constants b, c and d we describe as the coefficients of X, Z and W respectively. For this type of equation, the coefficients are always slopes, so that in the example above:

- b is the slope of the relationship between X and Y (when other variables are held constant);
- c is the slope of the relationship between Z and Y (when other variables are held constant);
- d is the slope of the relationship between W and Y (when other variables are held constant).

Relationships that are straight lines when plotted are referred to as linear relationships. If the coefficient or slope is larger then the line will be steeper, but if the coefficient is smaller then the line will be flatter – see Figure 2.2.

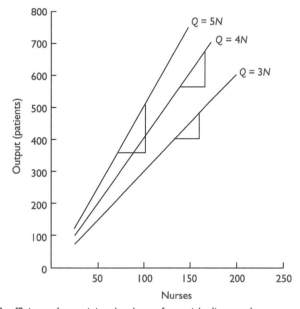

Figure 2.2 Coefficients determining the slope of a straight-line graph

The slope of a curved line

The nursing manager calculates the number of nurses she requires on the basis that each nurse can deal with four patients. However, when she puts it into practice she finds that there are not enough nurses to carry out all the work even though the number of new patients is the same as she predicted. She carries out a survey to find out how output varies according to the number of nurses that are hired. She calculates the output associated with each nursing level and plots this relationship on a graph – see Figure 2.3.

The nursing manager found that because the building is relatively small, the nurses were getting in each other's way. Hence as the number of nurses is doubled, output is less than doubled. In this case, there is not a linear (i.e. straight line) relationship

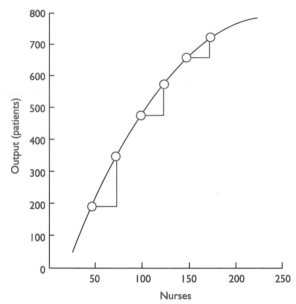

Figure 2.3 A curved-line relationship

between the number of nurses and output. As more nurses are added, output increases but by an ever-decreasing amount. This implies that the slope of output to nurses is decreasing as the number of nurses increases. The slope of this relationship can be estimated by measuring the slope of a straight line that connects two points on the curve. Table 2.2 shows how the slope falls as you move up the curve.

Table 2.2 The slope of a curved line

Movement	Slope of a straight line connecting the two points of an arc
50 nurses to 75 nurses	$\dfrac{\Delta Q}{\Delta N} = \dfrac{350 - 200}{75 - 50} = 6$
100 nurses to 125 nurses	$\dfrac{\Delta Q}{\Delta N} = \dfrac{580 - 480}{125 - 100} = 4$
150 nurses to 175 nurses	$\dfrac{\Delta Q}{\Delta N} = \dfrac{730 - 670}{175 - 150} = 2.4$

The formula $\dfrac{\Delta Q}{\Delta N}$ in these examples gives the slope of a straight line connecting two points on the curve. Thus, it measures the average responsiveness of output to a change in the number of nurses, over a *particular range* of nursing levels. You can also measure the slope at a *precise point* on the curve. The slope at this *point* on the curve is still $\dfrac{\Delta Q}{\Delta N}$ but ΔN is negligibly small (we say that it 'tends to zero'). According to calculus this is denoted as:

$$slope = \frac{dY}{dX} = \frac{\Delta Y}{\Delta X} \qquad \text{where } \Delta X \to 0$$

or in our specific example:

$$slope = \frac{dQ}{dN} = \frac{\Delta Q}{\Delta N} \qquad \text{where } \Delta N \to 0$$

The slope of the curve at a particular level of nurses, say 175, is equal to the slope of the straight line which is exactly tangential to the curve at that point. Tangential means that the line touches the curve without intersecting it – see Figure 2.4.

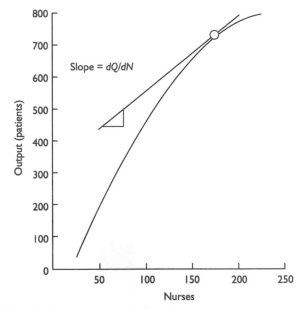

Figure 2.4 The slope of a curve at a particular point

Calculus can provide the mathematical formulae to enable you to calculate the slope of a curve for any value of X. Calculus will not be addressed in this book.

Marginal analysis

One of the most important concepts in economics is that of the margin. Health economists are not so much concerned with whether or not to provide a service but with whether to decrease or increase the scale of the service.

It's not just economists that make decisions at the margin. This evening you probably have the opportunity to do some studying or to spend some time with your friends and family. However, this is unlikely to be an all or nothing decision. It is more likely that you will you be able to spend some time studying and some time with your family.

If you spend the whole evening studying then you might find that over the course of the evening your concentration might decline, you are gradually taking in less and less of the reading and you miss having some company. Economists would say that your *marginal utility* from an hour of study is decreasing with each additional hour that you devote to studying. Similarly, if you spend the whole evening with your family, probably the first hour that you see them will be the most rewarding but this will gradually decrease with each additional hour that you are with them. The solution, assuming that you are trying to maximize your utility, is for you to split your time between the two activities, consuming both activities while the marginal utility is relatively high.

Marginal analysis is the study of the consequences of small changes in a variable or variables. This can be useful in identifying the point when a particular parameter is optimized. For example, in the production of a good or service, the profits of suppliers are maximized where marginal cost is equal to marginal revenue. In general, we can try to predict how choices will change by looking at changes in marginal costs and marginal benefits. The reason why marginal analysis is important is that many economic variables, including cost and utility, are not constant across every unit of output.

Now back to the previous example of nurses; the type of relationship that you have been looking at is referred to by economists as a *production function*. It is the relationship between an input (nurses) and output. The lines plotted in the graphs (Figures 2.1–2.4) are referred to as the total product (or output) curves.

Marginal product (*MP*) is the increase in total product (*Q*) from a one-unit increase in an input, in this case nurses (*N*):

$$MP_N = \frac{\Delta Q}{\Delta N} \quad \text{where } \Delta N = 1$$

Compare this with the slope:

$$slope = \frac{\Delta Q}{\Delta N} \quad \text{where } \Delta N \to 0$$

Although the slope of the total product function is not exactly equal to the marginal product (because the former is strictly measured as $\Delta N \to 0$ while the latter is measured for $\Delta N = 1$), they are usually so similar that for practical purposes they are considered identical. Thus the marginal product is approximately equal to the slope of the total product curve:

$$MP_N \approx \frac{dQ}{dN}$$

Note from Figure 2.4 that marginal product (as represented by the slope of the production function) is not constant. As the nursing level increases, so marginal product of nurses decreases, reflecting the decreasing productivity that was observed by the manager.

Increments and margins

Often, in practice, the increase in product associated with every 1 unit rise in an input is not known, although the overall increase for say a 10 unit rise in inputs might be known. If you measure the responsiveness of output relative to a 10 unit increase in inputs then you would describe this as the *incremental product* (IP):

$$IP_N = \frac{\Delta Q}{\Delta N} \quad \text{(where } \Delta N > 1\text{)}$$

Compare this with:

$$MP_N = \frac{\Delta Q}{\Delta N} \quad \text{(where } \Delta N = 1\text{)}$$

$$slope = \frac{\Delta Q}{\Delta N} \quad \text{(where } \Delta N \to 0\text{)}$$

Incremental product is, in essence, an approximate estimate of marginal product or, if you like, an approximate estimate of the slope of the total product curve. The slope estimates presented in Table 2.2 are all examples of incremental product.

Note that the production function you have been reading about is a very simple one. The production of the hospital is dependent not only on the number of nurses but also on a number of other factors. In economic analysis it is deliberately assumed that all other variables remain unchanged (*ceteris paribus*). This is necessary because, before you can make predictions in a complicated situation with many variables changing and interacting, you must understand the individual effects of each variable in isolation.

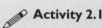 **Activity 2.1**

These questions will help you to see if you have understood the material covered in this chapter.

1   What is the slope in the following relationships?

   a) Q = 50P − 10 (Q = quantity supplied; P = price)
   b) the relationship shown in Figure 2.5 below.

2   Plot the following relationship on Figure 2.6: Q = 2P − 1.
3   Explain in words and formulae the concept of marginal product.
4   In Table 2.3 the relationships between cost (C) and output (Q) are listed. Match the formulae with the appropriate terminology in the table. (Note that terms may apply to more than one formula and that there is not necessarily a formula related to each term.)

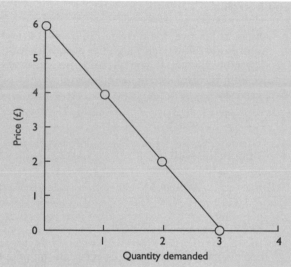

Figure 2.5 Calculate the slope

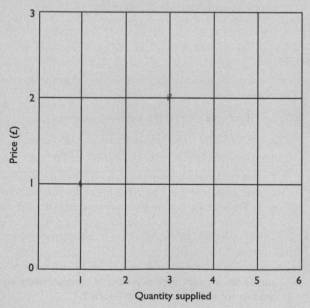

Figure 2.6 Q = 2P − 1

Table 2.3 Formulae and terms

Formula	Term
$\dfrac{\Delta C}{\Delta Q}$ (where $\Delta Q = 10$)	Slope of cost with respect to output
$\dfrac{\Delta C}{\Delta Q}$ (where $\Delta Q \to 0$)	Marginal cost
$\dfrac{\Delta C}{\Delta Q}$ (where $\Delta Q = 1$)	Average cost
$\dfrac{C}{Q}$	Incremental cost
$\dfrac{\Delta C}{\Delta Q}$ (where $\Delta Q = 100$)	Total cost

↻ Feedback

1 a) The slope of quantity supplied with respect to price is 50. This means that for every 1 unit increase in price there will be a 50 unit increase in quantity supplied.

   b) You can see that for every 2 unit decrease in price there is a 1 unit increase in the quantity demanded. This means that the slope of price with respect to quantity demanded is −2. Alternatively the slope of quantity demanded with respect to price is −0.5 because for every unit increase in price quantity demanded falls by half a unit.

2 In order to plot the graph, it is best to start off by plotting a number of points and then join them up:

If $P = 0$ then $Q = (2 \times 0) - 1 = 0 - 1 = -1$

If $P = 1$ then $Q = (2 \times 1) - 1 = 2 - 1 = 1$

If $P = 2$ then $Q = (2 \times 2) - 1 = 4 - 1 = 3$

If $P = 3$ then $Q = (2 \times 3) - 1 = 6 - 1 = 5$

Joining these points gives the line shown in Figure 2.7.

3 Marginal product is the increase in output associated with a 1 unit increase in an input. It is the change in output divided by the change in an input, where the change in input is equal to 1. Algebraically this is written as:

$$MP_N = \frac{\Delta Q}{\Delta N} \qquad (\text{where } \Delta N = 1)$$

where Q represents output and N the input (in this case nurses). Marginal product of nurses for a given level of nurses is approximately equal to the slope of the total product (of nurses) curve – see Figure 2.4.

4 Table 2.4 links the formulae to the correct terms.

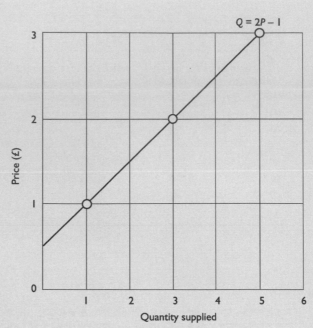

Figure 2.7 $Q = 2P - 1$ (solution)

Table 2.4 Formulae and terms (solution)

Formula	Term
$\dfrac{\Delta C}{\Delta Q}$ (where $\Delta Q = 10$)	Incremental cost
$\dfrac{\Delta C}{\Delta Q}$ (where $\Delta Q \to 0$)	Slope of cost with respect to output
$\dfrac{\Delta C}{\Delta Q}$ (where $\Delta Q = 1$)	Marginal cost
$\dfrac{C}{Q}$	Average cost
$\dfrac{\Delta C}{\Delta Q}$ (where $\Delta Q = 100$)	Incremental cost

Total cost is not represented by any of the above formulae. It is represented simply by C.

If you have followed the use of graphs and equations in this chapter then you should be well equipped to interpret the economic models you will come across over the course of this book. The mathematics you will encounter will be no more complicated than in this chapter.

Summary

You have learned how, in order to predict the effects of change, economists construct models which represent specific aspects of the real world. Economists test their models using experiments or observational studies, although experimental studies are often not feasible. Observational evidence is problematic as it is difficult to demonstrate cause. Models can be represented by words, graphs, diagrams or algebra.

SECTION 2

Supply and demand

3 A simple model of demand

Overview

In this and the next six chapters, you will be looking at market forces – supply and demand. In particular you will be thinking about how they influence activity and price in health care. You will start off in this chapter by looking at a simple model of demand and identifying which variables determine the demand for commodities. Later in the chapter you will move on to analyse why demand for health care is more complicated and what distinguishes it from the demand for other goods and services. You will see how information about demand can be used as an aid to the planning of health services.

Learning objectives

After working through this chapter, you will be able to:

- **define the term 'quantity demanded'**
- **show graphically how changes in demand factors influence the demand curve and therefore service use**
- **define consumer surplus and explain why it can be used as a measure of benefit**
- **list the factors which influence the demand for health care**
- **describe how demand theory can be used in health service planning**

Key terms

Complements Goods used along with an identified good.

Consumer surplus The difference between what a consumer pays for a good and the maximum they would be willing to pay for it.

Demand curve A graph showing the relationship between the quantity demanded of a good and its price when all other variables are unchanged.

Inferior goods Goods for which demand decreases as income increases.

Law of diminishing marginal utility A hypothesis that states that as consumption of a good increases so the marginal utility decreases.

Normal goods Goods for which demand increases as income increases.

Substitutes Goods that can be used in place of other goods.

The demand function

When you learned about the concepts of economics in Chapter 1, you learned that the term 'demand' is used to describe the amount of money purchasers are prepared to pay for a commodity. The following edited extract from Michael Parkin, Melanie Powell and Kent Mathews (2003) will introduce you to the determinants of demand.

 Demand

To demand something, you must:

- Want it
- Be able to afford it
- Have a definite plan to buy it

Wants are the unlimited desires or wishes that people have for goods and services. How many times have you thought that you would like something 'if only you could afford it' or 'if it weren't so expensive'? When we make choices, scarcity guarantees that many – perhaps most – of our wants will never be satisfied. Demand reflects our plans about which wants to satisfy.

The amount of any particular good or service that consumers plan to buy depends on many factors. The main ones are:

- The price of the good.
- The prices of related goods.
- Income.
- Expected future prices.
- Population.
- Preferences.

Let's start by modelling the relationship between the quantity demanded and the price of a good. To study this relationship, we hold constant all other influences on consumers' planned purchases. We can then ask: how does the quantity demanded of the good vary as its price varies?

The law of demand

The law of demand states: Other things remaining the same, the higher the price of a good, the smaller is the quantity demanded . . .

Demand curve and demand schedule

You are now going to study the demand curve, one of two parts of the most important model in economics.

Before going any further, you need to understand a critical distinction between *demand* and *quantity demanded*. The term *demand* refers to the entire relationship between the quantity demanded and the price of a good, illustrated by the demand curve and the demand schedule. The term *quantity demanded* refers to the exact quantity demanded at a particular price, or a particular point on a demand curve.

Figure 3.1 shows the demand curve for music tapes. A *demand curve* shows the relationship between the quantity demanded of a good and its price, when all other influences on

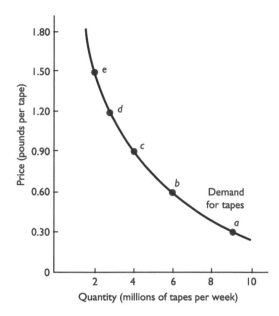

Figure 3.1 The demand curve

	Price (pounds per tape)	Quantity (millions of tapes per week)
a	0.30	9
b	0.60	6
c	0.90	4
d	1.20	3
e	1.50	2

Source: Parkin et al. (2003)

consumers' planned purchases remain the same. The table in Figure 3.1 is the demand schedule for tapes. A *demand schedule* lists the *quantities demanded* at each different price, when all the other influences on consumers' planned purchases – such as the prices of related goods, income, expected future prices, population and preferences remain the same. For example, if the price of a tape is 30 pence, the quantity demanded is 9 million tapes a week. If the price of a tape is £1.50, the quantity demanded is 2 million tapes a week. The other rows of the table show us the quantities demanded at prices between 60 pence and £1.20.

The demand curve is a graph of the demand schedule with quantity demanded on the horizontal axis and price on the vertical axis. The points on the demand curve labelled a through to e are plotted from the rows of the demand schedule.

Willingness and ability to pay

Another way of looking at the demand curve is as a willingness-and-ability-to-pay curve that measures marginal benefit. It tells us the highest price that someone is willing and able to pay for the last unit bought. If a small quantity is available, the highest price that someone is willing and able to pay for one more unit is high. But as the quantity available increases, the marginal benefit of each additional unit falls and the highest price offered falls along the demand curve.

In Figure 3.1, if 9 million tapes are bought each week, the highest price that someone is willing to pay for the 9 millionth tape is 30 pence. But if only 2 million tapes are bought each week, someone is willing to pay £1.50 for the last tape bought.

A change in demand

When any factor that influences buying plans changes, other than the price of the good, there is a change in demand. Figure 3.2 illustrates one such change – an increase in demand. When demand increases, the demand curve shifts to the right and the quantity demanded

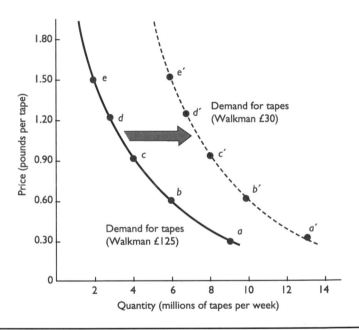

	Original demand schedule (Walkman £125)			New demand schedule (Walkman £30)	
	Price (pounds per tape)	**Quantity (millions of tapes per week)**		**Price (pounds per tape)**	**Quantity (millions of tapes per week)**
a	0.30	9	a′	0.30	13
b	0.60	6	b′	0.60	10
c	0.90	4	c′	0.90	8
d	1.20	3	d′	1.20	7
e	1.50	2	e′	1.50	6

Figure 3.2 An increase in demand

Source: adapted from Parkin et al. (2003)

is greater at each price. For example, at a price of £1.50 on the original demand curve, the quantity demanded is 2 million tapes per week.

On the new (dashed) demand curve, the quantity demanded is 6 million tapes per week. The quantity demanded is higher at every price.

Let's expand the model of demand to look at how these other factors influence demand.

1 Prices of related goods

The quantity of any goods and services that consumers plan to buy depends in part on the price of related goods and services. There are two types: substitutes and complements.

A substitute is a good that can be used in place of another good ... tapes have many substitutes – mini disks, CDs, radio and television broadcasts and live concerts. If the price of one of these substitutes increases, people economize on its use and buy more tapes ...

A complement is a good used in conjunction with another good ... Tapes have complements: Walkmans, tape recorders and stereo tape decks. If the price of one of these complements increases, people buy fewer tapes ...

2 Income

... Other things remaining the same, when income increases, consumers buy more of most goods, and when income decreases, they buy less of most goods ... Goods for which demand increases as income increases are called normal goods. Goods for which demand decreases when income increases are called inferior goods ...

3 Expected future prices

If the price of a good is expected to rise in the future, and if the good can be stored, the opportunity cost of obtaining the good for future use is lower now than it will be when the price has increased. So people substitute over time. They buy more of the good before the expected price rise and the demand for the good increases. Similarly, if the price of a good is expected to fall in the future, the opportunity cost of the good in the present is high relative to what is expected. So again, people substitute over time. They buy less of the good before its price is expected to fall, so the demand for the good now decreases.

4 Population

Demand also depends on the size and the age structure of the population. Other things remaining the same, the larger the population, the greater is the demand for all goods and services, and the smaller the population, the smaller is the demand for all goods and services. Also, other things remaining the same, the larger the proportion of the population in a given age group, the greater is the demand for the types of goods and services used by that age group.

5 Preferences

Finally, demand depends on consumer preferences. *Preferences* are an individual's attitudes towards and tastes for goods and services ... Preferences are shaped by past experience, genetic factors, advertising information, religious beliefs, and other cultural and social factors.

Movement along versus a shift of the demand curve

Changes in the factors that influence buyers' plans cause either a movement along the demand curve or a shift of the demand curve.

Movement along the demand curve

If the price of a good changes but everything else remains the same, there is a movement along the demand curve. For example, if the price of a tape changes from 90 pence to £1.50, the result is a movement along the demand curve, from point c to point e in Figure 3.1. The negative slope of the demand curve reveals that a decrease in the price of a good or service increases the quantity demanded – the law of demand.

A shift of the demand curve

If the price of a good remains constant but some other influence on buyers' plans changes, there is a change in demand for that good. We illustrate a change in demand as a shift of the demand curve . . . Figure 3.2 illustrates such a shift . . .

A change in demand versus a change in quantity demanded

A point on the demand curve shows the quantity demanded at a given price. A movement along the demand curve shows a change in the quantity demanded. The entire demand curve shows demand. A shift of the demand curve shows a change in demand.

Having learned about demand, the next activity provides an opportunity to apply the concepts to a health care example.

✎ Activity 3.1

1 Suppose that there is a health promotion programme advocating regular dental check-ups (for which people must pay directly). What do you think would be the effect on quantity demanded, *ceteris paribus*? Mark this effect on Figure 3.3, labelling it clearly.

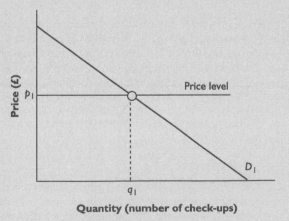

Figure 3.3 The demand for dental health checks

2 Suppose that the dental clinic relocates to an area outside the city such that it is far from the majority of the population, *ceteris paribus*. Mark this effect on Figure 3.3, labelling it clearly.

Feedback

1 The health promotion programme, if effective, will result in an increased preference for dental check-ups. This means that quantity demanded increases at each price level – that is, the demand curve shifts to the right (from D_1 to D_2 on Figure 3.4).

2 If the clinic becomes more distant from the people then this means that travel to the clinic becomes more expensive in terms of time and transport costs. Travel to the clinic can be considered a *complement* to the check-up. The increasing cost of travel will result in a decrease in quantity demanded for the check-up at all prices. The demand curve shifts to the left (from D_1 to D_3 in Figure 3.4).

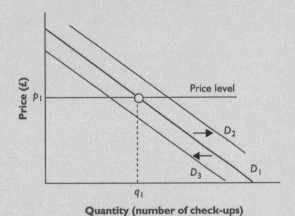

Figure 3.4 Changes in the demand for dental health checks

Activity 3.2

1 Suppose that the price charged for a dental check-up falls, *ceteris paribus*, from p_1 to p_2. Mark the effect on Figure 3.5.
2 If people's income falls, what would be the effect on demand for dental check-ups, *ceteris paribus*? Again mark the change on Figure 3.5.

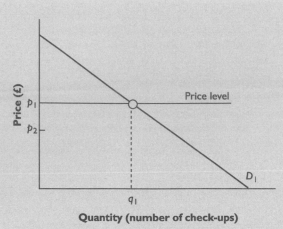

Figure 3.5 The demand for dental health checks

Feedback

1 This fall in price can be represented by a movement along the demand curve. As the demand curve slopes downwards, quantity demanded increases (from q_1 to q_2 in Figure 3.6).

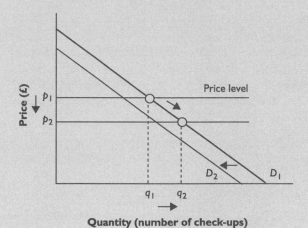

Figure 3.6 Changes in the demand for dental health checks

2 If a dental check-up is a *normal good* (and you have no reason to believe it is not) then the fall in income will result in a decrease in quantity demanded at all prices. Hence the demand curve shifts to the left (from D_1 to D_2 in Figure 3.6).

Demand and individual behaviour

So far, you have learned about demand in quite an abstract way. Demand has been interpreted either as:

- the quantity of a good that people plan to purchase at a given price; or
- the highest value (where value implies willingness to pay) placed on each unit of a good.

The next edited extract by Parkin *et al.* (2003) discusses the assumptions regarding the behaviour of individuals that underlie demand theory.

 Individual demand and market demand

An individual's consumption choices are determined by many factors, and we can model the impact of these factors using two new concepts: budget line and preferences.

Budget line

In this model of individual consumption, choices are constrained by income and by the prices of goods and services. We will assume that each individual has a given amount of income to spend, that everyone consumes all the goods they purchase within the relevant time period, and that individuals cannot influence the prices of the goods and services they buy.

The limits to individual consumption choices are described by a *budget line*. To make the concept of the individual's budget line as clear as possible, we'll consider a simplified example of one individual – Lisa – and her choice. Lisa has an income of £30 a month to spend. She spends her income on two goods – cinema films and cola. Cinema tickets cost £6 each; cola costs £3 for a six-pack. If Lisa spends all of her income, she will reach the limits to her consumption of films and cola.

In Figure 3.7, each row of the table shows affordable ways for Lisa to see cinema films and buy cola packs . . . These consumption possibilities are graphed as points *a* to *f* in Figure 3.7 . . .

Preferences and utility

How does Lisa divide her £30 between these two goods? The answer depends on her likes and dislikes or her preferences. Economists use the concept of utility to describe preferences. The benefit or satisfaction that a person gets from the consumption of a good or service is called utility. But what exactly is utility and in what units can we measure it? Utility is an abstract concept and its units are arbitrary. The concept of utility helps us make predictions about consumption choices in much the same way that the concept of temperature helps us make predictions about physical phenomena. It has to be admitted, though, that the marginal utility theory is not as precise as the theory that enables us to predict when water will turn to ice or steam.

Let's now see how we can use the concept of utility to describe preferences.

Total utility

Total utility is the total benefit or satisfaction that a person gets from the consumption of goods and services. Total utility depends on the person's level of consumption – more

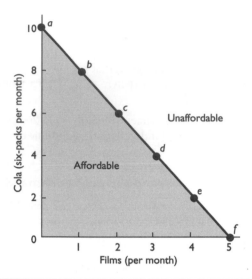

Possibility	Expenditure			
	Films		Cola	
	Quantity	Expensive (pounds)	Quantity (six-packs)	Expenditure (pounds)
a	0	0	10	30
b	1	6	8	24
c	2	12	6	18
d	3	18	4	12
e	4	24	2	6
f	5	30	0	0

Figure 3.7 Consumption possibilities

Source: Parkin et al. (2003)

consumption generally gives more total utility. Table 3.1 shows Lisa's total utility from consuming different quantities of cinema films and cola. If she does not go to the cinema, she gets no utility from seeing films. If she goes once a month, she gets 50 units of utility. As the number of visits in a month increases, her total utility increases so that if she sees 10 films a month, she gets 250 units of total utility. The other part of the table shows Lisa's total utility from cola. If she drinks no cola, she gets no utility from cola. As the amount of cola she drinks rises, her total utility increases.

Marginal utility

Marginal utility is the change in total utility resulting from a one-unit increase in the quantity of a good consumed. The table in Figure 3.8 shows the calculation of Lisa's marginal utility from seeing films. When her consumption of films increases from 4 to 5 a month, her total utility from films increases from 150 units to 175 units. Thus for Lisa,

Table 3.1 Lisa's total utility from films and cola

Films		Films	
Quantity per month	Total utility	Quantity (six-packs per month)	Total utility
0	0	0	0
1	50	1	75
2	88	2	117
3	121	3	153
4	150	4	181
5	175	5	206
6	196	6	225
7	214	7	243
8	229	8	260
9	241	9	276
10	250	10	291
11	256	11	305
12	259	12	318
13	261	13	330
14	262	14	341

Source: Parkin et al. (2003)

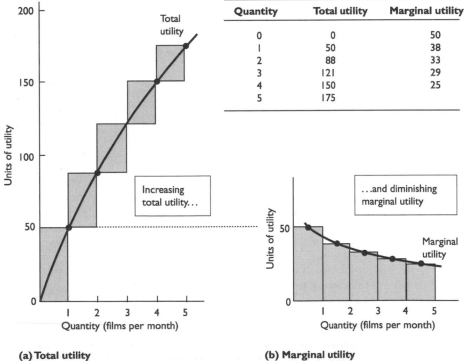

Quantity	Total utility	Marginal utility
0	0	50
1	50	38
2	88	33
3	121	29
4	150	25
5	175	

(a) Total utility

(b) Marginal utility

Figure 3.8 Total utility and marginal utility

Source: Parkin et al. (2003)

the marginal utility of seeing a fifth film each month is 25 units. Notice that marginal utility appears midway between the quantities of consumption. It does so because it is the *change* in consumption from 4 to 5 films that produces the marginal utility of 25 units. The table displays calculations of marginal utility for each level of film consumption.

Figure 3.8(a) illustrates the total utility that Lisa gets from seeing films. As you can see, the more films Lisa sees in a month, the more total utility she gets. Part (b) illustrates her marginal utility. This graph tells us that as Lisa sees more films, the marginal utility that Lisa gets from seeing films decreases. For example, her marginal utility from the first film is 50 units, from the second 38 units, and from the third 33 units. We call this decrease in marginal utility as the consumption of a good increases the principle of diminishing marginal utility . . .

Activity 3.3

Make notes on how diminishing marginal utility relates to various elements of health services. You could begin by thinking of the cases of surgical operations and care of the chronically sick.

Feedback

With surgical operations you might find that there is only a small amount of additional utility attributed to additional operations. An appendectomy, for example, yields a large amount of utility but it is a once-only intervention. With reconstructive plastic surgery, additional operations may provide additional utility but probably in ever-decreasing amounts.

Care of the chronically sick may provide one exception to the law in as much as after every day of care the next day's care is valued exactly the same. However, on any one day there will be diminishing utility associated with additional units of care given.

Consumer surplus

Now that you have an understanding of the concept of marginal utility, you need to consider the distinction between value and price. The following extract by Parkin *et al.* (2003) addresses this and introduces the concept of consumer surplus – the value placed on goods by consumers minus the cost to the consumers.

Efficiency, price and value

When Lisa allocates her limited budget to maximize utility, she is using her resources efficiently. Any other allocation of her budget would waste some resources.

We know that if Lisa allocates her limited budget to maximize utility, she will be on her demand curve for each good. A demand curve is a description of the planned quantity demanded at each price when utility is maximized. We also know that the demand curve shows Lisa's willingness to pay. It tells us her marginal benefit – the benefit from consuming an extra unit of a good. You can now see a deeper meaning in the concept of marginal benefit.

Marginal benefit is the maximum price that a consumer is willing to pay for an extra unit of a good or service when utility is maximized.

More than 200 years ago, Adam Smith posed a paradox: water, which is essential to life itself, costs little, but diamonds, which are useless compared with water, are expensive. Why? Adam Smith could not solve the paradox. Not until the theory of marginal utility had been developed could anyone give a satisfactory answer.

You can solve Adam Smith's puzzle by distinguishing between *total* utility and *marginal* utility. The total utility that we get from water is enormous. But remember, the more we consume of something, the smaller is its marginal utility. We use so much water that the marginal utility – the benefit we get from one more glass of water – diminishes to a tiny value. Diamonds, on the other hand, have a small total utility relative to water, but because we buy few diamonds, they have a high marginal utility.

When an individual has maximized total utility, he or she has allocated his or her budget in the way that makes the marginal utility per pound spent equal for all goods. That is, the marginal utility from a good divided by the price of the good is equal for all goods. This equality of marginal utilities per pound spent holds true for diamonds and water. Diamonds have a high price and a high marginal utility. Water has a low price and a low marginal utility. When the high marginal utility of diamonds is divided by the high price of diamonds, the result is a number that equals the low marginal utility of water divided by the low price of water. The marginal utility per pound spent is the same for diamonds as for water.

Another way to think about the paradox of value is through the concept of *consumer surplus*. Figure 3.9 explains the paradox of value using this concept. The supply of water (part a) is perfectly elastic at price Pw, so the quantity of water consumed is Qw and the consumer surplus from water is the shaded area. The supply of diamonds (part b) is perfectly inelastic at quantity Q_D so the price of diamonds is P_D and consumer surplus is the smaller shaded area. Water is cheap but brings a large consumer surplus, while diamonds are expensive but bring only a small consumer surplus.

Consumer surplus – an example

Consumer surplus is the value placed on goods by consumers minus the cost to the consumers. The area under the demand curve represents the value placed on the good by consumers. The area under the price line represents the cost to the consumers. Hence the consumer surplus is the area between the demand curve and the price line. The dotted area in the Figure 3.10 indicates the consumer surplus associated with the original position.

The consumer surplus after the health promotion programme is indicated by the enlarged dotted area shown in Figure 3.11. The gain in consumer surplus is therefore the dotted area to the right of D_1, the original demand curve.

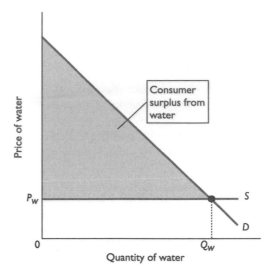

(a) Water

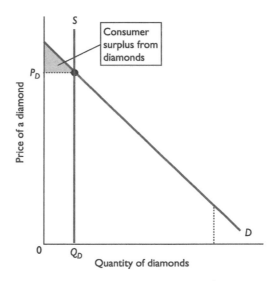

(b) Diamonds

Figure 3.9 The paradox of value

Source: Parkin et al. (2003)

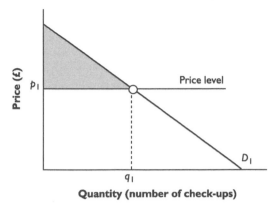

Figure 3.10 The demand for dental health checks showing consumer surplus

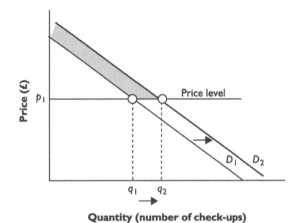

Figure 3.11 The demand for dental health checks after health promotion campaign

✏ Activity 3.4

Go back to Figures 3.4 and 3.6 and shade in the areas that represent the *changes* in consumer surplus as a result of:

1 The relocation of the dental clinic to an area outside the city (mark this on Figure 3.4).
2 The fall in the price charged for a dental check-up, *ceteris paribus*, from p_1 to p_2 (mark this effect on Figure 3.6).
3 Again on Figure 3.6, mark the change in consumer surplus if people's income falls.

Feedback

1 The *loss* of consumer surplus associated with the change of location (Figure 3.4) is indicated by the tinted area in Figure 3.12.

2 & 3 The *gain* in consumer surplus associated with the drop in price shown in Figure 3.6 is indicated by the dark tinted area in Figure 3.13, while the light tinted area indicates the *loss* of consumer surplus associated with the fall in income.

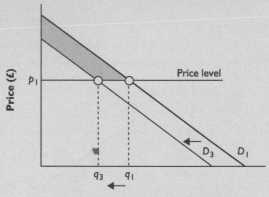

Figure 3.12 Changes in consumer surplus resulting from a change in demand

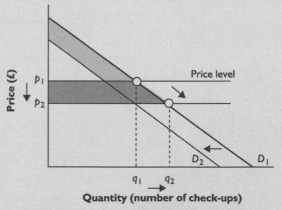

Figure 3.13 Changes in consumer surplus resulting from a change in demand

You will compare the different levels of consumer surplus associated with different types of market structure in Chapter 11. Besides its use in comparing market structures, the concept of consumer surplus is fundamental in cost–benefit analysis where benefits are defined as net increases in consumer surplus.

The demand for health care

As you have seen, demand requires that a person desires the service, that they can afford to pay for that service and that they are willing to pay for it. The (normative) need for health care is the care that practitioners believe is necessary for a person to remain or become healthy. On some occasions the patient decides they require health care (felt need) but their doctor decides that they could not benefit from such care. On other occasions, the doctor would have considered there to be a medical need but the patient does not consult their doctor because they prefer not to have treatment or do not recognize the need. Even if patients are as well informed as their doctor, it is quite possible that their demand is different from their need.

The use of services depends on the availability of services (the supply side) as well as the demand. In Chapter 4 you will see that when a market is 'in equilibrium' then demand equals use. Out of equilibrium it is possible for demand to exceed use. The following factors influence the demand for health care:

- need (as perceived by the patient);
- patient preferences;
- income;
- price/user charge;
- travel cost and waiting time;
- quality of care (as perceived by the patient).

Use depends on demand and accessibility. If planners allocate resources on the basis of need instead of demand then they may find that some services are under-used while other services are over-subscribed.

 Activity 3.5

From what you have read in this chapter and from your experience, in what ways do you think that the demand for health care is different from the demand for other goods and services?

 Feedback

Here are some ways in which the demand for health care is more complicated than the simple model of demand presented in this chapter:

1 One difference is that we demand health care not because we get satisfaction out of it *per se*. We demand it because we get satisfaction from the activities that we can do when we are healthy (that is, working and leisure activities). Demand for health services is therefore a *derived demand*.

2 The demand for health care is often for a single one-off intervention rather than multiple or repeated requests as occurs with the consumption of tapes.

3 Patients' perceptions of their need and of their capacity to benefit, both of which shape their demand, may be strongly influenced by their doctor – the supplier of health care.

4 It is generally assumed in economics that consumers are able to make informed decisions about their consumption patterns. Consumers are said to be 'sovereign'. However, in the case of health care, consumers often delegate this decision making power to health professionals who are much better informed.

5 Another complication relates to the fact that health care is extremely *heterogeneous*. Every patient has a slightly different combination of ailments and symptoms, and therefore every patient needs to buy a slightly different package of care. This means that effectively there is no overall market price.

6 A major difference is that payment for many health services comes, partly or wholly, from a third party (either an insurance company or a government).

Some aspects of health care may fit the simple demand model better than others. Consider, for example, the market for aspirin – a person with a headache knows with a relatively high degree of certainty the effects of consuming an aspirin. They can buy aspirins according to their preferences and without going through a third party. In Chapter 7 you will look at some more complicated models of demand but before that you will look at the supply of health care and at how prices are determined in markets.

Just from examining the simple model of demand it should be clear that the estimation of demand can sometimes be useful in health planning because:

- it allows you to predict, budget for, and possibly manipulate usage of health services;
- it gives you an estimate of the value of different health services to consumers (consumer surplus; cost–benefit analysis);
- it informs you about the effects, on different sections of the population, of imposing price changes, for example through user charges and taxes. (You will look at this in more detail in Chapter 6.)

A few final words on the subject of health service demand must be devoted to the subject of equity (or fairness). The provision of health care is seen as fundamentally important by many cultures. In particular, many health systems emphasize the need to supply health care regardless of people's incomes and ability to pay. It could be pointed out that shelter from the elements, warm clothing, nutritious food, clean water and clean air are all at least as important as health care in maintaining health. Nevertheless, equity plays an important part in health planning (this will be covered in Chapter 12). The ability of health systems to be equitable is inevitably restrained by the need to finance health services and achieve efficiency.

Summary

You have learned about the demand function, how to illustrate demand by way of a graph and the factors that influence demand (prices of related goods, income, expected future prices, population and preferences). You have seen how demand changes with changes in individual behaviour, influenced both by total and marginal utility. Finally you learned about consumer surplus. You will now learn about the other key function, supply.

Reference

Parkin M, Powell M and Mathews K (2003). *Economics* (5th edn). Harlow: Addison-Wesley.

4 Supply and price determination

Overview

In the previous chapter you looked at the determinants of demand. In this chapter you will look at the other side of the market, supply. You will identify the determinants of supply and discover how the forces of supply and demand interact to determine the market price. Finally, you will examine the consequences of government intervention (price regulation and subsidy) for the dental market that was introduced in Chapter 3.

Learning objectives

After working through this chapter, you will be able to:

- list the factors which influence the supply of a product
- show graphically how changes in supply factors influence supply
- explain how price is determined by the forces of supply and demand
- list some advantages of markets as a method of resource allocation
- give examples of health care markets
- describe the consequences of price regulation, subsidies and indirect taxation by the government

Key terms

Market equilibrium A situation where the price in a given market is such that the quantity demanded is equal to the quantity supplied.

Operational (technical, productive) efficiency Using only the minimum necessary resources to finance purchase and deliver a particular activity or set of activities (ie avoiding waste).

Quantity supplied The amount of a good that producers plan to supply at a given price during an identified period.

Subsidy A payment made by the government to a producer or producers where the level of payment depends on the exact level of output.

Supply curve A graph showing the relationship between the quantity supplied of a good and its price when all other variables are unchanged.

The supply function

In the previous chapter you were told that health service use is determined by supply as well as demand. The following extract by Martin Green (1995) starts by describing the influence of supply, using the example of osteopathy.

 ### The free market approach to health care

Supply – analysing sellers' behaviour

We assume that osteopaths want to maximise their profits. What are profits and how can they be maximised? Osteopaths earn money (revenue) by selling their services e.g. by massaging away muscular strains. Out of this revenue they need to pay for the factors they use to produce the treatment (costs) e.g. pay their receptionist, pay the rent or pay for a new ultrasound machine. Profit is the excess of revenue over costs.

Seeking to maximise profits leads each osteopath to want to sell more care at higher prices. There is a reliable and predictable positive relationship between price and quantity supplied. Formally, supply is defined as the quantity of a good or service that sellers are willing and able to sell at every conceivable price. This positive relationship is shown graphically by the supply curve. If the price changes there is a movement along the supply curve (Figure 4.1).

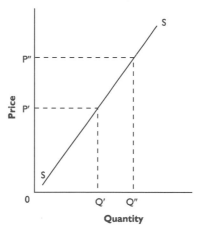

Figure 4.1 The supply curve for osteopathy treatments
SS is the supply curve for treatments. At price P′ osteopaths are prepared to sell Q′ treatments. When the price rises to P″ osteopaths are prepared to sell Q″ treatments.
Source: Green (1995)

If the level of factor costs change (e.g. nurses wages go up or rent becomes less expensive) then the supply curve will shift (Figures 4.2 and 4.3).

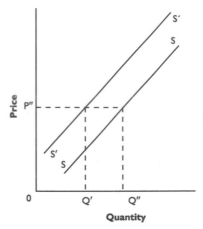

Figure 4.2 Nurses' wages rise
SS is the initial supply curve for treatments. Now nurses' wages rise, pushing up osteopaths'
costs. Osteopaths react by being prepared to supply less treatments at each price. The supply
curve shifts inwards to S"S". At a price such as P" osteopaths are now only prepared to sell Q'
treatments rather than Q".

Source: Green (1995)

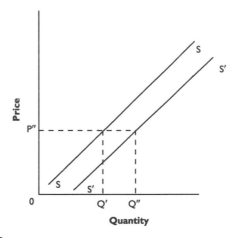

Figure 4.3 Rent falls
SS is the initial supply curve for treatments. Now rents fall and osteopaths react by being
prepared to supply more treatments at each price. The supply curve shifts outwards to S'S'. At a
price such as P' osteopaths are now prepared to sell Q" treatments rather than Q'.

Source: Green (1995)

The market

We can now put the demand and supply together to get a picture of the market for
osteopathy. This is shown by Figure 4.4. Notice that there is only one price at which the
quantity of treatments people want to buy is the same as the quantity the osteopaths want
to sell. This is called the equilibrium price (P' on Figure 4.4). Equilibrium means a state of
rest where there is no pressure for change.

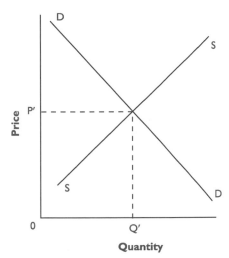

Figure 4.4 The market for osteopathy treatments
DD shows how many treatments consumers wish to purchase at each price while SS shows
how many osteopaths are prepared to sell. Q′, P′ are the equilibrium quantity and price.
Source: Green (1995)

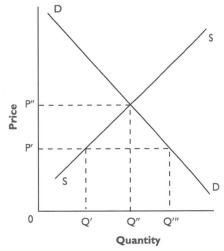

Figure 4.5 Excess demand
At P′ consumers demand Q‴ but osteopaths are only prepared to supply Q′. Excess demand
leads to the price being bid up to P″.
Source: Green (1995)

At any other price either buyers or sellers are dissatisfied and act to change the price.
Figures 4.5 and 4.6 illustrate this. If there is excess demand consumers bid up the price
while if there is excess supply sellers cut the price. Both these processes continue until
equilibrium is reached. So the free interaction of buyers and sellers in the market automatically leads to a single price at which the quantity traded 'clears' the market i.e. the
quantity supplied equals the quantity demanded.

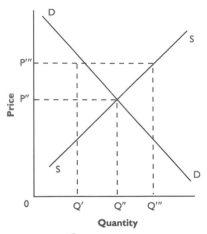

Figure 4.6 Excess supply
At P‴ osteopaths wish to sell Q‴ but consumers only wish to buy Q′. Excess supply leads to prices being cut to P″.

Source: Green (1995)

How the market responds to a shock

A shock is anything which moves a market out of equilibrium. Suppose people's incomes rise: how will the osteopathy market react? Figure 4.7 illustrates this situation. This process will occur whenever there is a shock leading to either a shift in demand or supply.

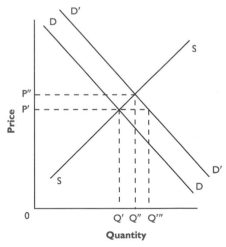

Figure 4.7 Impact of increase in income on market for osteopathy
DD and SS are the initial demand and supply curves and P′/Q′ is the initial equilibrium. The increase in income shifts the demand curve outwards (DD to D′D′) reflecting the fact that osteopathy is a normal good. This shift in demand throws the market out of equilibrium. Now people want to buy Q‴ treatments at price P′ but the osteopaths are still only prepared to sell Q′. The result is excess demand and unsatisfied buyers who react by 'bidding up' the price. The market regains equilibrium at price and quantity P″/Q″.

Source: Green (1995)

The market will move out of equilibrium with either excess demand or excess supply appearing. Price will adjust until equilibrium is regained.

Now, suppose you want to increase the quantity of dental services provided in your country. In the short term this will require dentists and their staff to work longer hours. Because they value their leisure time they might insist on a higher wage to work these longer, less sociable hours. The wage paid must reflect the opportunity cost of the lost leisure time. In the long term, you might be able to increase the number of dentists. To do this, you would have to raise dentists' wages to tempt people away from other career paths and into dental school. So in both the short term and long term the implication is that to increase output requires making use of more expensive resources. Therefore larger quantities can only be supplied at higher prices.

Activity 4.1

Figure 4.8 shows the supply curve for dental check-ups in a hypothetical city.

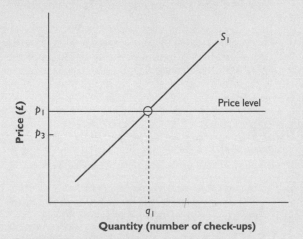

Figure 4.8 The supply of dental health checks

1 Suppose that there is an increase in the number of qualified dentists. What do you think would be the effect on quantity supplied, *ceteris paribus*? Mark and label this effect on Figure 4.8.
2 Now, suppose that the price charged for a dental check-up falls from p_1 to p_3, *ceteris paribus*. Mark the effect on Figure 4.8.

Feedback

1 The increase in dentistry graduates is an increase in the number of providers of dental services, including dental check-ups. Other things remaining equal, this means that quantity supplied increases at each price level – that is, the supply curve shifts to the right (a shift from S_1 to S_2 on Figure 4.9, resulting in an increase in quantity supplied at that price from q_1 to q_2).

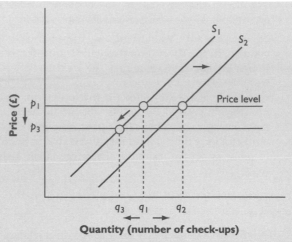

Figure 4.9 Changes in the supply of dental health checks

2 This fall in price can be represented by a downward movement on the supply curve. Dentists are willing to provide fewer check-ups at the lower price. This is shown in Figure 4.9 by the decrease in quantity supplied from q_1 to q_3.

Activity 4.2

Considering the dental practice described in Activity 4.1, what would be the effect on the supply curve in the following circumstances?

1 Suppose that there is a movement of dental clinics to an area that is outside the city. This means that dentists no longer have to pay the high rents of the city centre. Mark this effect on Figure 4.10, *ceteris paribus*.

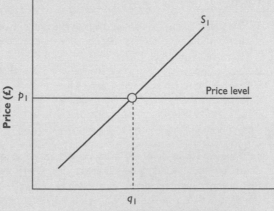

Figure 4.10 The supply of dental health checks

2 If receptionists' salaries increase, what would be the effect on supply of dental check-ups, *ceteris paribus*? Again mark the change on Figure 4.10.

 Feedback

1 The lower rent charge implies lower costs for all dental activities including check-ups. This means that the dentists will be prepared to supply more dental check-ups at each price level – that is, the supply curve shifts to the right (from S_1 to S_2 on Figure 4.11).

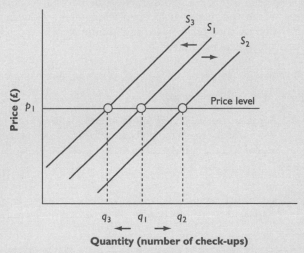

Figure 4.11 Changes in the supply of dental health checks

2 The higher wage of receptionists implies higher costs for all dental activity, including check-ups. This means that the dentists will be able to supply fewer dental check-ups at each price level – that is, the supply curve shifts to the left (from S_1 to S_3 on Figure 4.11).

The determination of price

You have read about how quantity demanded and quantity supplied respond to price changes. You will now learn how the forces of supply and demand interact to determine market price and market output.

Why do markets automatically move towards equilibrium? Suppose you have a situation where dentists are selling their services at charges above the market equilibrium charge. Here there will be a situation of excess supply. The quantity of dental services sold is less than the quantity dentists are willing to supply. The dentists still have to spend time in their surgery and pay their staff and rent but they are not selling many services so they find they are making a loss. The only way the dentist can sell extra services is to lower the charge. Gradually the charge will return to the equilibrium charge because only then are dentists selling the quantity of services that they want and making enough profit.

Suppose, alternatively, that dental charges are below the market equilibrium level. Here you have a situation of excess demand. The quantity of dental services supplied is less than the quantity demanded at current charge levels. Dentists find that they can sell all the services they want at the current charge level. There will be plenty of consumers who are prepared to pay more than the current charge level but are unable to buy because of the rationing caused by excess demand. Some consumers will offer the dentist a bribe in addition to the charge so that they can be seen quickly. Producers will realize that they can raise the charge and still sell all their output. Hence they increase dental charges and increase their profits. It is only when the market is in equilibrium that producers do not have an incentive to change their price. It is at equilibrium price that producers' profits (and consumers' utility) are maximized.

Activity 4.3

Suppose the market for dental check-ups is currently in equilibrium. What would happen to demand if the city's dental clinics were to relocate outside the city? Mark on Figure 4.12 the changes to the market equilibrium price and quantity.

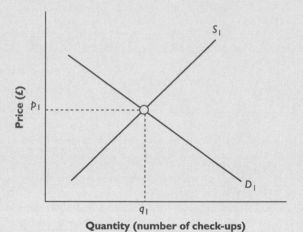

Figure 4.12 The market for dental health checks

Feedback

If the clinic becomes more distant from the people then this means that travel to the clinic becomes more expensive in terms of time and transport costs. The increasing cost of travel will result in a decrease in quantity demanded for the check-up at all prices. The demand curve shifts to the left.

In contrast, the effect of an increase in supply will be a fall in the equilibrium price (the dental charge) and so will be the effect of a fall in demand. Therefore the overall result of the relocation will be a fall in price. The overall effect on the quantity traded, however, is ambiguous because an increase in supply will, *ceteris paribus*, increase the quantity traded whereas a fall in demand, *ceteris paribus*, will decrease the quantity traded. One effect will partially offset the other. The overall result could be an increase, a decrease or no change in the quantity traded. It depends on the responsiveness of demand to the increase in travel costs and on the responsiveness of supply to the fall in costs. You will learn more about measuring and analysing responsiveness in the next chapter.

Markets for health care

Now that you have an idea of what determines supply and demand and of the concept of market equilibrium, you are going to consider the relevance of these theories to markets for health care.

The following extract by Martin Green (1995) discusses the key issues. Note that Pareto efficiency is the same as allocative efficiency. The term 'productive efficiency' is the same as operational efficiency and means that, for worthwhile programmes, the best use is made of the available resources to meet the programme's objective. This will be discussed more in Chapter 10.

The free market approach to health care (continued)

The market as allocation system

We have just demonstrated that our free market will automatically produce an equilibrium price and quantity. It is this which makes it a very powerful allocation system. This is what Adam Smith referred to as 'The Invisible Hand'.

Who decides how much osteopathy is to be produced? The answer is consumers. They go out and buy osteopathy treatments and the price they are prepared to pay sends signals to the osteopaths. The osteopaths respond by producing either more or less treatment. The market not only allocates resources automatically, it does so efficiently. Providing certain conditions are met, the free market will achieve a Pareto efficient allocation. How does price mechanism lead to a Pareto efficient allocation? For the consumer, the price measures the benefit or utility that the consumers expect to receive from consuming the unit. To be precise, the demand curve reflects the marginal utility (extra benefit) that consumers receive from consuming each unit. For the producer or seller, the price measures the cost of the resources involved in the production including the supplier's own time and effort. Again to be precise, the supply curve reflects the seller's marginal costs (the cost of producing one extra unit). Thus when a market is in equilibrium marginal benefit equals marginal cost. The benefit received from the last unit consumed will exactly equal the resource cost of producing that unit. This fulfils the condition for allocative efficiency. Producers chasing maximum profits will always choose the least cost combination of factors to produce a given output. Consequently, the free market will also be productively efficient.

Cosmetic surgery

How well does our theoretical model of a market explain what has been going on with cosmetic surgery? Clearly there is a demand – people are willing and able to pay for it [and there is] . . . evidence that the market is growing. Why is this happening? Firstly, changes in technology have reduced the costs of such treatment – shifting the supply curve outwards. Demand also seems to be growing. Why? A recent national survey found that one in four dislike their appearance suggesting that they would consider buying this kind of treatment if they could afford it. So consumers are likely to respond to the lower prices brought about by the shift in supply – a movement down the market demand curve. Another influence is almost certainly the growth in consumers' real income leading to an outward shift in the demand curve.

Suppliers have reacted to the growth of consumer demand in exactly the way our theory predicts . . . So our model has performed fairly well. But it suffers from being rather static.

A more dynamic view of the market

One thing the market is able to do very well is act as a powerful and efficient information system. Changes in consumers' tastes are quickly communicated to producers via market prices. The search for profits drives producers to offer new products or services and make them in more cost-effective ways. An example of this is the way in which consumers' concern over the link between high cholesterol and heart attacks has led to the appearance of cholesterol testing units at chemists and health food stores in the UK.

Competition and the need to respond to and, if possible, anticipate consumer demand lead to a system which provides the maximum choice for the lowest possible cost; a system which is flexible and dynamic but efficient.

Some economists such as Hayek, argue that in the real world most markets will be in a constant state of flux – adjusting towards equilibrium but rarely actually reaching it. In this analysis, it is the market's ability to act as an information system that is important rather than its ability to produce a single equilibrium price.

Take the market for cosmetic dental services. If the market was free and competitive, then different dentists would offer different mixes of service, and some dentists would be more skilful than others. The skilful dentists offering the services consumers want would have lots of customers and would be able to charge higher prices than their competitors. This would force the other dentists to modify the services they are selling to try to capture back the consumers. This process of competition would be continuous, particularly as other factors influencing demand and supply such as levels of income, or the state of technology are likely to be also changing.

 Activity 4.5

Try answering the following questions as fully as possible:

1   In this chapter, a hypothetical case study of a market for dental check-ups has been used. Can you think of any examples of markets for particular health services operating in your country?
2   What are the advantages of markets in the allocation of resources?
3   Are there ways in which the supply of health services in your country seems more complicated than the model given in this chapter?

⟲ **Feedback**

1 Markets tend to be used for services that are deemed non-essential, such as cosmetic surgery, or services that do not require the involvement of a health professional, such as simple drugs available in retail pharmacies, or for enhanced 'hotel' facilities when admitted to hospital.

2 Markets are a useful resource allocation mechanism for the following reasons:

a) In theory at least, markets automatically tend towards a situation of equilibrium where the output produced is exactly equal to the output used. You looked at this in the last activity.

b) Given a few specific requirements, markets will produce an output that is allocatively efficient – that is each unit of output is produced when the additional benefit it brings exceeds its cost. You will come back to allocative efficiency and the necessary conditions in Chapter 12.

c) The market is dynamic: it is a 'powerful and efficient information system'. Changes in people's preferences are quickly passed on to and acted on by producers. Likewise changes in the availability of and cost of resources are reflected in prices. Cheaper substitute resources are quickly opted for instead.

3 The supply of health services in practice is more complicated than the basic model of supply in the following respects:

a) The model of supply you have been reading about assumes that producers' sole aim is to maximize profits. However, producers of health care around the world include government agencies and non-profit organizations as well as profit-making firms.

b) Even where producers are largely private there is a lot of government intervention – subsidies, price regulation, public finance etc.

c) To talk of a supply of health care assumes that health care has an output that can be objectively measured. In fact, almost every individual patient receives a unique 'bundle' of services that makes up their treatment – health care is not a homogeneous product. It is very difficult to measure the inputs and the outputs of health care (especially quality of care).

d) Unlike manufactured goods, health care is provided by groups of professionals who provide training, regulations and ethical codes which will all affect the provision of health care.

Although these characteristics complicate the supply of health care, many of the implications of the basic model still hold. You will be returning to these complications from time to time during this book.

Regulating markets

You have seen that markets can be very dynamic and efficient mechanisms for the allocation of resources. You have also considered the ways in which markets are used to supply health services in your country. In the next couple of activities you will look at some of the ways in which governments can try to achieve policy objectives by manipulating or regulating markets.

Price regulation

As you have already seen, in market economies price is the mechanism through which markets achieve equilibrium. Using the example of the market for dental check-ups, suppose the Ministry of Health decides to limit the maximum price that can be charged (a *price ceiling*) so that poorer people can afford to go for a check-up. There are a number of possible consequences.

The effect of a price ceiling can be shown graphically as follows: a price ceiling (set below the market equilibrium) in the market for dental check-ups would cause the supply of check-ups (q_s on Figure 4.13) to fall as fewer dentists will want to provide them at the lower price.

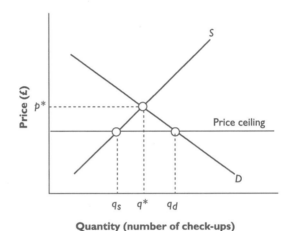

Figure 4.13 The market for dental health checks with a price ceiling

Quantity demanded, q_d, on the other hand, would increase as more people could afford them. This would result in excess demand, q_d–q_s. Patients would now have to incur additional search costs, looking for a dentist prepared to provide a check-up, and they would have to wait longer for an available appointment time. They might be faced with additional payments to the dentist, perhaps as under-the-table bribes or possibly as charges for hidden extras (waiting room use for example). These extra costs associated with consuming dental health checks might mean that poorer families are no more able to afford them than they were before the price ceiling was imposed.

One likely alternative is that instead of finding themselves faced with additional charges patients might find that the quality of the check-up diminishes. Perhaps the dentist spends less time on each check-up and is less thorough so that they can fit in more check-ups for the same cost. In health services where charges or budgets are held artificially low, quality of service is often found to be reduced.

Now assume that the Ministry of Health abandons its policy of dental charge ceilings. Suppose instead that the Ministry of Internal Affairs decides to impose a minimum wage for receptionists. Applying the same logic as in the example of price ceilings, what would be the consequences for dental receptionists and the market for dental services?

A minimum wage is an example of a *price floor*. A price floor is a law that restricts the price of a commodity falling below a specific level. A wage level is the price of labour. Its effects are shown in Figure 4.14.

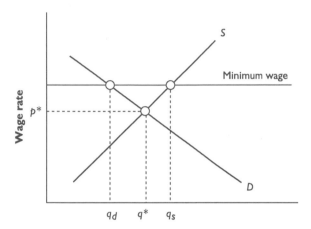

Figure 4.14 The market for dental receptionists with a price floor

You can see from the diagram that a price floor above the market equilibrium creates excess supply – far more people are prepared to work as dental reception-ists than dentists are prepared to hire. The effect is to reduce the number of receptionists employed or perhaps to reduce the number of paid hours. It will also impose search costs on individuals seeking receptionist work. It may also mean worse working conditions for those who are able to retain their positions. Perhaps they will be expected to work longer hours without additional pay. Some employers may illegally continue to pay wages that are below the minimum wage. If the minimum wage does effectively raise the costs of dental services then you would expect fewer services to be provided and the level of dental charges to rise.

The regulation of prices is problematic. Not only might a price ceiling have the opposite effect to the desired objective of raising service use, but it might also encourage corruption.

Taxes and subsidies

The Ministry of Health is still interested in increasing the number of check-ups. As a replacement for the unsuccessful price ceiling policy the Ministry is considering subsidizing dental health checks by £5 per check-up. A subsidy is a payment made by the government to a producer or producers (in this case dentists) where the level of payment depends on the exact level of output. A dentist providing 100 check-ups per month will receive a payment from the Ministry of £500 per month. The subsidy has the same effect as a fall in cost because from the perspective of the producer this is exactly what it is. Hence the supply curve shifts downwards (i.e. to the right) as a result of the subsidy. More precisely, the supply curve shifts downwards by exactly £5 at each output level – see Figure 4.15.

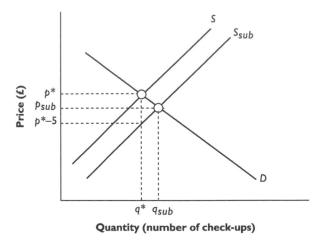

Figure 4.15 Effect of a subsidy on the market for dental health checks

Therefore the effect of the subsidy is to lower price and increase output. Note, though, that the fall in price is not as large as the subsidy. The benefits of the subsidy are distributed between the consumers of dental check-ups and the dentists.

By how much the price falls and by how much output increases depends upon the responsiveness of demand and supply to price. For example, Figure 4.16 shows a

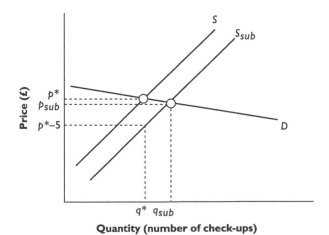

Figure 4.16 Effect of a subsidy on the market for dental health checks where demand is very responsive to price

market where demand is very responsive to price (i.e. the demand curve is relatively flat).

In this case, output increases considerably. Most of the subsidy is absorbed by the dentists so that the price does not increase very much. Alternatively if demand is much less responsive to price (i.e. the demand curve is relatively steep) as in Figure 4.17 then the number of dental checks does not increase very much although price drops substantially.

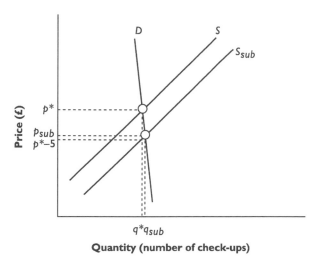

Figure 4.17 Effect of a subsidy on the market for dental health checks where demand is less responsive to price

The Ministry might want to collect some data to try to estimate the responsiveness of demand. If demand is very responsive then only a small per unit subsidy is required to substantially increase the number of dental health checks taken every year.

Activity 4.6

The Ministry of Health has conducted a survey which suggested that dental check-ups are highly responsive to price. They decide to go ahead with the subsidy but the minister of finance insists that a new sales tax will have to be levied to pay for the subsidy. A sales tax is a payment extracted from producers by the government that depends on the level of output. The minister of health decides to levy a tax on sweets arguing that this can be justified because sweets are responsible for much tooth decay.

1   Show graphically, in Figure 4.18, the effects of the sales tax in the market for sweets, assuming that this tax will deter the consumption of sweets.
2   Considering your graph, do you think taxing sweets is an effective policy? Make your answer as full as possible, giving reasons for your conclusion.

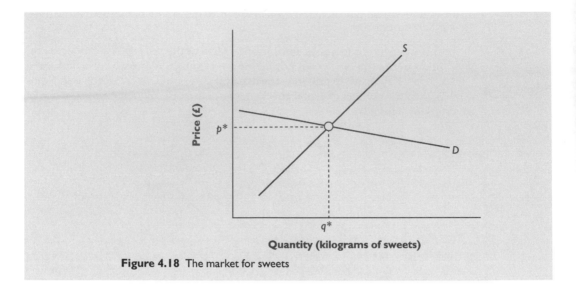

Figure 4.18 The market for sweets

↻ Feedback

1 The sales tax has exactly the opposite effect of a subsidy – that is, it shifts the supply curve upwards (to the left), as in Figure 4.19.

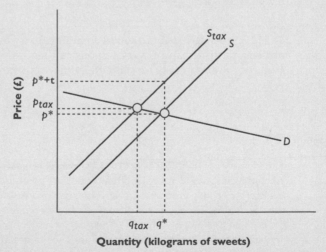

Figure 4.19 The market for sweets – effect of a sales tax

2 Quantity traded decreases and price increases. In this example you can see that demand is very responsive to price. This is not really surprising. Sweets have many close substitutes (chocolate, cake, biscuits, fruit etc.) so when the price rises people find a

substitute. Because demand is so responsive, price changes little so that producers have to absorb the tax and quantity traded falls dramatically. Such a tax is highly distortionary; the tax causes a major change in the allocation of resources. Such a sales tax introduced for the purposes of raising revenue should only be levied on commodities that are less responsive to price. Whether the government decides to go ahead with the tax or not may depend on where the sweets are manufactured. If most sweets are imported then a policy that is hard on the sweet industry will not be too unpopular with the government. There may be health benefits although these would be offset by increased consumption of close substitutes such as cakes.

There is another reason why economists might urge caution in deciding to impose a sales tax. People do get utility from consuming sweets. The act of imposing the tax reduces consumption of sweets and lowers consumer surplus. In general terms, at the aggregate level of the economy, taxes and subsidies may distort the allocation of resources, lower welfare and therefore reduce allocative efficiency. Of course this may be a price worth paying if it means that policy objectives are met. Economists employ a tool called cost–benefit analysis to decide if the costs associated with a policy are fully compensated by the associated benefits. You will learn more about cost–benefit analysis in Chapter 18.

You have seen that the responsiveness of supply and demand are important determinants of the effectiveness of government regulation of markets. In the next chapter you will look at how economists measure responsiveness and how these measures can be used for policy analysis.

Summary

In this chapter you have learned about the supply function and the effect various factors have on the supply curve. You also learned how prices are determined and about the concept of market equilibrium. Finally you learned about the ways governments can regulate markets through price regulation and the imposition of taxes and subsidies.

Reference

Green M (1995) *The economics of health care*. London: Office of Health Economics.

5 Elasticity of demand

Overview

In Chapter 4 you looked at the determinants of demand and supply. In this and the next two chapters you will take a more in-depth look at demand. First, in this chapter, you will find out how to measure the responsiveness of demand to changes in price. Then in Chapter 6 you will look at how such measurements can be used to inform the levying of taxes for health promotion purposes and the setting of user charges. In Chapter 7 you will learn about the concepts of risk and uncertainty, and how to model the demand for health care.

Learning objectives

After working through this chapter, you will be able to:

- **define price elasticity of demand (PED)**
- **calculate PED over a portion of the demand curve**
- **describe the relationship between PED and revenue**
- **decide when an increase in price will increase revenue**

Key terms

Cross-elasticity of demand The percentage change in quantity demanded of the commodity divided by the percentage change in the price of another related commodity.

Income elasticity of demand The percentage change in quantity demanded of the commodity divided by the percentage change in population income.

Price elastic When quantity demanded is relatively responsive to price changes. When price elasticity of demand is greater than one.

Price elasticity of demand The relative responsiveness of the quantity demanded of a good to a change in its price. It is the percentage change in quantity demanded divided by the associated percentage change in price.

Price elasticity of supply The percentage change in quantity supplied of a commodity divided by the percentage change in the commodity's price.

Price inelastic When quantity demanded is relatively unresponsive to price changes. When price elasticity of demand is less than one.

The responsiveness of demand

In Chapter 2 you learned how economists use models to estimate the response to changes in certain factors. The example used was the production function of a hospital. You learned how such a relationship could be represented by equations and graphs. You also learned how the slope is a measure of responsiveness. If you are not comfortable with this material it will help to go over it again before continuing with this chapter, where you will learn about another measure of responsiveness, elasticity, and you will see how it can be applied to the demand function.

 Activity 5.1

The following edited extract from Michael Parkin and colleagues (2003) explains about elasticity of demand, taking oil and the oil producers' organization, OPEC, as an example. While you are reading, try to answer the following questions:

1 Slope and elasticity are both measures of responsiveness to change. How are they different?
2 What is the relationship between revenue and price elasticity of demand?

 Price elasticity of demand

OPEC's economists, like you, know that when supply decreases, the equilibrium price rises and the equilibrium quantity decreases. But does the price of oil rise by a large amount and the quantity decrease by a little? Or does the price barely rise and the quantity decrease by a large amount? The answer depends on the responsiveness of the quantity demanded to a change in the price. You can see why by studying Figure 5.1, which shows two possible scenarios in the world oil market where prices are always quoted in dollars. Figure 5.1(a) shows one scenario and Figure 5.1(b) shows the other.

In both cases, supply is initially S_0. In part (a), the demand for oil is shown by the demand curve D_a. In part (b), the demand for oil is shown by the demand curve D_b. Initially, in both cases, the price is $10 a barrel and the quantity of oil produced and consumed is 40 million barrels per day.

Now suppose OPEC decides to cut production whatever the price. The supply curve shifts leftward to S_1. In case (a), the price of a barrel of oil rises by an enormous $20 to $30 a barrel and the quantity decreases by 17 to 23 million barrels per day. In contrast, in case (b), the price rises by only $5 to $15 a barrel and the quantity decreases by 25 to 15 million barrels per day.

The different outcomes arise from differing degrees of responsiveness of the quantity demanded to a change in the price. But what do we mean by responsiveness? One possible answer is slope. The slope of demand curve D_a is steeper than the slope of demand curve D_b.

In this example, we can compare the slopes of the two demand curves. But we can't always do so. The reason is that the slope of a demand curve depends on the units in which we measure the price and quantity. And we must often compare the demand curves for

(a) Large price change and small quantity change

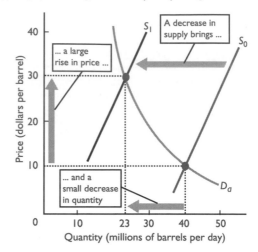

(b) Small price change and large quantity change

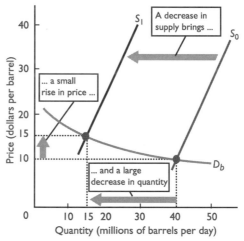

Figure 5.1 How a change in supply changes price and quantity

Source: Parkin et al. (2003)

different goods and services that are measured in unrelated units. For example, an oil producer might want to compare the demand for oil with the demand for natural gas. Which quantity demanded is more responsive to a price change? This question can't be answered by comparing the slopes of two demand curves. The units of measurement of oil and gas are unrelated. The question can be answered with a measure of responsiveness that is independent of units of measurement. Elasticity is such a measure.

The price elasticity of demand is a units-free measure of the responsiveness of the quantity demanded of a good to a change in its price when all other influences on buyers' plans remain the same.

Calculating price elasticity

We calculate the price elasticity of demand by using the formula:

$$\text{Price elasticity of demand} = \frac{\text{Percentage change in quantity demanded}}{\text{Percentage change in price}}$$

To use this formula, we need to know the quantities demanded at different prices when all other influences on buyers' plans remain the same. Suppose we have the data on prices and quantities demanded of oil and calculate the price elasticity of demand for oil.

Figure 5.2 enlarges one section on the demand curve for oil and shows how the quantity demanded responds to a small change in price. Initially the price is $9.50 a barrel and 41 million barrels a day are sold – the original point in the figure. Then the price increases to $10.50 a barrel and the quantity demanded decreases to 39 million barrels a day – the new point in the figure. When the price increases by $1 a barrel, the quantity demanded decreases by 2 million barrels a day.

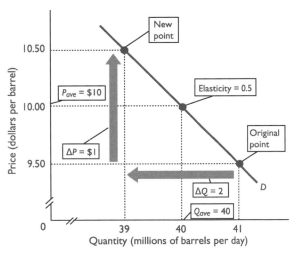

Figure 5.2 Calculating price elasticity of demand (PED)

Source: Parkin *et al.* (2003)

To calculate the elasticity of demand, we express the changes in price and quantity demanded as percentages of the *average price* and the *average quantity*. By using the average price and average quantity, we calculate the elasticity at a point on the demand curve midway between the original point and the new point. The original price is $9.50 and the new price is $10.50, so the average price is $10. The $1 price increase is 10 per cent of the average price. That is:

$$\Delta P/P_{ave} = (\$1/\$10) = 10\%$$

The original quantity demanded is 41 million barrels and the new quantity demanded is 39 million barrels, so the average quantity demanded is 40 million barrels. The 2 million barrel decrease in the quantity demanded is 5 per cent *of* the average quantity. That is:

$$\Delta Q/Q_{ave} = (\$2/\$40) = 5\%$$

So the price elasticity of demand, which is the percentage change in the quantity demanded (5 per cent) divided by the percentage change in price (10 per cent), is 0.5. That is:

$$\text{Price elasticity of demand} = \frac{\%\Delta Q}{\%\Delta P}$$

$$= \frac{5\%}{10\%} = 0.5$$

Interpreting the value of price elasticity of demand

Now that you have calculated the value of price elasticity of demand, you need to know what it means. The value of 0.5 for the price elasticity of oil is telling you that a 1 per cent rise in the price of oil will lead to a 0.5 per cent fall in the quantity demanded. Alternatively, a 1 per cent fall in price will lead to a 0.5 per cent rise in quantity demanded.

Inelastic and elastic demand

Figure 5.3 shows three demand curves that cover the entire range of possible elasticities of demand. In Figure 5.3(a), the quantity demanded is constant regardless of the price. If the quantity demanded remains constant when the price changes, then the elasticity of demand is zero and demand is said to be perfectly inelastic. One good that has a low elasticity of

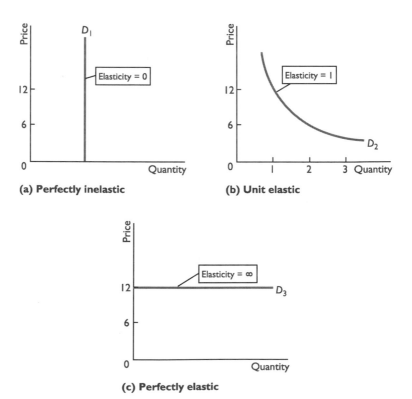

Figure 5.3 Inelastic and elastic demand

Source: Parkin et al. (2003)

demand is insulin. Insulin is of such importance to some diabetics that they will buy the quantity that keeps them healthy at almost any price.

If the percentage change in the quantity demanded equals the percentage change in price, the elasticity of demand is 1 and demand is said to be unit elastic. The demand curve in Figure 5.3(b) is an example of unit elastic demand.

Between the examples shown in parts (a) and (b) of Figure 5.3 are the more general cases when the percentage change in the quantity demanded is less than the percentage change in price. In these cases, the price elasticity of demand lies between zero and one and demand is said to be inelastic. Bread and tobacco are examples of goods with inelastic demand.

If the quantity demanded is infinitely responsive to a price change, then price elasticity of demand is infinity and demand is said to be perfectly elastic. The demand curve in Figure 5.3(c) is an example of perfectly elastic demand . . .

Between the examples shown in parts (b) and (c) of Figure 5.3 are the general cases when the percentage change in the quantity demanded *exceeds* the percentage change in price. In these cases, price elasticity of demand is greater than 1 and demand is said to be elastic. Wine and fresh meat are examples of goods with elastic demand.

Elasticity along a straight-line demand curve

Elasticity and slope are not the same but they are related. To understand how they are related, let's look at elasticity along a straight-line demand curve – a demand curve that has a constant slope. Figure 5.4 illustrates the calculation of elasticity along a hypothetical straight-line demand curve for oil.

Let's calculate the price elasticity of demand for oil when the price rises by $20 from

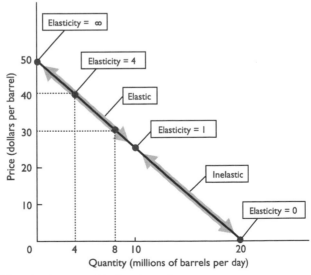

Figure 5.4 Elasticity along a straight-line demand curve

Source: Parkin *et al.* (2003)

$30 to $50 a barrel. The average price in this case is $40 and so the proportionate change in price is:

$\Delta P/P_{ave} = \$20/\$40$

When the price rises from $30 to $50 a barrel, the quantity falls by 8 million barrels per day from 8 to zero and the average quantity demanded is 4 million barrels. So the proportionate change in quantity is:

$\Delta Q/Q_{ave} = 8/4$

Now divide the proportionate change in the quantity demanded by the proportionate change in the price to calculate price elasticity of demand:

$$\frac{\Delta Q/Q_{ave}}{\Delta P/P_{ave}} = \frac{8/4}{20/40} = 4$$

. . . On a straight-line demand curve, the price elasticity is always 1 at the midpoint. Above the midpoint demand is elastic, and below the midpoint demand is inelastic. Demand is perfectly elastic (infinity) where the quantity demanded is zero and perfectly inelastic (zero) where the price is zero.

Elasticity and total revenue

Total revenue from the sale of a good equals the price of the good multiplied by the quantity sold. So can oil producers like OPEC increase total revenue by cutting supply and raising price? When a price changes, total revenue changes. But a rise in price does not always increase total revenue. The change in total revenue depends on the elasticity of demand.

- If demand is elastic, a 1 per cent price rise decreases the quantity sold by more than 1 per cent and total revenue decreases.
- If demand is unit elastic, a 1 per cent price rise decreases the quantity sold by 1 per cent and so total revenue does not change.
- If demand is inelastic, a 1 per cent price rise decreases the quantity sold by less than 1 per cent and total revenue increases.

Figure 5.5 shows how we can use this relationship between elasticity and total revenue to estimate elasticity using the total revenue test. The total revenue test is a method of estimating the price elasticity of demand by observing the change in total revenue that results from a price change (other things constant).

- If a price rise decreases total revenue, demand is elastic.
- If a price rise increases total revenue, demand is inelastic.
- If a price rise leaves total revenue unchanged, demand is unit elastic.

Figure 5.5(a) shows the same hypothetical demand curve for oil as in Figure 5.4. Over the price range from $50 to $25, demand is elastic. Over the price range from $25 to zero, demand is inelastic. At a price of $25, demand is unit elastic. In Figure 5.5(b) you can see how total revenue changes. At a price of $50, the quantity sold is zero so total revenue is also zero. At a price of zero, the quantity demanded is 20 million barrels a day, but at a zero price, total revenue is again zero. A price rise in the elastic range brings a decrease in total revenue – the percentage decrease in the quantity demanded is greater than the percentage increase in price. A price rise in the inelastic range brings an increase in total revenue – the percentage decrease in the quantity demanded is less than the percentage increase in price. At the point of unit elasticity, total revenue is at a maximum.

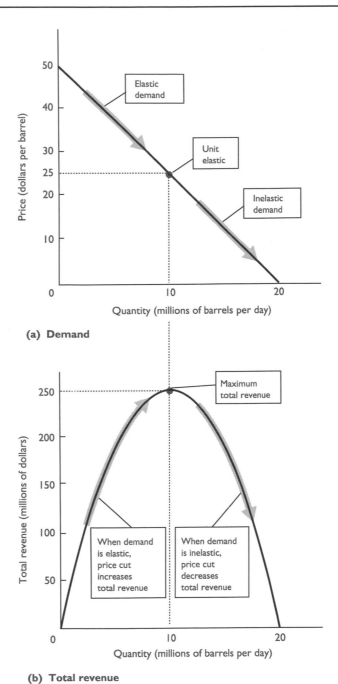

(a) **Demand**

(b) **Total revenue**

Figure 5.5 Elasticity and total revenue

Source: Parkin et al. (2003)

So if when the price of any good rises and you spend less on it, your demand for that good is elastic; if you spend the same amount, your demand is unit elastic; and if you spend more, your demand is inelastic.

Feedback

1 Slope measures the *absolute* change in one variable given an *absolute* change in another variable. Elasticity, on the other hand, measures the *relative* (or proportional or percentage) change in one variable given a *relative* change in another variable. So the *slope of demand* with respect to price is the consequent change in quantity demanded divided by an initial change in price, whereas the *elasticity of demand* with respect to price is the consequent *percentage* change in quantity demanded divided by an initial *percentage* change in price.

Elasticities are most useful when you want to compare the responsiveness of demand in different markets because slopes are dependent on the unit in which the good or service is measured. Consider a demand curve for aspirins that has quantity in terms of number of grams of aspirin. This will be much steeper than a similar demand curve that has quantity measured in tonnes of aspirin. However, for each price level the elasticity will be the same for both curves.

2 The following statements are always true by definition:

• if demand is price *elastic* then revenue will *decrease* if the price is increased
• if demand is price *inelastic* then revenue will *increase* if the price is increased

Total revenue is equal to price multiplied by quantity demanded. Therefore if price increases then total revenue can only decrease if there is a corresponding decrease in quantity demanded which is proportionally greater than the increase in price.

If PED is elastic then, by definition, an increase in price will lead to a proportionally greater decrease in quantity demanded. Hence, the increase in revenue on each unit sold is more than offset by the decrease in revenue caused by the fall in the number of units sold. Alternatively, if PED is inelastic then, by definition, an increase in price will lead to a proportionally smaller decrease in quantity demanded. Hence, the increase in revenue on each unit sold is not fully offset by the decrease in revenue attributed to the fall in the number of units sold.

Activity 5.2

The next extract from Parkin and colleagues (2003) considers which factors influence the elasticity of demand. As you read, make notes on the factors that determine the responsiveness of quantity demanded to price for a particular commodity.

The factors that influence the elasticity of demand

Actual values of elasticities of demand have been estimated and some examples for the United Kingdom are set out in Table 5.1. You can see that these real world elasticities of demand range from 1.4 for fresh meat, the most elastic in the table, to zero for bread, the

Table 5.1 Some real-world price elasticities of demand

Good or service	Elasticity
Elastic demand	
Fresh meat	1.4
Spirits	1.3
Wine	1.2
Unit elasticity	
Services	1.0
Cereals	1.0
Inelastic demand	
Durable goods	0.9
Fruit juice	0.8
Green vegetables	0.6
Tobacco	0.5
Beer	0.5
Bread	0.0

Source: Parkin et al. (2003)

least elastic in the table. What makes the demand for some goods elastic and the demand for others inelastic? Elasticity depends on three main factors.

1 Closeness of substitutes

The closer the substitutes for a good or service, the more elastic is the demand for it. For example, tobacco and housing have few real substitutes. As a result, the demand for tobacco and housing is inelastic. In contrast, fresh meat has many substitutes (fish, cheese, vegetables, and prepared meats), as do metals (carbon fibre and plastics), so the demand for these goods tends to be elastic.

In everyday language we call some goods, such as food and housing, *necessities* and other goods, such as exotic vacations, *luxuries*. Necessities are goods that have poor substitutes and that are crucial for our well-being, so generally they have inelastic demands. Luxuries are goods that usually have many substitutes and so have elastic demands . . .

2 Proportion of income spent on the good

Other things remaining the same, the higher the proportion of income spent on a good, the more elastic is the demand for it. Think about your own elasticity of demand for crisps and textbooks. If the price of a packet of crisps doubles, you'll consume nearly as many crisps as before. Your demand for crisps is inelastic. But if the price of textbooks doubles, you'll really notice and you'll use the library more and share books with your friends. Your demand for textbooks is more elastic than your demand for crisps. Why the difference? Textbooks take a large proportion of your budget while crisps take only a tiny portion. You don't like either price increase, but you hardly notice the higher price of crisps, but the higher price of textbooks puts your budget under severe strain . . .

3 Time elapsed since price change

The greater the time lapse since a price change, the more elastic is demand. When a price changes, consumers often continue to buy similar quantities of a good for a while. But given enough time, they find acceptable and less costly substitutes. As this process of substitution occurs, the quantity purchased of an item that has become more expensive gradually declines. When a price falls, consumers buy more of the good. But as time passes they too find more creative ways of using less expensive substitutes and demand becomes more elastic.

 Feedback

Parkin *et al.* (2003) identify three factors that are likely to mean that demand for a commodity is highly elastic.

- if there are many close substitutes for the commodity then quantity demanded will be very responsive to a change in price
- if expenditure on the commodity takes up a large proportion of income then an increase in price will be very noticeable and substitutes will be eagerly sought – again demand is likely to be very responsive, all other things being equal
- it may take some time to find suitable substitutes – therefore the longer the time period looked at, the more responsive will be quantity demanded, all other things remaining equal.

 Activity 5.3

In this exercise you can check your understanding by calculating price elasticity for a hypothetical demand curve.

Figure 5.6 shows a hypothetical demand curve for cigarettes. In some countries, the levying of taxation on cigarettes is used to reduce cigarette consumption and

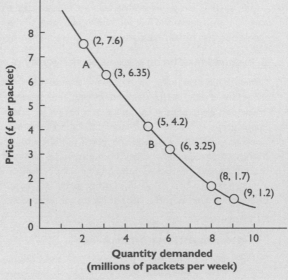

Figure 5.6 The demand for cigarettes

consequently improve the health of the population. It is also popular with governments as a means of raising government revenue. In this exercise you will find out what tax level would maximize government revenue.

1 Calculate the price elasticity of demand (PED) between the two points marked at section A of the demand curve. Do the same for sections B and C. Use the following equation:

$$PED = \frac{\Delta Q/Q_{ave}}{\Delta P/P_{ave}}$$

2 At present there is no tax on cigarettes. Assume that producers currently charge £1.45 per packet of cigarettes and the supply curve is horizontal at this price. This implies that a tax of £1 will raise price by £1 to £2.45. The impact of a tax depends on the slopes of the demand and supply curves. Policy makers are considering tax levels up to £6 per packet. At what tax level, very approximately, will *total revenue* be maximized?

Feedback

1 Calculations are as follows.

For section A:

$\Delta Q = 3 - 2 = 1$ $\Delta P = 7.6 - 6.35 = 1.25$

$Q_{ave} = (2 + 3)/2 = 2.5$ $P_{ave} = (6.35 + 7.6)/2 = 6.98$

$PED = (\Delta Q/Q_{ave})/(\Delta P/P_{ave}) = (1/2.5)/(1.25/6.98) = \mathbf{2.23}$

For section B:

$\Delta Q = 6 - 5 = 1$ $\Delta P = 4.2 - 3.25 = 0.95$

$Q_{ave} = (5 + 6)/2 = 5.5$ $P_{ave} = (3.25 + 4.2)/2 = 3.73$

$PED = (\Delta Q/Q_{ave})/(\Delta P/P_{ave}) = (1/5.5)/(0.95/3.73) = \mathbf{0.71}$

For section C:

$Q = 9 - 8 = 1$ $P = 1.7 - 1.2 = 0.5$

$Q_{ave} = (8 + 9)/2 = 8.5$ $P_{ave} = (1.2 + 1.7)/2 = 1.45$

$PED = (Q/Q_{ave})/(P/P_{ave}) = (1/8.5)/(0.5/1.45) = \mathbf{0.34}$

2 Demand is price inelastic (that is, the magnitude of PED is less than 1) at points B and C. This means that the price can be increased beyond £3.73 without a consequent fall in total revenue. At point A demand is price elastic (that is, the magnitude of PED is greater than 1). This implies that raising price beyond £6.97 will reduce total revenue.

Total revenue will be maximized where PED = 1, at a price level between £3.73 (P_{ave} at B) and £6.97 (P_{ave} at A). This would correspond to a tax level between £2.27 (that is, £3.73 − £1.45) and £5.52 (that is, £6.97 − £1.45).

By measuring the elasticity at more places on the demand curve, you could find out more precisely what price level maximizes total revenue. Figure 5.7 shows the changes in revenue associated with moving from section C to section B.

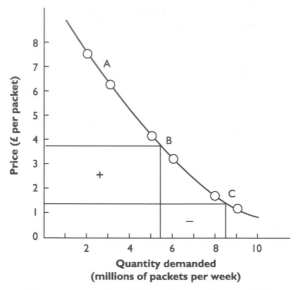

Figure 5.7 Increase in revenue associated with an increase in price of cigarettes

The rectangle indicated by the '+' symbol shows the increase in revenue associated with the increase in price. The rectangle indicated by the '–' symbol shows the loss of revenue associated with the decrease in quantity demanded. The revenue gained is clearly larger than the revenue lost: therefore total revenue has increased. This concurs with the finding that this part of the demand curve is price inelastic. Figure 5.8 shows the changes in revenue associated with increasing the price beyond A.

Again the rectangle indicated by the '+' symbol shows the increase in revenue associated with the increase in price, whereas the rectangle indicated by the '–' symbol shows the loss of revenue associated with the decrease in quantity demanded. This time the revenue gained is clearly less than the revenue lost, therefore total revenue has decreased. Again this concurs with the earlier finding that this part of the demand curve is price elastic.

You have seen that, if the demand function for a particular commodity has been estimated, then the measurement of elasticities can be used to find the tax level that maximizes government revenue. In the next chapter you will read about a study that estimated empirically a demand function and calculated price elasticity.

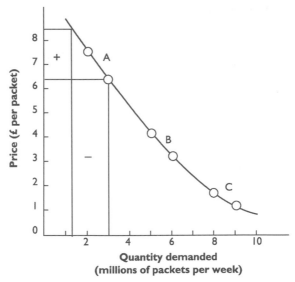

Figure 5.8 Decrease in revenue associated with an increase in price of cigarettes

Some other elasticities

Elasticities are not just used to measure the responsiveness of quantity demanded to price. They can be used to measure the responsiveness of any variable to any other variable. In addition to price elasticity of demand the following elasticities are often calculated:

- *Cross-elasticity of demand* is the percentage change in quantity demanded of the commodity divided by the percentage change in the price of another related commodity. If the related good is a complement then the cross-elasticity of demand is less than zero because a positive change in price brings about a negative change in quantity demanded. If the related good is a substitute then the cross-elasticity of demand is more than zero because a positive change in price brings about a positive change in quantity demanded.
- *Income elasticity of demand* is the percentage change in quantity demanded of the commodity divided by the percentage change in population income. If an increase in income brings about an increase in quantity demanded then income elasticity of demand is positive and the commodity is described as a 'normal good'. If an increase in income brings a decrease in quantity demanded then income elasticity of demand is negative and the commodity is described as an 'inferior good'.
- *Price elasticity of supply* is the percentage change in quantity supplied of a commodity divided by the percentage change in the commodity's price. Supply is generally more responsive to price in the long term than it is in the short term.

Summary

You have learned about what is meant by price elasticity of demand and how to calculate it. You also learned about the relationship between elasticity and total revenue and the factors that influence elasticity of demand – closeness of substitutes, proportion of income spent on the good and time elapsed since a price change.

Reference

Parkin M, Powell M and Mathews K (2003). *Economics* (5th edn). Harlow: Addison-Wesley.

6 | Applying elasticity of demand to health policy

Overview

In Chapter 5 you found out how to measure the responsiveness of demand to changes in price. Now you will look at how such measurements can be used to inform the levying of taxes for health promotion purposes and the setting of user charges.

Learning objectives

After working through this chapter, you will be able to:

- **discuss issues concerning imposing (or increasing) tax on cigarettes**
- **discuss issues concerning imposing (or increasing) health service charges**

Key terms

Progressive tax A tax that takes an increasing proportion of income as income rises.

Proportional tax A tax that takes a constant proportion of income regardless of income level.

Regressive tax A tax that takes a decreasing proportion of income as income rises.

Levying taxes to promote health

As was noted in Activity 5.3, the levying of tax on cigarettes is sometimes used to reduce cigarette consumption, thus improving health and raising government revenue. You investigated the effects of different tax levels on government revenue. In this chapter you will examine some of the other consequences of imposing cigarette taxation, in particular the way taxation can impact on different social groups. A particular concern is to avoid regressive taxation – that is, a tax that takes a decreasing proportion of income as income rises.

 Activity 6.1

Read the following edited extract of an article by Pim Borren and Mathew Sutton (1992). Although it is somewhat dated, it serves as a good example of the way economics can be used to inform governments as to possible strategies to reduce a major public health danger, smoking. The social class system referred to in the text is defined as:

Class I – professionals (non-manual)
Class II – managers (non-manual)
Class III – skilled workers (non-manual and manual)
Class IV – semi-skilled workers (manual)
Class V – unskilled workers (manual)

As you read, consider the following questions:

1 What is the study question being addressed by the paper?
2 How did the authors try to investigate this problem?

Are increases in cigarette taxation regressive? (aims and methods)

Tobacco taxation as a policy tool has received much attention in the empirical literature. However, whilst much has been written on the *efficiency* of a pricing policy, little attention has been paid to the *equity* implications of such a policy.

Cross-sectional surveys of smoking behaviour indicate that patterns of smoking in different occupational groups have become increasingly diverse since the 1950s. This increasing divergence in smoking behaviour may have significant implications for policy makers planning to control the level of tobacco consumption through taxation policies and health education programmes.

Large-scale British studies of smoking behaviour . . . estimated that the price elasticity of tobacco differed significantly over different time periods and different occupational groupings. In particular, employed non-manual households were found to have a lower price elasticity than manual households over the period 1970 to 1984, although the difference between these groups had narrowed considerably from 1982 onwards . . . Atkinson et al. (1984) suggested that price elasticity estimates varied across different socio-economic groups, suggesting a price elasticity of −0.6 for manual households who did not own their own homes, and −0.46 for professional owner-occupying households . . .

Addressing the argument that increases in cigarette taxation were regressive, Townsend (1987) estimated the price elasticity of demand for cigarettes by men in the five social classes over the period 1961–1977. Having found a significant price gradient in the point estimates, with lower social classes being more sensitive to changes in price, Townsend calculated the additional tax burdens that would be expected to fall on the different social groups as a result of a range of tax-induced price increases. Finding that all social groups faced approximately the same nominal increase in tax burdens, Townsend suggested that increasing the levy on cigarettes was not a regressive policy, since the consumption of cigarettes by men from the lower social classes was more sensitive to price changes.

This finding is of fundamental importance since, if these conditions exist, targets to reduce the level of smoking in these groups (where smoking is becoming increasingly concentrated) can be achieved equitably through sustained taxation increases. If these conditions do not exist, however, then sustained increases in cigarette taxation will place a heavier tax burden on individuals with, on average, lower incomes. Given that the vast majority of studies suggest that the demand for cigarettes is price inelastic, the reduction of smoking in lower social classes may only be achieved at considerable cost to these individuals' welfare and a widening of welfare differentials . . .

There has been considerable interest in the modelling of the effects of economic factors on smoking behaviour. The purpose of this paper is not to attempt to judge the validity of the competing approaches but rather to see whether the particular approach adopted by Townsend still supports the same conclusions.

Data

Surveys of the consumption of tobacco in Great Britain . . . provided sales-adjusted figures for the average weekly consumption of manufactured cigarettes per person by sex and by social class. These surveys interviewed approximately 10,000 people about their smoking habits, and the samples were nationally representative in terms of sex, age, social class, regional and occupational groupings . . . Social class figures were available for the periods 1977–1985 and 1986–1987.

The implicit price series for cigarettes was obtained by dividing expenditure on cigarettes at current prices by expenditure valued at 1980 prices. A real price series was then obtained by deflating the implicit cigarette price index by an all items index, calculated by dividing total consumers' expenditure in current terms by total consumers' expenditure valued at 1980 prices . . . The series was converted into real terms using the implicit price deflator derived from the total consumers' expenditure series, and into a per adult figure by the mid-year estimate of the UK population aged 15 years and over.

Estimation procedure

The demand functions for each social class were estimated . . . The results . . . do not provide parameter estimates for those variables which were not found to have a significant influence on the consumption of cigarettes in that group. The estimates which are included are those for which a significant effect was estimated, or whose omission would suggest serial correlation or functional form problems.

Feedback

1 Borren and Sutton are estimating a cigarette demand function for each of five social classes in the UK. They want to compare the responsiveness of these different classes to rises in cigarette taxation and they want to see where the burden of increased taxation is at its highest. They want to find out whether or not the policy of increasing taxation on cigarettes is *regressive*.

2 They built a model of demand using time series data from a number of UK sources including data on the quantity demanded, price (relative to other prices in the economy) and income. They estimated separate demand curves for each of ten groups of the population. For each of these groups, they estimated price elasticities. The burden of taxation was calculated for each group.

Activity 6.2

Now read the results they obtained and their implications for policy. While you are reading, try to answer the following questions:

1   What do the numbers in Table 6.1 mean?

Table 6.1 Price elasticities of demand for men (1961–85) and for women (1958–87). All significantly different from zero except for men in Class V

	Class I	Class II	Class III	Class IV	Class V
Men	−0.69	−0.48	−0.84	−0.89	−0.31
Women	−1.04	−0.93	−0.65	−0.85	−0.45

Source: Borren and Sutton (1992)

2   What groups are likely to reduce their smoking the most?
3   Who is likely to bear the burden of higher levels of taxation?

Are increases in cigarette taxation regressive? (results and discussion)

To ensure the consistency of the data set with that used by Townsend, the model was initially estimated over the same time period (1961–1977) and for males only. The estimation results concurred with those that were published, showing an increasing pattern of price elasticity from social class one through to social class five, although few, if any, of the coefficients were significant at the 5 per cent level.

To test the stability of Townsend's results, extensive sensitivity analyses were carried out on each of the variables included in the model. As may have been anticipated given the lack of significance, the coefficients for all of the variables were highly sensitive to even the slightest adjustments to any of the annual data series. A 5 per cent change to a single data value was sufficient to alter the entire set of results. Given the use of some very general proxies, particularly the average real income variable, such sensitivity makes the results highly suspect . . . Given both the insignificance and sensitivity of the estimates of price and income elasticities, the authors of this paper could not find any justification for the conclusion drawn from the results by Townsend, that increases in cigarette taxation would fall less heavily on lower social groups.

The model was then estimated using the full data set (1961–1987) . . . The price elasticity of demand for cigarettes is found to be significantly different from zero for four of the five social class groups (Table 6.1). However, there is no obvious pattern of increasing price elasticity across the classes. This is contrary to the findings of Townsend, where price responsiveness rose consistently between social classes one and five. Indeed, social class two, which is made up of managers and administrators, and is consistently the highest income group, together with social class five, the lowest income group, seem to be the two groups least influenced by price. The middle income social classes three and four seem to be most influenced by the price of cigarettes . . .

For women, cigarette prices were again highly significant for all groups. Although there were no obvious patterns between social classes in terms of the magnitude of the price-elasticities, it is noted that the elasticities for social classes one and two are higher than the other social classes, and considerably higher than those of their male counterparts. Women in class three are less price responsive while class four is relatively similar for both sexes. In social class five womens' demand is once again considerably more price elastic than that of men. Trends in price elasticity clearly do not follow a consistent pattern . . .

There is little evidence of any significant differences in the responsiveness of the different social classes to changes in the price of cigarettes. Almost all of the price elasticity estimates are significantly different from zero, but do not appear to be significantly different from each other. These results offer no evidence of a systematic gradient in the responsiveness to price increases across the social classes and therefore contradict Townsend's findings.

Policy implications

At the outset, it should be made clear that the subject of this article . . . relates to the *marginal* impact of cigarette taxation. The main focus of this debate has been to establish whether the pursuance of a policy of concerted increases in cigarette taxation is a regressive measure. In terms of the absolute impact of the levy on the sale of tobacco, it is clear that in 1987, cigarette taxation was regressive in terms of the total tax bill and as a proportion of income. Furthermore, despite Townsend's predictions, the continual real price rise in cigarettes over the period 1980 to 1987 actually *widened* the gap between the amount of taxation paid by each social class, although this observation may reflect other factors.

To highlight the effect of our results on the implications for cigarette tax paid for each social class, the effects of various increases in cigarette tax have been calculated (1987 quantities and prices) . . . The implications of these results on the extra tax burden faced by each social class are that cigarette tax increases are regressive in nature, for both men and women (Figure 6.1). The distributive effects of increased cigarette tax are such that men in social class five could expect to pay over eight times more in increased tax than their

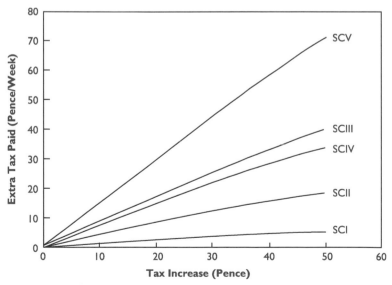

Figure 6.1 The extra tax burden faced by women in each social class as a result of cigarette tax increases   SC = social class

Source: Borren and Sutton (1992)

counterparts in social class one. Women in social class five could expect to pay almost eleven times more in increased tax than their counterparts in social class one. On average men would pay one third more in increased tax than women . . .

Conclusions

These results suggest that price and time are the two most significant influences on cigarette smoking across all social classes. Income did not prove to be as significant and was rarely retained in our final estimations. One-off health 'shocks' surrounding the publicity attached to reports published by the Royal College of Physicians were also not significant in influencing consumption. One possibility is that the health awareness and education programmes over the entire period have affected tastes, and, in the form of the time trend, appear to have reduced smoking significantly. The results suggest that men have been influenced more strongly than women. Traditionally, men have smoked more heavily than women and early anti-tobacco campaigns may have targeted men more strongly. As stereotypes have declined, the historical gap between male and female smokers has closed. It remains clear, that since the lower classes have the highest smoking-averages, reducing smoking-rates amongst these groups has the greatest potential for reducing tobacco-related health problems.

These results also suggest that price increases through increased taxation will be successful in reducing smoking in all social classes. However, the redistributive effects on tax paid and welfare are regressive on average. Since income is not a major influence on smoking, any adverse effects on equity between social classes caused by increased cigarette taxation could be corrected through changes in other forms of taxation or subsidies.

 Feedback

1 These are the *price elasticities of demand* (PED) for each class-sex group. For each group, PED is constant across the demand curve because this is the functional form the investigators have assumed. All of the elasticities have a minus sign in front of them. This is perfectly normal – it reflects the fact that the change in quantity demanded is in the opposite direction to the change in price (that is, the demand curve slopes downwards). Technically speaking, estimates of PED should always be preceded by a minus sign. However, since PED is always negative economists have developed the lazy convention of omitting the sign. For other types of elasticity, signs should always be indicated appropriately to show the direction of change (as well as the magnitude of the change).

2 You get this answer directly from the price elasticities. The elasticities with the largest magnitude indicate large percentage reductions in cigarette consumption relative to the price change. They indicate that men in Classes III and IV and women in Classes I, II and IV will be most responsive in relative terms (Table 6.1). However, these groups have different starting points in terms of initial smoking consumption. A large percentage change in a low smoking group might represent a smaller absolute change in consumption than a small percentage change in a high smoking group.

3 The model was used to predict the increased tax burden associated with various tax levels for each group. Figure 6.1 presents these predictions graphically for women. It seems that increasing tax levels on cigarettes will increase the tax burden of social Class V more than social Class I. The authors conclude that the policy of imposing taxation on cigarettes is regressive. This conclusion contradicts the results of the earlier study by Townsend referred to in the paper.

Activity 6.3

In the final activity of this chapter you are asked to think about the wider issues arising from the imposition of a sales tax on cigarettes.

You have looked at how cigarette taxation can be used to raise government revenue. You also observed that the burden of this taxation may be distributed unequally and arguably unfairly. In addition to the health gain, the revenue gain and the tax distribution, what other considerations should policy makers bear in mind in deciding this issue? Make brief notes as to the issues that you would wish to raise in a discussion of the problem.

 Feedback

Health is one aspect of quality of life and there is no doubt that reducing smoking will improve people's health. However, there are other aspects of quality of life. One consideration might be the loss of quality of life from people smoking less. People smoke because they choose to and because they get some utility from smoking. By heavily taxing cigarette smoking and reducing cigarette consumption, governments deprive people of this utility and reduce consumer surplus. This loss partially offsets the health gains of the initiative. However, the freedom of people to smoke may be argued against on at least two grounds. First, some people become addicted and as such probably should be discouraged, but the addictiveness obviously affects people's responsiveness to price. Second, smoking has adverse health effects on people who do not smoke through passive smoking and for this reason perhaps policy makers should discourage smoking.

Taxes levied on cigarettes will have an adverse effect on the tobacco industry. Profits will be reduced, the market will contract and probably workers will be made redundant. Policy makers in countries with a large tobacco industry may feel that these costs outweigh the health benefits (though redundant workers might be able to be retrained and redeployed in other industries).

There may be consequences for health service utilization resulting from the policy. If people stop smoking, then they will live longer. This might mean that they will place a larger burden on the health service and on pensions over the duration of their extended lives. Alternatively, it might mean that they place a smaller burden on health services because they will require less treatment for smoking-related diseases.

Weighing it all up

When a policy has several different consequences, economists try to put a value on each of the costs and each of the benefits. If the aggregate value of the benefits is greater than the aggregate value of the costs, then the policy should be implemented. Sometimes it is appropriate to weigh benefits and costs according to who incurs them. The method used is called cost–benefit analysis and will be looked at in Chapter 18.

Godfrey and Maynard (1988) evaluated the different effects of cigarette taxation in Britain. They were positively in favour of increasing cigarette taxation. However, at the time of their study the evidence of the regressive nature of the tax was not yet available.

Health service user charges

The factors that influence a policy maker's decision whether or not to introduce or raise user charges for health services are similar to the factors relevant to cigarette taxation:

- The user charge should not be raised if prices are elastic because this will entail a loss of revenue (unless there is some other benefit of increasing charges).
- Some economists have advocated the use of charges to eliminate unnecessary consultations. Whether such consultations are really 'unnecessary' is highly questionable, though.
- The charge, if it reduces necessary demand, will have a detrimental effect on the health of the population, more so if demand is highly price elastic.
- The distribution of the financial burden of the charges may be uneven. Poorer, sicker people may be paying a lot more (especially as a portion of their income).
- Charges will increase inequality in the health of the population if they prevent relatively poorer, sicker people from taking the treatment that they need.
- If the increase in charge allows a decrease in taxation then the result might be a boost to other sectors of the economy. This would count as a benefit of the policy. However, it is questionable to what extent this would happen, if at all. You will look at the issue of charging patients in more detail later.

Summary

You have learned about the impact of taxation on demand for cigarettes and the various factors policy makers should take into account when deciding about imposing cigarette taxation. Similarly you learned about the factors to consider when deciding health service user charges.

References

Atkinson A, Gomulka J and Stern N (1984) *Household expenditure on tobacco 1970–1980: evidence from the family expenditure survey*. Economic and Social Science Research Council Programme.

Borren P and Sutton M (1992) Are increases in cigarette taxation regressive? *Health Economics* 1:245–53.

Godfrey C and Maynard A (1988) Economic aspects of tobacco use and taxation policy. *British Medical Journal* 297:339–43.

Townsend, J (1987) Cigarette tax, economic welfare and social class patterns of smoking. *Applied Economics* 19:355–65.

7 Risk, uncertainty and modelling demand

Overview

In Chapter 1 you learned about some of the determinants of demand and in Chapters 5 and 6 you looked at the responsiveness of demand to these variables. At the end of Chapter 1, however, it was observed that health care had some interesting characteristics such that it did not entirely fit the simple model of demand. In this chapter you will find out about three, more complicated, models (the insurance model, the agency model and the health production model) which do take into account the special characteristics of health care. You will also examine incentive structures for doctors and consider the implications of correcting health inequalities.

Learning objectives

After working through this chapter, you will be able to:

- explain why people take out health insurance
- explain why the relationship between doctor and patient could be described as an 'agency' type relationship
- discuss possible ways of encouraging doctors to act as perfect agents
- explain why taking up exercise could be considered an 'investment in human capital'
- describe the health production model and its theoretical implications for health inequalities

Key terms

Agent A person who acts on behalf of another (the principal).

Asymmetry of information A market situation where all participants do not have access to the same level of information.

Expected utility The benefit or satisfaction that an individual anticipates getting from consuming a particular good or service.

Health production function The relationship between consumption of health inputs and subsequent health status.

Principal A person on whose behalf an agent acts.

Risk aversion The unwillingness of an individual to take on an identified risk.

Living in an uncertain world

Up to this point, the models of demand that you have studied have been abstract representations of the real world. The readings that you will do for Activity 7.1 introduce the concepts of risk and uncertainty and examine the ways in which people make economic decisions when they're unsure of the consequences.

Activity 7.1

Read the following extract by Cam Donaldson and Karen Gerard (2005), and then try to answer the following questions:

1 Why do people take out insurance?
2 Why do people take out health insurance?
3 Under what circumstances are individuals more likely to take out insurance?

The article refers to 'actuarily fair premiums'. This means the amount (premium) an individual pays for insurance reflects their personal likelihood of needing to use health care.

Uncertainty and the demand for insurance

For the individual, illness is unpredictable. In general terms, it may be possible to predict the prognoses associated with various chronic conditions and to predict in probabilistic terms how people of varying ages, circumstances, and pre-existing conditions will fare in terms of their future health status. But, at the level of the individual, future health status is likely to be uncertain.

It follows from this that one cannot plan one's future consumption of health care in the way that one could do so for commodities like food. As a result of this inability to plan when a future event will occur, an unregulated market would respond by developing insurance mechanisms, whereby an individual, or family, could make payments to some risk-pooling agency (usually an insurance company) for guarantees for some form of financial reimbursement in the event of illness leading to the insured person incurring health care expenses. Some insurance against loss of income may be taken out by the insured person, but, despite the desirability of doing so, it is difficult to insure against anxiety, pain and suffering resulting directly from illness. This is because of difficulties in valuing anxiety, pain and suffering in monetary terms, and because insurance companies could never obtain reliable and objective estimates of how much anxiety, pain and suffering an illness leads to. On the other hand, health care expenditures incurred are a fairly reliable signal that an illness has occurred and they are more readily quantifiable. Therefore, it is *health care* insurance which is mostly taken out by insured people, although it is commonly referred to as *health* insurance. People cannot insure against ill-health itself but rather the financial costs of ill-health. Thus, health care insurance embodies the wider concept of income maintenance.

If insurance policies are actuarially fair, premiums paid will equal health care expenditure incurred. However, this assumes that insurance companies make no profit and incur no administration costs. These assumptions do not hold, but people still take out (actuarially unfair) insurance, paying premiums which are 'loaded' so as to cover administration and profit. The reason for this is that, in general, people are risk-averse; they do not like risk and gain utility from covering the uncertainty of large financial losses. This is a utility gain for which they are willing to pay.

For example, in a community of ten people it might be known that each person has a one-in-ten chance of incurring health care expenditures of £1000 per annum. If all are risk averse, each would take out an insurance policy, paying £100 per annum each if it were actuarially fair. However, if administrative costs were £10 per annum, would each person be willing to pay the actuarially unfair premium of £101 each? The answer is probably 'yes'.

People are also more likely to insure against larger losses which are unpredictable than against smaller losses which occur more regularly and therefore more predictably. For instance, of those people who visit a dentist every six months for a check-up, some may not find it worth their while insuring against the predictable and inexpensive check-up itself, but would rather insure against the unpredictable and more expensive consequence of requiring treatment subsequent to the check-up. This does not mean, of course, that no one will insure against relatively small potential losses; many people do insure against such losses. The reason for this may be related not only to uncertainty itself, but also to the anxiety associated with incurring financial costs. However, as one would expect, the value of insurance is in providing cover against the uncertainty of financial losses – especially large ones.

↻ Feedback

1 People who are risk averse are likely to take out insurance because insurance reduces the risks that they have to face. They will take out insurance if the expected utility associated with taking out insurance is more than the expected utility associated with bearing the risk themselves.

If you found some of the concepts difficult to grasp, the following example may help: suppose that you work in a company where you have two options for your end of year bonus. If you choose option A, you get a lump sum of £1000. If you choose option B, you get 1000 company shares. You do not know how much they will be worth at the end of the year. Suppose that you know that there is a 50 per cent chance they will be worth £1500 and a 50 per cent chance they will be worth only £500. The expected value of this option is £1000 (£1500 × 0.5 + £500 × 0.5). Therefore both options (A and B) have the same *expected value*.

A person who does not mind which of these two options they get would be described as *risk neutral*. They are only interested in the amount of money not in the associated risk. A person who prefers option A would be described as *risk averse*. They do not like risk and would rather have the lump sum option. The empirical evidence seems to show that most people are risk averse.

2 As Donaldson and Gerard point out, health insurance is not insurance against poor health *per se*. Health insurance is insurance against health treatment costs. If a person pays a health insurance premium then when they are ill they will not have to pay their health care charges. Alternatively, if they do have to pay then they pay at a much reduced rate.

3 Several factors influence whether an individual will take out insurance or not:

- the more risk averse they are the more likely they are to take out insurance
- also, they are more likely to take it out if the potential loss is large – modern health care can cost vast amount so, in high income countries at least, many people take out health insurance
- the larger the risk of loss the more likely they are to take out insurance – so people who perceive themselves as very healthy are unlikely to take out health insurance
- the cheaper the premium, the more likely they are to take out the insurance
- other things remaining equal, the poorer they are, the less likely they are to take out insurance because they cannot afford the premiums; however, rich people may not insure either, because any loss they could incur might be perceived as small next to their entire wealth

Insurance markets evolve as a natural response to the burden of risk. That they exist certainly complicates the model of demand you looked at in Chapter 1. Consumers, instead of demanding health care, demand health insurance. The insurance companies then demand the health care or else the individuals demand it and the insurers pay for it. The ability of either individuals or insurers to exert their sovereignty over health providers is the subject of the next activity. You will also consider it in Chapter 11.

The agency relationship

You will now learn more about the effects of asymmetry of information in the doctor–patient relationship. Economists often describe doctors as 'agents' because they act on behalf of the patient. The doctor (agent) is informed about a patient's health and their treatment options. The patient (principal) is relatively uninformed about these matters and therefore has to rely on the doctor to act in their (the patient's) best interests. A person will employ the services of an agent if they believe that their utility afterwards will be greater than without the help of the agent.

But what makes a perfect agent? There are several different views on the matter:

- the doctor gives the patient all the information they require and the patient makes the decision, to maximize the patient's health (Williams 1988);
- the doctor gives the patient all the information but then the doctor makes the decision, to maximize the patient's health (Culyer 1988, 1989);
- the doctor acts in a way that maximizes the utility of the patient (Evans 1984);
- the doctor acts in a way that maximizes social welfare (Mooney 1994).

All of these definitions could be suffixed with the phrase 'subject to resource constraints'. This distinguishes all these views from the view of medical ethicists who probably would not acknowledge such a constraint. From an individual perspective, a perfect agent would maximize a patient's utility. The factors that contribute to a patient's utility are:

- their health;
- information about their health and treatments;
- an appropriate level of participation in the decision making process;
- process utility – respect from staff, pleasant environment, etc.;
- utility from non-health care consumption.

In contrast, a perfect agent from a societal perspective occurs when *social welfare* is maximized. And social welfare is a concept that incorporates not just the total level of utility in society but also the distribution of utility. Just what allocation of utility gives the highest social welfare depends on a particular society's attitude to inequality.

Activity 7.2

1 What do you think would encourage doctors to be perfect agents?
2 Consider what might be the major factors which feature in the utility function of a doctor.

Feedback

1 You might have suggested:

* their own income (and consumption)
* their own leisure time
* the utility of their family and friends
* their professional prestige
* their patients' utility

Although patients' utility features in the doctor's utility function, it is only one of several influences. The maximization of the doctor's utility is unlikely to occur at the same point as when patients' utility is maximized.

2 The factors that would limit the doctor from acting in their own (personal) interest (besides the doctor's own interest in their patients' welfare) are:

* if patients are relatively well informed
* the existence of peer review and other forms of professional regulation – the thought of being found out and embarrassed by their colleagues might be a very strong incentive
* their belief in a set of medical ethics
* financial incentives in their contracts which encourage them to act in the interest of the patients

The key thing is to design employment contracts and monitoring mechanisms in such a way that the agents' interests are the same as their principals. In the case of business executives who are the agents of business owners, payment is often profit-related so that both the owners and the executives have an interest in increasing the profits of their firm. In the case of doctors, additional payments might be made for carrying out certain services like screening or domiciliary visits. Alternatively there could be financial penalties associated with patient complaints. If possible, payments should reflect the most important outcomes of care.

An alternative or supplementary policy might involve increasing patient information. In relatively uncomplicated medical areas with unambiguous evidence the government could disseminate evidence on effectiveness to the general public. The government could also publish data on the performance of health care providers.

This would help consumers of health care to monitor their doctors. It would provide incentives for doctors to act in their patients' interests. The implications of the doctor–patient relationship for efficiency in health care markets will be discussed in Chapter 11.

Health production

Health care is not the only factor that promotes good health. Other determinants of good health include good diet, plenty of exercise and personal hygiene. Some economists like to think of individuals as deliberately combining all these factors to *produce* good health. An example is the health production model which assumes that individuals or households invest in health *inputs* to *produce* a *return* of healthy days (Grossman 1972, 2004).

For example, it is known that lack of exercise is bad for the health: among other things, it raises the risk of coronary heart disease. People who work in offices often do not get much exercise in their work. Some of them decide to take-up some form of exercise, perhaps running or swimming. Economists might refer to this action as investing in human capital. This is because the exercise programme is seen as an investment (the person is investing time and money) in health. When a firm increases or improves its machinery it is said to be investing in *capital*. Households or individuals, when they increase their skills or health, are said to be investing in *human capital*.

Seven assumptions underlie the health production model:

* people value their health (along with other things);
* people produce health using health inputs;
* neither health production nor other activities are without cost;
* individuals have fixed incomes;
* there is diminishing marginal utility for health and other activities (i.e. the healthier a person becomes the less they value each additional increase in health);
* there is diminishing marginal product of health inputs (i.e. the more a person invests in health the less they gain from each successive input);
* education increases the efficiency of health production (i.e. an educated person gets more health gain from a given health input than a less educated person).

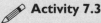 **Activity 7.3**

According to the health production model, how might inequalities in health be addressed?

 Feedback

The model suggests that as an individual's income increases so their health increases because they will be buying more health inputs. But as income increases by x per cent, health will increase by less than x per cent. This is because of the assumption that there is *diminishing marginal product*. (Diminishing marginal product is believed by economists to be present for all inputs and all production functions.) This has consequences for the distribution of income. Suppose you take some money from one individual and give it to an individual on a lower income. It happens that the loss of health to the first individual will be less than the gain in health to the poorer individual. This means that redistributing income will not only reduce health inequality but will also increase the average health of the population.

Subsidies of health inputs for poorer people would be another effective way of reducing health inequality according to the model. Lower input prices result in a substitution to health inputs and therefore an increase in health for the individuals incurring the lower prices.

Finally, the assumption that education means that people will be able to use health inputs more effectively implies that, as a proportion of income, educated individuals will spend less on health inputs but will be healthier. This means that, in theory, health inequality can be reduced through health education programmes and through improving the education of the population.

All of these strategies involve the use of additional resources. While they may be effective at reducing health inequality, the additional cost means that there is a cost in terms of reduced efficiency. Whether policy makers decide to go ahead with any of these policies or not will depend on how much weight they place on equality of health. You will look at the issues surrounding equality and fairness in more detail in Chapter 12.

 Activity 7.4

Do you perceive any inconsistency between the investment model and the agency model of health demand?

 Feedback

There is a paradox concerning the assumptions that each model makes about the information available to consumers of health. The agency model assumes that people have little information about how to improve their own health. Alternatively, the health production model assumes that people know how to use health inputs to improve their health.

The contradiction may not be so great when you remember that the agency model concerns only health care whereas the production model is concerned with all types of health inputs. It is possible that people may have a greater awareness of the effectiveness of other health inputs than they have with regard to health care. For example, most people are aware that smoking is detrimental to health, that too much fatty food is detrimental, that too little exercise is detrimental. Few people, however, would know exactly what is the best way of treating hypertension.

Like many economic models, the health production model is largely theoretical. You should therefore treat such models with caution as empirical studies have failed to find strong evidence of the relationship between education and health production postulated by the model.

Summary

You have learned why people take out health care insurance, the role of health care professionals as agents and the reasons why they may not function as perfect agents. You have also seen how models may help to describe and explain economic relationships though they remain theoretical until empirical evidence can be prove them right.

References

Culyer AJ (1988) Inequality in health services is, in general, desirable, in Green DG (ed) *Acceptable inequalities*. London: Institute of Economic Affairs.

Culyer AJ (1989) The normative economics of health care financing and provision. *Oxford Review of Economic Policy* 5:34–58.

Donaldson C and Gerard K (2005) *Economics of health care financing. The visible hand* (2nd edn). Basingstoke: Palgrave Macmillan.

Evans RG (1984) *Strained mercy: the economics of Canadian medical care*. Toronto: Butterworth.

Grossman M (1972) On the concept of health capital and the demand for health. *Journal of Political Economy* 80:223–55.

Grossman M (2004) The demand for health, 30 years later: a very personal retrospective and prospective reflection. *Journal of Health Economics* 23:629–36.

Mooney G (1994) *Key issues in health economics*. Hemel Hempstead: Harvester.

Williams A (1988) Priority setting in public and private health care: a guide through the ideological jungle. *Journal of Health Economics* 7:173–83.

8 Production and costs in the short and long run

Overview

You have now learned quite a bit about the demand for health care. In this and the next chapter you will return to the theory behind the supply curve and then to apply that theory to the supply of health care. In this chapter you will learn about the constraints which producers are under, the relationship between inputs and outputs and the relationship between output and cost. You will use this theory in Chapter 9 to discuss the advantages and disadvantages of large-scale production of health care.

Learning objectives

After working through this chapter, you will be able to:

- **explain when it might be better to substitute between production inputs**
- **estimate and graph simple cost functions**
- **define efficient and inefficient production**
- **describe the relationship between scale of production and cost**

Key terms

Diminishing returns to scale As the quantity of one factor (input) increases, *ceteris paribus* output increases but by ever-diminishing quantities.

Diseconomies of scale Technological conditions under which long-run average cost increases as output increases.

Economies of scale Technological conditions under which long-run average cost decreases as output increases.

Fixed cost A cost of production that does not vary with the level of output.

Returns to scale The proportional increase in output that occurs when all inputs are increased by the same percentage.

Variable cost A cost of production that varies directly with the level of output.

Production in the short run

Suppose you are the manager of a community nursing service in a rural area. You have two cross-country vehicles at your disposal. At the end of the year, the Ministry may provide more vehicles or else it may reallocate the ones you have already. For now you can only influence the number of patients treated by varying the amount of nurse time. Hence, vehicles represent a fixed cost and nurses a variable cost. Table 8.1 shows the short-run production function of your service. It shows the *total product* (in terms of patient contacts per day; column 2) achievable with two vehicles (total fixed cost; column 5) for different numbers of nurses (column 1). It also shows the *marginal product* (column 3), that is the extra output achieved for each additional input (i.e. each additional nurse).

Table 8.1 Short-run production function for community nursing service

Number of nurses	Total product	Marginal product	Total variable cost	Total fixed cost (i.e. vehicle cost)	Total cost	Average (total) cost
1	15	15	30	50	80	5.33
2	30	15	60	50	110	3.67
3	70	40	90	50	140	2
4	100	30	120	50	170	1.7
5	130	30	150	50	200	1.54
6	150					
7	170					
8	180					
9	190					
10	200					

 Activity 8.1

1 Complete the marginal product column of Table 8.1. This has been started for you. Are there diminishing returns associated with increasing the number of nurses (i.e. does the number of patient contacts per day for each nurse decrease as the number of nurses increases)? What might explain this relationship?

2 Suppose that a nurse is paid £30 per day and vehicles cost £25 per vehicle per day and assume that there are no other costs. Calculate the total variable cost (number of nurses × cost per nurse), total fixed cost (number of vehicles × cost per vehicle) and the total cost (total variable cost + total fixed cost) columns in the table. These calculations have also been started for you.

3 Finish calculating average total cost. Plot average cost against total product in Figure 8.1.

4 Explain the shape of the short-run average cost curve.

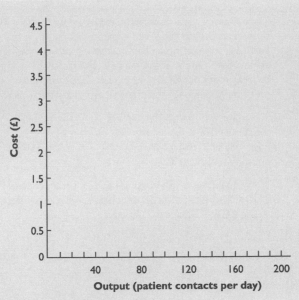

Figure 8.1 Short-run average cost

↻ **Feedback**

1 Marginal product is the total product associated with *x* number of nurses minus the total product with one less nurse. For the third nurse this is 70 − 30 = 40. The rest are shown in Table 8.2.

Table 8.2 Short-run production function for community nursing service (solution)

Number of nurses	Total product	Marginal product	Total variable cost	Total fixed cost (i.e. vehicle cost)	Total cost	Average (total) cost
1	15	15	30	50	80	5.33
2	30	15	60	50	110	3.67
3	70	40	90	50	140	2
4	100	30	120	50	170	1.7
5	130	30	150	50	200	1.54
6	150	20	180	50	230	1.53
7	170	20	210	50	260	1.53
8	180	10	240	50	290	1.61
9	190	10	270	50	320	1.68
10	200	10	300	50	350	1.75

Marginal product starts at 15, increases to 40 and then decreases gradually down to 10 extra visits per day. From this you can say that there are increasing marginal returns at first and then diminishing marginal returns thereafter.

The increasing returns might be explained by specialization of the nurses. Perhaps, with three nurses, each can visit a separate village or perhaps each nurse can specialize in a particular disease area. The decreasing returns might be explained by geographical spread. Each time an extra nurse is added they have to travel further and further away to treat more patients. They have to spend more time travelling and have less time to meet patients. Hence the marginal product diminishes.

2 The variable cost is the number of nurses multiplied by £30. For two nurses this is 2 × £30 = £60. The fixed cost is the number of vehicles, 2 × £25 = £50. Total cost is fixed cost + variable cost. For two nurses total cost is £60 + £50 = £110. The rest of the costs are shown in Table 8.2.

3 Average cost is total cost divided by total product. For two nurses average cost is £110 ÷ 30 = £3.67. The other results are shown in Table 8.2 and the curve is plotted in Figure 8.2.

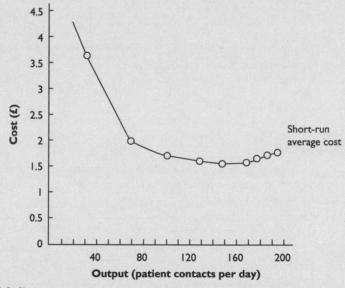

Figure 8.2 Short-run average cost (solution)

4 The short-term average cost curve is U-shaped (it falls at first then gradually levels out before beginning to rise). The falling average costs at the start of the curve are explained by two factors:

- increasing returns to nurses (this implies decreasing average variable costs as output rises)
- the spreading of fixed costs over a larger output – for example, average fixed costs are £1.67 when output is 30, but only £0.50 when output is 100

Average fixed costs are continually diminishing as output rises. However, the increasing returns to nurses eventually give way to diminishing returns. This implies increasing average variable costs. Eventually the increase in variable cost exceeds the decrease in average fixed cost and at this point the average cost curve starts rising.

Production in the long run

You will now consider production in the long term. Imagine it is the end of the financial year. As the manager of the community nursing service you are required to assess your potential for increasing total product. This is so that the Ministry can make an assessment of capital requirements for the forthcoming year. Together with your nursing staff you estimate your potential production to be as shown in Table 8.3.

Table 8.3 Total product (patient contacts per day)

Vehicles	Nurses									
	1	2	3	4	5	6	7	8	9	10
0	5	10	15	20	22	24	26	28	29	30
1	15	20	25	30	35	45	60	75	90	100
2	15	30	70	100	130	150	170	180	190	200
3	15	30	100	150	180	200	200	200	200	200
4	15	30	100	180	195	200	200	200	200	200
5	15	30	100	180	200	200	200	200	200	200

The table shows the maximum output achievable for a given combination of inputs. You will see, for example, that the third row (two vehicles) shows the same information as the second column in Table 8.1. Your concern is to ensure the service is *operationally efficient* which, as you learned in Chapter 4, means that no input can be decreased without also decreasing output.

Activity 8.2

Shade the items in Table 8.3 that are operationally inefficient.

Feedback

There are several combinations of vehicles and nurses that are operationally inefficient. For example, seven nurses and three vehicles is operationally inefficient because you can decrease the number of nurses to six and still have a total product of 200 contacts per day. Similarly the combination of six nurses and four vehicles is operationally inefficient because you can decrease the number of vehicles to three and still have an total product of 200 contacts per day. The operationally inefficient combinations are shaded in Table 8.4.

Table 8.4 Total product (patient contacts per day) (solution)

Vehicle	Nurses									
	1	2	3	4	5	6	7	8	9	10
0	5	10	15	20	22	24	26	28	29	30
1	15	20	25	30	35	45	60	75	90	100
2	15	30	70	100	130	150	170	180	190	200
3	15	30	100	150	180	200	200	200	200	200
4	15	30	100	180	195	200	200	200	200	200
5	15	30	100	180	200	200	200	200	200	200

Another concern you will have as a manager is what output you gain for each successive increase in input. Is the impact (or return) constant or does it vary with the overall size of the service?

Returns to a factor indicates the addition to output by increasing only *one factor*. *Returns to scale*, on the other hand, indicates the addition to output attained by increasing *all factors* by the same proportion. People talk about returns to a factor in the short term because at least one factor is fixed. Returns to scale is a long-run phenomenon because only in the long term can all factors be increased proportionally.

Increasing returns to scale are explained in the same way as increasing returns to factor – by improved division of labour and increased specialization. In the long term there is less constraint on specialization because the quantity of all factors is variable. Hence there may be increasing returns to scale over ranges where there were decreasing returns to a factor.

Decreasing returns to scale are usually explained by the difficulties involved with managing and coordinating all the decisions that need to be made to run a large organization.

 Activity 8.3

Compare the total product associated with one vehicle and one nurse with that for two vehicles and two nurses and so on. Are there constant returns to scale? What might explain the pattern you observe?

 Feedback

The output added by one nurse and one vehicle is 15 visits (see Table 8.5). If you add another nurse and another vehicle then you get 15 more visits. Over this range you can say that there are constant returns to scale. As you add another nurse and another vehicle you get an additional 70 visits. This means there are increasing returns to scale. If you do so again you get even more (80 visits) but afterwards the extra product from one nurse and one vehicle is only 20 visits. Therefore there are decreasing returns to scale. This may be explained by the geographical spread of the population and the fact that the population and therefore output is limited.

Table 8.5 Returns to scale

Input combinations	Total product	Extra product
1, 1	15	15
2, 2	30	15
3, 3	100	70
4, 4	180	80
5, 5	200	20

Now continue with your analysis of the long-term options for the community nursing service.

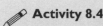 **Activity 8.4**

1   In Table 8.6 finish filling in the total cost associated with each input combination using the factor prices mentioned in Activity 8.1 – ignoring the operationally inefficient combinations. Also calculate the average cost for each combination and enter it between the parentheses.
2   What is the lowest cost for the following output levels: 20, 30, 100, 180, 200?

Table 8.6 Total cost (average cost) in £ per day

Vehicles	Nurses									
	1	2	3	4	5	6	7	8	9	10
0	30	60	90	120	150	180	210			
	(6)	(6)	(6)	(6)	(6.82)	(7.5)	(8.08)	( )	( )	( )
1	55	85	115	145	175	205	235			
	(3.67)	(4.25)	(4.6)	(4.83)	(5)	(4.56)	(3.92)	( )	( )	( )
2		110	140	170	200	230	260			
		(3.67)	(2)	(1.7)	(1.54)	(1.53)	(1.53)	( )	( )	( )
3			165	195	225	255				
			(1.65)	(1.3)	(1.25)	(1.28)				
4				220	250					
				(1.22)	(1.28)					
5					275					
					(1.38)					

 Feedback

1   Total cost is equal to the number of nurses multiplied by £30 plus the number of vehicles multiplied by £25. For two nurses and two vehicles this is $(2 \times 30) + (2 \times 25) = £110$. Average cost is total cost divided by output (output is given in Table 8.3). For two nurses and two vehicles this is $110 \div 30 = £3.67$. The full set of total and average costs is shown in Table 8.7.

2   There are three input combinations that give an output of 30: 2N2V, 4N1V and 10N. These have costs of £110, £145 and £300 respectively. Therefore the lowest cost method of producing 30 visits is two nurses and two vehicles. The other minimum cost points are given in Table 8.8. Every point in this table is *economically efficient* because at these points output cannot be increased without incurring extra cost. Or, put another way, they are situations where cost cannot be reduced without reducing the total product.

Table 8.7 Total cost (average cost) in £ per day (solution)

Vehicles	Nurses									
	1	2	3	4	5	6	7	8	9	10
0	30	60	90	120	150	180	210	240	270	300
	(6)	(6)	(6)	(6)	(6.82)	(7.5)	(8.18)	(8.57)	(9.31)	(10)
1	55	85	115	145	175	205	235	265	295	325
	(3.67)	(4.25)	(4.6)	(4.83)	(5)	(4.56)	(3.92)	(3.53)	(3.28)	(3.25)
2		110	140	170	200	230	260	290	320	350
		(3.67)	(2)	(1.7)	(1.54)	(1.53)	(1.53)	(1.61)	(1.68)	(1.75)
3			165	195	225	255				
			(1.65)	(1.3)	(1.25)	(1.28)				
4				220	250					
				(1.22)	(1.28)					
5					275					
					(1.38)					

Table 8.8 Long-run costs

Total product	Input combination	Total cost (£)	Average cost (£)
20	2 nurses, 1 vehicle	85	4.25
30	2 nurses, 2 vehicles	110	3.67
100	3 nurses, 3 vehicles	165	1.65
180	4 nurses, 4 vehicles	220	1.22
200	6 nurses, 3 vehicles	255	1.28

Another concern you will have as a manager is how the average cost of a nurse visit varies with the size of the service. In other words, are there *economies* (or *diseconomies*) *of scale*? Generally, economies of scale (i.e. average costs falling as output increases) are explained by three factors:

- increasing returns to scale;
- falling factor prices with increased scale;
- spreading of fixed costs.

Likewise, diseconomies of scale (i.e. increasing average costs with respect to output) are explained by:

- decreasing returns to scale;
- increasing factor prices with increased scale.

Table 8.9 summarizes the relationship between cost and output in the long run compared to the short run. Returns to scale have already been discussed. Factor prices might decrease with scale because the firm is able to negotiate a better deal with the suppliers of inputs – for example, the vehicle supplier might give discounts for multiple purchases. On the other hand, factor prices might increase with scale perhaps because the factor becomes harder to find. For example, it might be harder to find more than three nurses available for work in the local area and

Table 8.9 Causes of trends in average cost with respect to total product

	Short run	Long run
Average cost falls as output rises (economies of scale)	1 Increasing returns to *factor* (specialization)	1 Increasing returns to *scale* (specialization)
	2 Spreading of fixed costs	2 Decreasing factor prices
		3 Spreading of fixed costs
Average cost rises as output rises (diseconomies of scale)	Decreasing returns to *factor*	1 Decreasing returns to *scale* (i.e. bureaucracy)
		2 Increasing factor prices

therefore employing more will involve advertising or perhaps increased pay to lure nurses away from their current employment. For Figure 8.3, however, factor prices are assumed to be stable and the relationship between cost and output is caused by returns to scale alone.

It was stated that in the long run all factors are variable. However, there may be costs that are fixed with respect to output even in the long run. For example, marketing costs or research and development costs may be entirely unconnected to output. Therefore as output is increased, these costs are spread over a larger number of units.

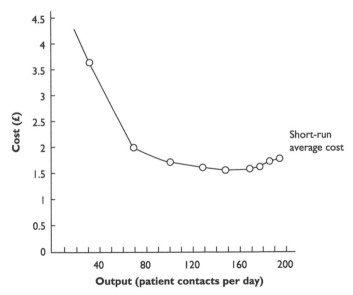

Figure 8.3 Short-run average cost

 **Activity 8.5**

1 For which input/output combination are average costs at their lowest?
2 In Figure 8.3, plot the long-run average cost curve alongside the short-term curve (from Activity 8.1). Does it display economies of scale? Why?
3 Consider what would happen if factor prices, such as the price of vehicles or of nurses, were to change.

Feedback

1 The output level with the lowest average cost (from Table 8.8) is 180 visits per day using four vehicles and four nurses. This is described as *scale-efficient* because at this output level the cost per visit is minimized. Therefore the size of the operation is optimal.

2 Figure 8.4 shows the long-run average cost plotted next to the short-run average cost curve that was plotted in Activity 8.1. The long-run curve has the same shape as the short-run curve – U-shaped. At higher levels of output the long-run cost curve is below the short-run curve. This is because the use of two vehicles is an inefficient technique for producing this level of output. The U-shaped long-run cost curve implies economies of scale initially followed by diseconomies of scale for higher levels of output.

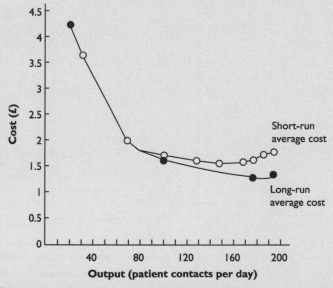

Figure 8.4 Long-run and short-run average cost

3 If the vehicle costs were higher, say £35 per day, then all input combinations with one or more vehicles would be more costly. The greater the number of vehicles the more would be the additional cost. A rise in the cost of vehicles, if the rise is large enough, will cause a cost-efficient provider to substitute from vehicles to nurses. For example,

Table 8.10 shows the cost of producing 180 visits a day using different input combinations. It shows the effect of an increase in the price of vehicles from £25 to £35. At £25, four nurses and four vehicles will be the least-cost method of producing 180 visits. However, at £35 five nurses and three vehicles will be the least-cost method of producing 180 visits. Hence the increase in vehicle price causes a substitution from vehicles to nurses. The change from £25 to £35 shifts the long-run average cost curve upwards. The substitution means that costs do not increase as much as they would have if the input levels had remained unchanged.

Table 8.10 Total cost of 180 visits (£)

Input combination	Cost if vehicle price is £25	Cost if vehicle price is £35
4 nurses, 4 vehicles	220	260
5 nurses, 3 vehicles	225	255
10 nurses	300	300

A rise in the price of *nurses*, on the other hand, will cause a cost-efficient provider to substitute nurses for vehicles. A country where the price of labour is high relative to the price of capital is likely to have more capital-intensive production. A country where the price of labour is low relative to the price of capital is likely to have more labour intensive production.

What do you think are the implications of the above cost analysis for community nursing service resource allocation? You can look at this question from two perspectives. First, the perspective of the producer (or provider) and second, the perspective of the service as a whole.

As far as the producer goes, the analysis does not tell us very much about the appropriate output level, although it does tell us which input combinations are economically efficient for each output level. The actual output level has to depend on the budget as well as the cost. If the budget of the community nursing service is £110 a day then they will be able to make 30 visits a day – see Table 8.8. Alternatively, if the budget is £275 a day then they will be able to produce 200 patient visits each day.

Summary

You have learned how the production function describes the relationship between inputs and output (or product) and the cost function describes the relationship between output and cost. You went on to learn about marginal outputs and economies of scale. In the short run this is because of increasing returns to factor (due to increased specialization) and the spreading of fixed costs. In the long run this is because of increasing returns to scale (due to increased specialization) and because input prices might decrease as output rises. Eventually average cost may get larger – diseconomies of scale. Finally you saw that when average costs are at their long-run minimum, the provider is not only technically efficient and economically efficient but also scale-efficient.

Costs: the broader service perspective

Overview

Now that you know more about the theory behind the supply curve, you will use this theory to discuss the advantages and disadvantages of large-scale production of health care.

Learning objectives

After working through this chapter, you will be able to:

- **diagnose whether economies or diseconomies of scale exist**
- **discuss the advantages and disadvantages of hospital mergers**

Key terms

Scale efficiency A situation where the provider is producing at an output level such that average cost is minimized.

Diagnosing economies of scale

You have looked at the implications of cost analysis for health care providers. Now you will find out about cost and efficiency analysis carried out on hospitals. In Chapter 8 you learned about average cost curves (Figure 8.4). Similarly you can plot a marginal cost curve. A marginal cost curve always intersects the average cost curve at its minimum. An example is shown in Figure 9.1.

If the marginal cost is lower than average cost, then average cost must be falling (i.e. there are economies of scale). Conversely, if marginal cost is greater than average cost then average cost must be rising (i.e. there are diseconomies of scale). If you add one unit of output and the cost of this extra unit is more than the average cost of all the other units then of course it must increase the average cost. Conversely, if you add one unit of output and the cost of this extra unit is less than the average cost of all the other units then it must pull down the average cost.

The implication of all this is that if you know a provider's marginal and average cost then you can say whether they are experiencing economies or diseconomies from their current scale. Economists estimate cost functions using regression

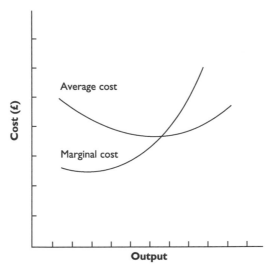

Figure 9.1 Marginal and average cost

analysis on hospital data in much the same way as they estimate demand functions (see Chapter 6). From the cost function, the marginal cost can be estimated for different output levels. Comparing these estimates of marginal costs with average cost estimates from the same data set allows the diagnosis of economies or diseconomies of scale.

There are several ways in which hospitals might seek to improve the efficiency of their operations:

- length of stay could be reduced;
- staff productivity could be increased;
- equipment could be fully utilized and maintained regularly;
- over-prescribing of drugs could be avoided;
- drug ordering and storage could be managed properly to avoid wastage and pilfering;
- nurses could replace doctors when appropriate;
- low-cost equipment could replace staff when appropriate;
- day surgery could replace inpatient stays.

If you have worked in a hospital, perhaps you have already experienced or attempted some of these measures. Were they successful? Implementation might be difficult, although some measures will be harder to enforce than others. To encourage efficient use of resources, hospitals should collect financial data and managers should be trained to carry out cost analyses. There is also a need for staff to be aware of the financial constraints of the hospital if implementation is to be effective.

Economies of scale: a case study

Suppose you are a regional director of community nursing services. You have 50 provider units spread across the region and each one has produced a cost analysis for the end of year financial report. You have to decide whether to redistribute vehicles between the different units. You also have the power to create additional units or merge current units. The situation at present is that every patient who needs treatment is being treated – if a patient is not being visited by one unit then they are being visited by a neighbouring unit instead. This amounts to 5000 patient visits per day. However, the government is cutting the budget and therefore cost savings are imperative. You want to cut costs without rationing care.

There are two possibilities for making the cost savings:

1 Encourage providers to be efficient by reviewing their choice of inputs and substituting between factors where necessary.
2 Change the scale of provider units in order to exploit economies of scale.

You carry out the first strategy but you still need to make more cost savings, so now you have to carry out the second strategy.

Suppose that every provider has the cost function outlined in Table 8.8 and each is producing 100 visits at least cost. You can work out how much cost can be saved by changing the scale of providers as follows.

There is a demand of 5000 patient visits a day across the region being produced at a total cost of £8250 a day (i.e. 5000 × £1.65). But if every unit was scale-efficient and produced 180 visits a day then only 28 units would be needed to supply the 5000 visits. The total cost of these 28 units would be £6100 (5000 × £1.22). The cost saving would therefore be £8250 – £6100 = £2150 each day.

Now see if you can estimate the cost savings if the scenario is slightly different.

Activity 9.1

1 Suppose again that each provider has the same cost function but instead of there being 50 units each producing 100 visits per day, there are 25 units each producing 200 visits a day. What cost savings can be made?
2 Suppose this time that there are 10 units producing 200 visits a day and 30 producing 100 a day. Again, what cost savings can be made?

Feedback

1 The cost of current production is 5000 × £1.28 = £6400. The cost of the scale-efficient output you know is £6100. Therefore there is a potential cost saving of £300 per day (£6400 – £6100).

2 The cost of the 10 units is 10 × 200 × £1.28 = £2560. The cost of the 30 units is 30 × 100 × £1.65 = £4950. Therefore the total cost of current production of £2560 + £4950 = £7510 per day. The potential cost saving is £7510 – £6100 = £1410.

When provider units are producing below the scale-efficient output then there are potential cost savings from merging. When provider units are producing above the scale-efficient output then there are potential cost savings from decentralizing production. If some provider units are above and some are below then there will be cost savings from transferring production between provider units.

Do hospital mergers achieve greater efficiency?

Does the size of a hospital affect its efficiency? The evidence suggests that only for small hospitals are there economies of scale and larger hospitals may actually have diseconomies of scale. Evidence from the USA suggests that the optimal size of a hospital is around 190 beds. This suggests that, purely on grounds of cost, large hospitals should not be constructed. Of course, other relevant considerations, such as feasibility of staffing, might outweigh concern about efficiency.

When inefficiency is exhibited it may not be a result of the size of the hospital but operational inefficiency in the system. For example, bed days could be reduced and output maintained. This highlights one of the difficulties encountered when trying to assess the efficiency of hospitals – to assess whether a hospital is scale-efficient you have to assume that it is operationally and economically efficient, which need not be the case.

Another reason why it is difficult to assess the relative efficiency of different providers is that you need to make sure that output is measured consistently across providers. It is difficult to quantify hospital output in a single measure. For example, should outpatient visits receive the same weighting as inpatient visits? Furthermore, when comparing the efficiency of different hospitals, you should adjust for differences in the types of patient they are treating and, even more importantly, take into account the health outcomes being achieved. Inputs should be measured consistently across providers as well. This is not always the case in practice because hospitals may have different methods of calculating capital costs and because the hospital may not be responsible for (and therefore may not record) all of its costs.

✎ Activity 9.2

In the British National Health Service (NHS), all secondary and tertiary care (i.e. hospitals) is provided by publicly-owned autonomous organizations called 'trusts'. There has been a tendency for these trusts to merge with each other to form larger trusts. The following abridged article by Nigel Edwards and Duane Passman (1997) discusses the economic and management consequences of these mergers. They consider not only economies of scale but also economies of scope (i.e. there may be economic benefits for an organization that originate from the scope or range of services it provides).

When you have finished reading, write notes in response to the following questions.

1 Why might management costs *not* be halved when two hospitals merge?
2 Besides management cost savings, what other arguments are there for and against hospital mergers?

All mixed up

Mergers have generally been proposed as a means of reducing management costs, or as a major element in programmes of strategic change or service rationalisation. But the evidence to support a policy of widespread mergers appears weak. There has been no evaluation of the results of trust mergers, nor is there any systematic study of the advantages and disadvantages of integrated trusts or multi-site acute trusts. A review of the international literature found that merged hospital systems in the US did not have lower costs than others. It also suggests that economies of scope and scale are unlikely to be exploited by merged organisations, which may actually experience significant diseconomies with increased size. This appears to be consistent with some of the evidence from both manufacturing and service industries, where there is an increasing trend towards de-merger.

It is not always clear what problem mergers are expected to address. But several plausible reasons for pursuing them can be identified: reducing management costs; a mechanism for replacing the current management team; implementing or promoting strategic change; improving service integration.

. . . They should: have measurable benefits for patients (even if only indirectly by allowing reductions in overhead costs); act as a catalyst for change and improvement in services – for example, allowing a critical mass of services or skills; provide benefits in cost or service terms that outweigh any loss of contestability; demonstrate long-term benefits that clearly outweigh any inevitable disruption.

Reducing costs

The idea that mergers reduce management costs is based on the theory that duplication can be eliminated. For example, at first sight it appears that the number of executive and non-executive directors and their support structures could be halved and other departments combined. But even if this is the case, the savings associated with top management are not very significant in the context of total trust turnover. Estimates of the available savings range from £200,000–£250,000, though some argue they could be as high as £400,000–£500,000. However, these figures may not be achieved in the short term: the increased size and complexity of the organisation means that structures cannot simply be halved.

This is a particular issue in mergers that bring together different activities, such as acute/community or acute/community/mental health, where it may still be necessary to retain very senior managers with specialist knowledge. Even in mergers of similar organisations, communication and co-ordination problems may increase exponentially with size (Sheldon et al. 1996). Second, in industry top managers' pay is related to turnover not to performance, and it would be reasonable to expect some pay inflation in the new merged trust for most director and second-in-line posts, if not beyond.

There are also significant implementation costs, including redundancy, which, if they involve early retirement, can have major long-term implications. If the elimination of duplication or management cost reductions are needed, other actions could be taken that would be less disruptive, are more certain of success and are less likely to divert the trust from the main business of managing its services. They may also be more rapidly achieved as mergers take at least 18 months to two years to execute.

Changing the team

Some believe there is a strong case for using mergers to change poorly performing trust management. This idea has its attractions, although more for purchasers than providers. Such a policy could provide a new set of incentives to improve efficiency, although it may also encourage undesirable purchaser micro-management of trusts . . .

Achieving strategic change

Trust mergers can play a crucial part in programmes of strategic change by aligning trust structures to fit new patterns of service, and by 'internalising the problem' of duplication and difficulties in rationalising services resulting from competition between trusts and their desire for organisational survival. Mergers also provide opportunities to address medical staffing/critical mass issues.

They can provide a catalyst for change, too – private sector mergers have been found to promote more wide-reaching change. The main mechanisms operating are the introduction of new managers and the engendering of a culture in which previous practice is questioned. One of the most significant effects of mergers of acute trusts is that they reduce the power of vested interests seeking to protect a particular site or service. It is significant that some of the most successful site rationalisation programmes have taken place within multi-site trusts, which have more options for change than a single-site institution.

Mergers may also reduce the inertia that can result from purchasers being locked into particular sites or services. Large trusts with multiple sites and different services can reallocate overheads more easily if purchasers shift work between services.

In these cases the cost savings, quality or improved efficiency gains come from the rationalisation of services rather than the merger. The implication is that mergers must follow strategy and cannot take place in isolation from plans for wider change. It is not clear that these strategies exist in all cases where mergers are being considered.

In these circumstances a decision is being made to trade the advantages of contestability for major – but probably one-off – cost savings, improved quality or efficiency from rationalisation. If contestability is lost it may be that new methods will be required for ensuring that efficiency and quality can continue to be tested.

Improving service integration

Mergers are not necessarily the best way to achieve improved integration of services between secondary, primary and social care . . . Issues of professional culture and approaches to patient management may have a more significant influence than management structure on whether services are integrated across the secondary-community/primary interface, and management intervention may only be able to affect this indirectly . . .

Implementation issues

The financial and non-financial costs of merger will often be an important factor in whether or not to go ahead, since any other advantages appear not to be particularly significant. Planning and carrying out a merger takes time and will inevitably divert management attention from strategic and operational issues. Such a loss of focus can have adverse effects on many of the activities so important in ensuring the smooth operation of a complex organisation. As a result, any benefits of a merger could be wiped out by the lost opportunities for change in other areas.

Public opinion is also relevant. Mergers may be associated with hospital rationalisation and redundancies. If trusts have a high profile locally, their disappearance could cause public anxiety. Little research exists on the role of health care providers in the local political economy. Though it is not possible to say whether this anxiety is valid, it is certainly worthy of more investigation.

Experience from industry and the NHS suggests that mergers based on a shared vision of the future, and by consent rather than hostile takeovers, are more likely to succeed, take less time to produce benefits, and cost less.

Mergers will not perform well against the criteria unless they are based on clear objectives about the direction of change rather than the search for short-term cost savings. Even then the costs need to be carefully weighed against the benefits. Caution is needed before trusts embrace mergers as the solution to reducing management costs or reconfiguring services . . .

Where there is a well developed strategy for site or service rationalisation, mergers can help by providing a catalyst for change and reducing the commitment to the maintenance of particular sites or services. Ideally, mergers in this context should be by consent and have the support of clinicians. A plan for mergers is not a substitute for a strategic plan for provision, it is merely a way to see it through . . .

Though in some cases mergers will be appropriate, a case-by-case approach is needed and a blanket policy of promoting them without further thought and research is likely to have more costs than benefits.

 Feedback

1 Management costs are not necessarily halved because:

- the organization to be managed has increased in size and complexity; communication and coordination problems may be much larger in the new structure
- if the two hospitals had different activities then managers with the appropriate expertise need to be retained from both
- senior managers' pay may have to be increased to reflect their increased responsibilities
- there may be substantial costs associated with the implementation of the merger; for example, if redundancy payments have to be made then these costs will offset the cost savings gained by the merger

The authors conclude that there may be more effective ways of reducing short-term costs.

2 Edwards and Passman suggest the following potential benefits of mergers:

- they can be used to remove poorly performing staff
- they can be used to implement major strategic changes (hopefully leading to cost savings in the long run)
- they can be used to improve service integration (although there is no evidence that this is the case)

The major disadvantage is that the merger might 'divert management attention from [other] strategic and operational issues'. It may also cause public anxiety if the hospitals involved have a high public profile.

Edwards and Passman do not rule out substantial cost savings from merger but they believe that they will arise only in the long term and only if the merger fosters the implementation of major strategic change. They feel that there may be better ways of achieving the benefits without the use of slow and costly merger. When considering merging or decentralizing hospitals or other health programmes, health planners should always bear in mind the implementation costs as well as the potential benefits.

Summary

You have learned that health service planners should organize their provider units such that each one is scale-efficient. This entails mergers if there are economies of scale and decentralization if there are diseconomies of scale. The empirical evidence seems to show that only in hospitals with fewer than 200 beds will there be economies of scale. Hospital mergers may offer various advantages but cost savings may not be one of them.

Having considered supply and demand functions over the past seven chapters, in the next two chapters you will learn about markets and their failings in health care.

References

Edwards N and Passman D (1997) All mixed up. *Health Service Journal* June 30th: page 1.
Sheldon T, Ferguson B and Posnett J (1996) *Concentration and choice in the provision of hospital services*. York: University of York.

SECTION 3

Markets

So far you have looked at the behaviour of providers of health care and of patients and have seen some ways in which knowledge of this behaviour can be used to inform health planning. However, you might still be wondering: 'why the fascination with markets?' In this and the next two chapters you will consider issues relating to markets and market failure. In this chapter you will learn why markets, when they are working well, are a highly effective system for the production and distribution of goods and services. You will also find out exactly what the necessary conditions are and you will consider whether these conditions can ever be met in the area of health care. In Chapters 11 and 12 you will look in more detail at the aspects of health care which together imply that a health care market will fail to allocate resources efficiently, before going on to consider questions of equity in the health care market.

After working through this chapter, you will be able to:

- **list and describe the assumptions of the perfectly competitive market**
- **give examples of markets which are highly competitive and those which are less so**
- **explain why perfectly competitive markets are efficient**
- **compare health care markets with the model of perfect competition**

Consumer efficiency A situation where consumers cannot increase their satisfaction by reallocating their budget.

Exchange efficiency Is achieved when the price at which a good or service is exchanged is equal to both the marginal social cost and the marginal social benefit of that good or service.

Market failure The failure of an unregulated market to achieve an efficient allocation of resources.

Perfect competition A market in which there are many suppliers, each selling an identical

> product and many buyers who are completely informed about the price of each supplier's product, and there are no restrictions on entry into the market.
>
> **Price taker** A supplier that cannot influence the price of the good or service they supply.

Highly competitive markets

In Chapter 4 you learned that markets are useful resource allocation mechanisms because they are automatic, responsive to changes in consumer preferences and, *under the right conditions*, allocatively efficient. You will now find out exactly what conditions are required for a market to be allocatively efficient.

A free market is one in which there is *perfect competition*. It is characterized by four features:

- many producers selling the same product to many purchasers;
- no restrictions on potential producers entering the market;
- existing producers have no advantage over the new producers;
- producers and purchasers are well informed about prices.

The following extract by Michael Parkin, Melanie Powell and Kent Mathews (2003) describes how perfect competition arises.

 **Activity 10.1**

While you are reading, make notes in response to the following questions:

1 Why are firms in perfectly competitive industries unable to influence their commodity's price?
2 Do you think health services in your country are perfectly competitive? Explain why.
3 Give some examples of highly competitive industries.

 How perfect competition arises

First, perfect competition arises if the minimum efficient scale of a single producer is small relative to the demand for a good or service. The minimum efficient scale is the smallest quantity of output at which long-run average cost reaches its lowest level. Where the minimum efficient scale of a firm is small relative to the demand, there is room for many firms in the industry.

Second, perfect competition arises when consumers don't care which firm they buy from. This usually happens when the goods and services produced by any one firm has no distinctive characteristics which differentiate it from the output of other firms in the industry.

Price takers

Firms in perfect competition make many decisions, but the one decision they never make is the price at which to sell their output. Firms in perfect competition are said to be price takers. A price taker is a firm that cannot influence the price of a good or service.

The reason why a perfectly competitive firm is a price taker is that it produces a tiny fraction of the total output of a particular good or service and buyers are well informed about the prices of other firms.

Imagine for a moment that you are an apple farmer in Brittany in France. You have a thousand acres under cultivation – which sounds like a lot. But when you take a drive around Brittany you see thousands more acres like yours full of apples. Your thousand acres is just a drop in an ocean of apples.

Nothing makes your fruit any better than any other farmer's, and all the buyers of apples know the price at which they can do business. If everybody else sells their apples for €0.5 a kilogram, and you want €0.6, why would people buy from you? They can simply go to the next farmer, and the one after that, and the next, and buy all they need for €0.5 a kilogram. You are a price taker. A price taking firm faces a demand curve that is perfectly elastic.

The market demand for apples is not perfectly elastic. The market demand curve is downward-sloping, and its elasticity depends on the substitutability of apples for other fruits such as pears, bananas and oranges. The demand for apples from farm A is perfectly elastic because apples from farm A are a *perfect substitute* for apples from farm B. A price taker faces a perfectly elastic demand curve.

Feedback

1 This question was illustrated by the example of the apple farmer. Because there are many suppliers of the commodity, any farmer raising their price above the market equilibrium price will find that they cannot sell their product. They cannot sell it because every buyer is fully informed about the prices suppliers are charging. The buyers are also fully informed that the quality of the good does not vary between suppliers. Suppliers could reduce their price below the market price but this would only result in reduced profits because they could already sell as much as they wanted at the higher price.

This leads on to two more assumptions associated with the model of perfect competition that were not stated by Parkin and colleagues but are implicit:

- all firms are profit maximizers
- all consumers are utility maximizers (it is sometimes said that 'consumers are rational' which means the same thing)

2 There are several ways that health services are not perfectly competitive.

a) For some areas of health care there may be many suppliers but for others not. Generally, primary care is provided by a large number of individual doctors and small group practices whereas specialist services often have few providers.

b) There are barriers to entry into the health care system. Doctors, nurses and other health professionals (quite rightly) need qualifications and a licence before they can provide health care.

c) Different providers are not selling an identical product. The quality (or at least the reputation for quality) of care and service is known to vary between providers.

d) For a lot of health care, consumers are not fully informed about what services they need and they cannot be sure about differences in quality between providers.

The health system in your country might feature these characteristics to a different extent but it will probably include most or all of them. For some services there might be only one provider.

3 Most agricultural industries are highly competitive. For although producers can be very large, each one only provides a small proportion of the world market. Although agricultural products may vary in quality to some extent, they will still remain close substitutes for each other.

Some manufacturing industries are competitive while others are not. These industries tend to be highly competitive when the following conditions hold:

• there are no patents
• manufacture is simple and cheap
• quality is obvious at the time of purchase

Likewise some service industries are competitive while others are not. Unless they are extremely specialized there may be many providers but consumers may not be fully informed about the quality of the service. For example, painting and hairstyling are competitive services because the results can be easily judged by the purchaser. With car or building maintenance on the other hand, shoddy workmanship may not show up for years or even decades.

Efficiency and competitive markets

You will now find out what constitutes allocative efficiency and why the perfectly competitive markets you have just read about attain allocative efficiency. You will sometimes find differing uses of particular economic terms describing efficiency. Table 10.1 provides a guide for interpreting these terms.

Given the imperfections of the health care market, can efficiency be achieved within a given health care system? This question is addressed by Cam Donaldson and Karen Gerard (2005) in the following extract from their book.

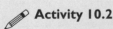 **Activity 10.2**

While reading, consider the following questions:

1 What is allocative (or social) efficiency?
2 Why is it a good thing for markets to be allocatively (socially) efficient?

Efficiency

Given the imperfections of the health care market, can social efficiency be achieved within a given health care system? The short answer is probably no, and the question then becomes how close can systems get to this outcome. In principle, social efficiency is an

Table 10.1 Different types of efficiency

Category	Definition	Necessary (but insufficient) conditions
Operational efficiency Also known as: • Technical efficiency • Producer efficiency • Scale efficiency • Technological efficiency	1 Producer's output cannot be increased without increasing one or more input; producer is on a production function 2 Each producer is producing output at minimum average cost; producer is at the bottom of its average cost curve	
Economic efficiency	Producer's output cannot be increased without increasing cost; producer is on its average cost curve	Operational efficiency
Allocative efficiency Also known as: • Pareto efficiency • Exchange efficiency • Social efficiency	Commodities traded at prices where social marginal cost equals social marginal benefit. No person's utility can be increased without reducing the utility of someone else. Demand equals supply; social costs equal private costs; social benefits equal private benefits	Operational efficiency Economic efficiency

uncontentious objective of any health care system because the objective seeks the greatest improvements in health from available resources. This is synonymous with what economists term minimising 'opportunity cost', i.e. minimising the cost to society of achieving these health benefits.

Minimising opportunity cost is derived from the notion of scarcity and the need to make choices between competing claims on resources. In economic terms, the decision to commit resources to tackling a health problem denies society the opportunity of using these resources to tackle other health problems. Therefore, some opportunities for improving health remain unfunded. The gains forgone are called opportunity costs. It follows that costs are inextricably linked with benefits. The optimum, social goal in any health care market – regulated market – can be defined as: maximise benefits and minimise costs. To have resources deployed inefficiently would mean that these resources could be reallocated to increase output and thereby social welfare.

Achieving efficiency is therefore about comparing the costs (or resources spent) and benefits (or well-being produced) of competing health care interventions and ensuring that resources are allocated in such a way as to maximise health gains to society.

There are two levels of efficiency: 'operational' efficiency and 'allocative' efficiency. Each of these is based on 'effectiveness'. These two types of efficiency and effectiveness represent different breadths of perspective, effectiveness being the narrowest and allocative efficiency the broadest. It is easier to talk about these levels because they apply to health care provision but it should be noted that they are important for evaluating changes in financing arrangements.

Effectiveness

Effective health care does not necessarily imply efficiency. It simply means that production or consumption of something will yield satisfaction (or utility). Thus, effective health care is about improving health status. Both operational and allocative efficiency, however, are necessarily conditional upon effectiveness. An example of effectiveness would be a drug with a proven beneficial impact on a health condition. The focus is limited to the production of health gains.

Operational efficiency

Operational efficiency asks the question, 'Given that some activity is worth doing, what is the best way of providing it?' This perspective brings costs into the calculus alongside effectiveness. Operational efficiency involves the selection between alternative means of achieving the same ends and may, therefore, be interpreted as the pursuit of maximum output for a given level of resources or minimum cost for a given level of output.

An example of operational efficiency would be if there was a choice between an effective drug therapy and a surgical operation to treat a given condition. Assessment of the costs and effectiveness of each option determines which is the more operationally efficient. If drug therapy is both less costly and more effective then it is clearly to be preferred. The difficult judgement is if one treatment modality is both less costly and less effective than the other. In such a situation, the cost-effectiveness ratios of the alternatives determine which is most efficient; the lower ratio indicates greater operational efficiency.

The 'rules' for achieving operational efficiency are thus:

- If one means of achieving a given end is less (more) costly and produces the same amount of output then this option should (should not) be preferred;
- If one means of achieving a given end is less costly and produces more output then this should be preferred;
- If one means of achieving a given end is less costly and produces less output then cost-effectiveness ratios should be computed, the lower ratio indicating greater efficiency . . .

Allocative efficiency

Allocative efficiency judges whether an activity is worthwhile doing and, given that much health policy is about the scale at which programmes should operate, allocative efficiency may also address the question of scale, or as economists term it, marginal analysis. Just as operational efficiency infers effective health care, so allocative efficiency infers operational efficiency. If something is deemed worth doing then it must be carried out in a way which ensures the optimum use of scarce resources. The social perspective is fundamental to allocative efficiency. This perspective ensures that due account is taken of all costs and benefits of interventions, regardless of whether they fall within or outside the health care sector (e.g. on families and patients or on the productive capacity of the economy) . . .

The rules of allocative efficiency capture the utilitarian ethic, the maximisation of satisfaction for the greatest number of individuals who collectively form society. It is important, however, to recognise the harm that over-zealous pursuit of allocative efficiency may lead to. It may create a pattern of resource and benefit distribution which discriminates against certain members of society; maximising health, or utility, from health care resources may not be conducive with a 'fair' distribution of health.

Feedback

> 1 *Allocative efficiency* describes a situation where resources are allocated and commodities distributed in a way that maximizes social welfare. *Social welfare* is total benefit minus total cost. For a particular market, social welfare is represented by the area below the *marginal social benefit curve* and above the *marginal social cost curve*. Social welfare is maximized at the point where marginal social benefit (MSB) equals marginal social cost (MSC). If MSB is greater than MSC then you can increase social welfare by increasing quantity because the extra benefit is greater than the extra cost. And vice versa: if MSB is less than MSC then you can increase social welfare by decreasing quantity because the benefit lost is less than the cost saved. A free market will be allocatively efficient if demand is equal to MSB and supply is equal to MSC. This will only be the case if there are no *market failures*.
>
> 2 It is a good thing for a market to be allocatively efficient because it means that total benefit to society is maximized. This means that the sum of the utilities of every person is maximized. However, this might mean that some people have a very large amount of utility but others have a relatively small amount. An allocatively efficient allocation might be considered to be unfair. In this case there is scope for government intervention even though there is efficiency. Equity is another objective of economics and is discussed in Chapter 12.

Competitive markets in health care

Now you will investigate whether competitive and efficient markets are present in the health sector or not. For patients to be *sovereign* in the health care market they must:

- judge the costs and benefits of health care;
- bear the costs and receive the benefits;
- purchase those treatments where benefits exceed costs.

For many areas of health care, these conditions do not hold. Patients find it very difficult to judge the benefits of health care. First, they are unsure of the possible benefits of the different treatment options. Second, after they have received treatment, they cannot be sure whether the treatment has worked or whether some other contributing factor cured the disease. They rely on health care professionals to help them make decisions. The professionals, however, are also suppliers and therefore may not act in the best interest of the patient even if they are fully informed about the preferences of the patient.

There are situations where patients are more knowledgeable. Where treatment options are relatively uncomplicated and purchase is a common event for individuals then they might have a clear idea of benefits. If there is a time gap between diagnosis and treatment then people might have time to gather the relevant information. An example is childbirth. Mothers can gather information about services that they might need. They will have an even better idea if they have been through childbirth before. The notion that patients bear all of their health care costs can also be disputed where there is health insurance. In this case they only indirectly bear the cost, with their premiums or taxes, and this does not directly reflect the cost of treatment. Similarly, patients do not always incur all the benefit. If the treatment is for an infectious disease then there will be benefits to the wider community from the reduced infection.

The last condition, that people make a choice over their own treatment, also does not hold in all areas of health care. Some patients will be incapable of making a decision. Also, people might become anxious as a result of having to make a decision about their health.

All of these examples would suggest that patient sovereignty is, to some extent, quite limited.

There clearly are failings in the market for health care but there are problems involved with government intervention as well. Government intervention will inevitably require some public funding (probably from taxation). If the government goes as far as taking over the health care market then huge amounts of finance will be required. Taxes are distortionary, whether they are on goods and services or on incomes. They change the equilibrium price and quantity and reduce social welfare in these markets. It is the *extent* of the market failure that is the important consideration. If market failures associated with health care are relatively minor then health care should probably be left to the market. In the next chapter you will assess the severity of market failures in health care. Then, in Chapter 12, you will look again at the arguments for and against government intervention.

Now, in the final activity of this chapter you will see an alternative view of the health care market. In the following extract, Martin Green (1995) presents the case made by supporters of a free market for health care. (Note: he is not related to David Green, whose views he describes.)

Activity 10.3

When you have finished reading, answer the following question:

What might a government do to try to make the health care market more competitive?

 ### The case for a free market in health care

What would happen if all health care was bought and sold in the market? The answer to this question is fiercely debated. Free market economists such as David Green argue that the market would deliver the best possible care at the lowest possible cost. He supports his view by using evidence from the USA. In 1986, he looked at the performance of the health care market in the USA and came to the conclusion that the introduction of a more effective free market in the early 1980s resulted in the emergence of a flexible, cost-effective system. He claimed that problems often associated with the American health care system were the result of a failure of the free market to operate.

Green argues that the problems of US health care in the 1960s and 1970s were the result of the doctors' monopoly power over supply. The doctors achieved this partly by restricting entry to the medical profession through limits on medical schools and partly by keeping consumers in ignorance. The doctors association, the American Medical Association (AMA), 'was able to keep a tight grip on the number of doctors trained and hence to limit the supply of doctors in active practice'. They also maintained the monopoly by preventing doctors from advertising which prevented consumers from gaining the information they needed to make a rational market choice.

This monopoly power was fatally undermined in 1982 when the US Supreme Court outlawed the AMA's ban on advertising. The Federal Trade Commission had already enforced a number of other pro-competition policies on the doctors such as making price fixing by the Michigan State Medical Society illegal. Combined with a significant expansion in the number of doctors, this led to the effective emergence of competition. Green argues that the emergence of this effective competition in the health care market has led to exactly the results predicted by the free market model. What are these results? A perfectively competitive free market will provide an allocation which is allocatively efficient. This means health care which accurately reflects consumer demand. It will also be productively efficient and deliver the health care for the lowest possible cost.

Green believes that American consumers now have a much greater choice of where to get their medical treatment and that increased competition has led to the producers of health care becoming more responsive to consumer demand. Another result of the increase in competition, Green argues, has been a significant fall in costs. In other words he claims that American health care has become more productively efficient. He cites as evidence the fall in hospital use and the fall in visits to doctors' surgeries between 1981 and 1985 – 'the producers are on the defensive as competition cuts costs and promotes high quality'. In particular, he notes that some day surgery centres are able to carry out over 750 medical procedures at savings of between 30% and 50% of hospital in-patient charges. He also cites the AMA's contention that as a direct result of increasing competition, the real purchasing power of doctors' incomes fell in 1984.

Green believes that the extension of the free market in health care in the US in the early 1980s brought substantial benefits, and in particular delivered exactly the kind of result that the free market model predicts. He does not claim that the American health care system is without problems but he does believe that those problems stem from the effects of state interference rather than the failure of the market.

 Feedback

The government should carry out policies that make restrictive practices illegal and which increase the knowledge of patients. Policies carried out in the USA to reduce monopoly power in the health care market have included:

- outlawing the ban on advertising (which had suppressed consumer information)
- banning price setting by professional bodies – price setting implies that doctors are not competing in terms of price
- increasing the number of medical graduates

Markets are not the only way that efficiency can be fostered. In public (and sometimes private) provision of health care, individual programmes are financed by setting budgets (rather than charging a fee for every service). In these cases economic evaluations can be carried out so that resources are allocated efficiently. Services are provided if they yield a large health benefit compared to their resource use. Services for which this is not the case are not provided.

In this chapter you have looked at whether health care markets are efficient, and a number of market failures were identified. In the next chapter you will look at these market failures in more detail and consider some remedial policies.

Summary

You have learned about the circumstances necessary for a perfectly competitive market in which patients would be sovereign and firms are price takers. You also saw how allocative efficiency is when social welfare is maximized – that is, marginal social benefit is equal to marginal social cost. Perfectly competitive markets are allocatively efficient because marginal social benefit equals demand and marginal social cost equals supply. However, most areas of health care are not highly competitive, which you will learn more about in the next chapter.

References

Parkin M, Powell M and Mathews K (2003) *Economics* (5th edn). Harlow: Addison-Wesley.
Donaldson C and Gerard K (2005) *Economics of health care financing. The visible hand* (2nd edn). Basingstoke: Palgrave Macmillan.
Green M (1995) *The economics of health care*. London: Office of Health Economics.

Market failure

Overview

In the previous chapter you found out about the characteristics required in order for a market to operate efficiently. It was concluded that health care markets are not inherently efficient. In this chapter you will look in more detail at the ways in which markets fail. You will also look at the options that are available to governments who want to make resource allocation in these markets more efficient.

Learning objectives

After working through this chapter, you will be able to:

- **categorize and describe the activities of government**
- **describe why monopoly power, externalities and information asymmetries constitute market failures**
- **explain the consequences for price, output and efficiency for each market failure**
- **explain how monopoly power, externalities and information asymmetries manifest themselves in the health care market**
- **suggest some possible government strategies for each health care market failure**

Key terms

Adverse selection When a party enters into an agreement in which they can use their own private information to the disadvantage of another party.

Barriers to entry Factors which prevent a firm from entering a market.

Deadweight loss The loss in allocative efficiency resulting from the loss of consumer surplus is greater than the gain in producer surplus.

Externality Cost or benefit arising from an individual's production or consumption decision which indirecly affects the well-being of others.

Fee-for-service (FFS) A means of paying health care staff on the basis of the actual items of care provided.

Monopoly power Ability of a monopoly to raise price by restricting output.

Moral hazard A situation in which one of the parties to an agreement has an incentive, after the agreement is made, to act in a manner that brings additional benefits to themselves at the expense of the other party.

Natural monopoly A situation where one firm can meet market demand at a lower average cost than two or more firms could meet that demand.

Price discrimination Offering the same product at different prices to different people.

Public good A good or service that can be consumed simultaneously by everyone and from which no one can be excluded.

Social cost Private cost plus external cost.

Supplier-induced demand Increased demand as a result of a provider (e.g. a doctor) exploiting an asymmetry of information.

Transaction costs The costs of engaging in trade – i.e. the costs arising from finding someone with whom to do business, of reaching an agreement and of ensuring the terms of the agreement are fulfilled.

Market failure and the economic theory of government

According to economic theory, there are three main areas of government activity:

- redistribution of wealth and income;
- stabilization of the macroeconomy (to keep unemployment, inflation and economic growth at reasonable levels);
- correction of microeconomic market failure.

As regards the last of these, there are four circumstances in which governments can and should get involved:

- ensuring and protecting public goods;
- controlling monopoly power;
- reducing externalities;
- reducing asymmetry of information.

You will consider each of these in turn before looking at market failure in health care.

Public goods

A public good is 'a good or service that can be consumed simultaneously by every-one and from which no individuals can be excluded. If the provider of a public good tries to ask people how much they are willing to pay to receive it, consumers say they don't want it. Why? Because the consumers know that once the good is provided they can consume it even if they don't pay for it. This is called the free-rider problem' (Parkin *et al.* 2003).

So, is health care a *public good*? It isn't. For one thing, it is *rival*. If one person consumes a drug (or a consultation) then there is one drug (consultation) fewer available for others to consume. Health care is also excludable – providers can easily prevent individuals from consuming it.

There are public health examples of public goods though. Mills and Gilson (1988) cite the case of malarial management through environmental control. They give the example of pond cleaning. Everyone in the community can benefit from having a malaria-free water supply without stopping anyone else from benefiting – it is non-rival. Furthermore no one can be excluded from this benefit. Such programmes will be under-provided by the market because people hope to benefit without having to contribute to the cost. In other words, there are incentives for *free-riding*.

Monopoly power

In Chapter 10 you learned that allocative efficiency was achieved only when there were many firms (providers) in the market. You now need to consider the consequences for price, output and efficiency when there is only one supplier in the market.

A producer should produce at the output where marginal cost equals marginal revenue because this is the output level where profits (total revenue minus total cost) are maximized. For a monopoly producer, marginal revenue is below the demand curve. This is because a one unit increase in output increases revenue by the amount of the price of that unit (indicated by the demand curve) *minus* the loss in revenue on the other units caused by the associated fall in price. However if, as sometimes happens, a monopoly producer price discriminates then marginal revenue is the same as the demand curve. Price discrimination means offering the same product at different prices to different people. For example, railways and airlines often charge lower prices to students, young people and elderly people. This is not an act of generosity. Quite the opposite, it is a way of maximizing profits. Parkin and colleagues note that 'by charging the highest price for each unit of the good that each person is willing to pay, a monopoly perfectly price-discriminates and captures all the consumer surplus'. In practice, monopolies are never able to perfectly price discriminate but they can discriminate between different groups of people where each group has a different elasticity of demand.

 Activity 11.1

Drawing on your own knowledge and understanding of health care, can you think of any features that are characteristic of a monopoly? You need to consider aspects such as whether alternative providers are feasible and available, and whether any barriers to entry exist to stop new providers (either individual practitioners or organizations such as hospitals).

 Feedback

In some cases there are *close substitutes* to health care but in most cases there are probably not. For example, if someone has influenza then they could take drugs for symptomatic relief. They could alternatively just spend some time in bed until the symptoms stop. In this case rest is a substitute for medication. However, with a disease like appendicitis there is no real substitute for surgical treatment.

Health care professionals require a licence to practise. This licence is an example of a *barrier to entry* in the health care market. Patents are also barriers to entry because they prevent other manufacturers from producing a particular good. Patents are very common in the pharmaceutical industry. There may be examples of legal monopolies in health care in some countries as well.

Health care providers are not usually considered to be *natural monopolies*. It was noted in Chapter 8 that economies of scale exist only for small hospitals. It is unlikely, therefore, that a single provider can operate at a lower cost than would be achievable by several competing providers. However, in rural areas travel to other providers may be prohibitively expensive such that the local hospital is in effect a monopoly supplier for the local population.

✎ Activity 11.2

For many years a cervical cancer screening programme based on examining slides under a microscope has existed. In 2003 the government decided that private laboratories should carry out the laboratory work. There were 100 laboratories competing for this business. Since there are no significant economies of scale in this work, the firms carrying it out can be described in terms of the classic perfect competition model (see Figure 11.1).

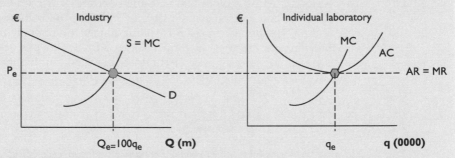

Figure 11.1 Hypothetical market for cervical screening before the introduction of new technology – a perfectly competitive market

However, in 2005 it was agreed that this technology was no longer appropriate and it was decided that the manual reading of slides should be replaced by automated reading, which was found to be much more accurate. Since a patent exists on this technology and there are great economies of scale, the result will be that the (single) firm that holds the patent will provide all services. The simple monopoly model in Figure 11.2 describes the new situation.

Compare the pattern of price, cost and output in the two scenarios. Why is monopoly provision against the interest of users?

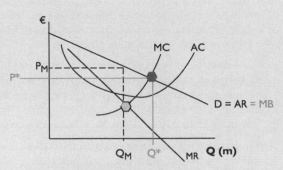

Q_M = Monopolist's profit-maximizing output
Q^* = Allocatively efficient output

Figure 11.2 Hypothetical market for cervical screening after the introduction of new technology – a monopoly market

↻ **Feedback**

If we assume there are no externalities, then MC = marginal social cost (MSC) and MB = marginal social benefit (MSB). This means that the competitive market was allocatively efficient. But with the new technology, a single provider could produce at a lower cost than multiple providers. This producer, if it was a profit maximizer, would have an incentive to produce at Q_M, which is below the allocatively efficient output (Q^*, where MC = MB). (Remember that there is no supply curve in the case of a monopoly, since quantity and price are determined by the interaction of demand and cost functions.) This is against the interests of consumers because units of output where the benefit exceeds the cost (MB > MC) would not be provided.

The advantage of the new technology is that *potentially* we can reduce costs, increasing the supply of the service. The disadvantage is that it allows a single provider to exert monopoly power. There are steps that the government can take to make sure that monopoly power is curbed and service provision is increased:

- they could make the market contestable – offering the monopoly to the provider that offered to cut prices the most; or
- they could put a ceiling on the price to bring it down to the social optimum price, P^* – where there is a monopoly, a price ceiling can lead to increased output (this is unlike a price ceiling in a competitive market, which will reduce the quantity supplied).

There is a particular problem when patent protection is involved. In this case, a supplier is allowed to be the sole provider of a good because it has developed the technology itself. Without patents, suppliers would not have the incentive to develop new more efficient technologies because their competitors could adopt the new technology immediately without the expense of research and development costs. The down side of patents is that the firm is able to restrict output and raise price during the period that the patent is in operation.

Why are monopolies inefficient? Monopolies transform consumer surplus into producer surplus. However, the loss in consumer surplus is less than the gain in producer surplus. Therefore, there is an overall loss to society – the *deadweight loss* – a measure of loss in allocative efficiency.

It is sometimes suggested that monopolies are less able to achieve technical and allocative efficiency. It is argued that their incentive to reduce cost is diminished because monopolies have very large profits already. On the other hand, the vast majority of research and development comes from very large suppliers, implying that these firms pay considerable attention to cost reduction.

You have seen that markets with many suppliers tend to be very efficient (given that certain conditions are met) but that markets with only one supplier are allocatively inefficient. So what is the situation when there are a few suppliers? (Such a system is called an oligopoly.) Well, the decisions of suppliers become very complicated when there are only a few suppliers. This is because the decisions of any one producer in the market will have consequences for all the other firms. Although the situation is complicated, it is safe to assume that the smaller the number of producers, the easier it is for them to restrict output and raise price, and therefore the less efficient is the market.

The factors that lead to (inefficient) monopoly power are:

- few providers;
- few close substitutes;
- barriers to entry.

The existence of professional bodies might imply that supply of these professionals is restricted and this in turn implies higher salaries than there would be if there were perfect competition – i.e. that there is allocative inefficiency.

In rural areas the scarcity of hospitals might mean that hospital services are priced artificially high. Again this is inefficient. However, monopoly pricing may not occur if providers are non-profit-making.

Externalities

You may have heard the term 'externalities' but exactly what does it mean? Parkin and colleagues (2003) describe it as follows:

> An externality is a cost or a benefit arising from an economic transaction that falls on people who do not participate in the transaction. They cannot partici- pate because there is no market for the cost or benefit. For example, when a chemicals factory (legally) dumps its waste into a river and kills the fish, it imposes an externality – in this case, an external cost – on the fisherman who lives downstream. External costs and benefits are not taken into account by the people whose actions create them if there are no markets – and no prices – for these costs and benefits. For example, the chemicals factory does not take the damaging effects on the fish into account when deciding whether to dump waste into the river because there is no market for waste water.

The normal interactions in the market take personal benefits into account, since private demand functions reflect self-assessed benefits to individuals. However, in the case of vaccinations, one person's consumption also yields benefits to other people but these additional benefits are not taken into account when an individual makes their decision whether or not to purchase – hence they are external benefits. We can represent this graphically by showing that the value placed by society on each unit of output (MSB) is greater than that the value placed by the individual purchaser (marginal private benefit, MPB), as indicated by the demand curve in Figure 11.3.

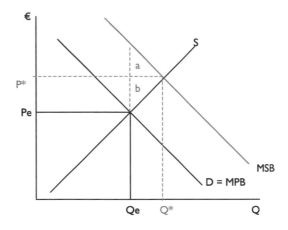

P*, Q* = Allocatively efficient price and output level
Pe, Qe = Profit-maximizing price and output level
D, S = Demand and supply
MPB = marginal private benefit (= demand)
MSB = marginal social benefit
Area a + b = the deadweight loss to society due to the market failure associated with external benefits

Figure 11.3 An example of external benefits: the market for vaccination against measles

To increase the consumption of vaccinations up to the social optimum, the government could consider a voucher scheme, a price subsidy or perhaps there could be state provision of vaccinations.

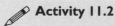 **Activity 11.2**

Write down your responses to the following questions:

1 What is the defining characteristic of an externality?
2 Can you think of any examples of health-related external costs and benefits?

Feedback

1 An externality is a cost or benefit arising from an individual's consumption or production decision which indirectly affects the well-being of others. The most obvious

example of an external cost is that associated with industrial pollution. A power station releases chemicals into the atmosphere. These chemicals create costs in terms of reduced agricultural production in the surrounding area and reduced health. These costs are not incurred by the power station, they are incurred by the nearby community. If the costs were incurred by the power station then it would produce less pollution.

2 The external benefits of health care are the benefits to the population as a whole (in terms of risk reduction) of removing and preventing infectious diseases. You will learn more about this later in the chapter.

Many forms of production and consumption may have external health costs. An example is the consumption of cigarettes. There is now good evidence that passive smoking (the involuntary inhalation of smoke from cigarettes) harms people's health. Therefore there is an external cost associated with smoking. When someone decides how many cigarettes to consume they weigh up the benefits against their own private costs (the price plus the costs to their own health). They are unlikely to consider the costs incurred by the people around them.

Asymmetry of information

Asymmetry of information exists when one person in an economic transaction has more relevant information than the other person. It requires that the cost to the uninformed person of accessing this information is prohibitively high. If the informed person has an appropriate incentive then, after their transaction has been agreed, they might use it to the disadvantage of the uninformed person. This is called *moral hazard*. Under normal circumstances, the uninformed person would gather information so that they can minimize their loss. In this circumstance, the cost of information-gathering is so expensive that it would completely offset any benefits gained from the original transaction. As such it is a market failure. It is inefficient because the result will not reflect the costs of the uninformed person and hence, as with externalities, private costs do not equal social costs.

Someone who is insured may have an incentive to act recklessly. If they do so then it is the insurer who is likely to suffer financially. The insurer could build a clause into the contract that disallowed such behaviour but it would be too costly to monitor all those they insure to see if they are adhering or not. Hence you are left with a situation where the insured acts in a way such that the benefit of their action (the reckless behaviour) is less than the social cost of this action.

Information asymmetry can be used to one's advantage not only after an agreement has been made but also at the agreement stage. Informed people who will benefit most from an agreement (to the detriment of the uninformed person) are more likely to enter the agreement. The uninformed person cannot tell whether the agreement will be to their own disadvantage or not because they do not have the necessary information. This is *adverse selection*.

In the case of insurance, if someone thinks they are a low risk then they are less likely to take-up insurance than someone who believes themselves to be a high risk. This will mean that only high-risk people will pool their risks and low-risk people will not. However, the insurer will not be able to tell if those they insure are high or low risks. If the insurer could afford to gather information on the risk level of each person they insure then they could offer a premium that was beneficial to each person. As things stand there will be a sub-optimal level of insurance.

The best way of correcting an informational asymmetry is to create a contract whereby the informed party has an incentive to behave in a way that benefits the uninformed party. You may recall that this was discussed in Chapter 7 regarding the doctor–patient relationship. There are two methods used by insurance companies to reduce moral hazard.

The first method involves reducing premiums for people who have made no claims in previous similar transactions. This method helps to distinguish low-risk from high-risk persons and therefore gives the insurer the ability to offer premiums that reflect the risk levels of each group. The method will not be perfect, however, because some high-risk clients will not have made a claim yet whereas some unfortunate low-risk clients will have already had to make a claim. Furthermore this cannot be applied when someone has never taken out a policy before or if it is not possible to verify whether they have made a claim or not. The strategy will provide insured people with an incentive to minimize their risk because if they do not and they then need to make a claim it will cause their future premiums to be increased.

The second method is to charge deductibles. That is, the insured has to pay out a certain amount every time they make a claim. This means that the insured has an incentive not to act recklessly. As with the first method the insurer can use this to distinguish high and low risks. A policy with relatively high deductibles and low premiums will be attractive to low risks but not to high risks. A policy with relatively low deductibles and high premiums will be attractive to high risks but not to low risks.

In the case of health insurance, the idea that high-risk people (notably the chronically sick) have to pay higher premiums is unacceptable to many people. This could be described as unfair but it is not a 'market failure'. Government intervention to promote fairness is considered in Chapter 12. Before that, you will learn more about market failures as they occur in the area of health care.

Market failure in health care

An alternative approach to categorizing reasons for market failures to that described earlier in this chapter is to distinguish between three causes of failure:

- failure of the health insurance market (including asymmetries of information and monopoly power);
- health care externalities;
- failure of the health care market (including asymmetries of information and monopoly power).

These are the categories used in the rest of this chapter.

Health insurance market failures

When considering health insurance market failures, you need to consider three questions:

* Why is there a lack of competition in the health insurance market?
* What policies are used to counteract moral hazard in the health insurance market?
* What groups of people are likely to be without health insurance?

The reason for the lack of competition in the health insurance market is the existence of economies of scale. Larger firms are able to operate at a lower average cost than smaller firms. These larger firms can therefore charge lower premiums than their smaller rivals. Hence, there will be a tendency for small firms to go out of business. Equilibrium will occur where there are a few large firms. The economies of scale exist because insurance companies incur substantial fixed costs – marketing costs. Larger firms have smaller average costs because the fixed costs are spread over a larger output. There may also be returns to scale associated with processing bills and collecting premiums. These returns to scale contribute further to the economies of scale. The situation with health insurance is very different from the case of hospitals. You may recall that the evidence suggests that economies of scale are not significant for hospitals.

As there are few suppliers in the market there is potential for the exploitation of market power. The insurance companies may be able to restrict output and raise price (compared with the perfectly competitive equilibrium). This increases the insurers' profits but constitutes a market failure because the loss of consumer surplus more than offsets the gain in profit. Adverse selection in the health insurance market also implies under-provision. This will occur if the insurers use community rating. If they use experience rating then adverse selection will be avoided. The market will be efficient but many high-risk people will not be able to afford health insurance – which one might consider to be unfair. In either case there can be an argument for a compulsory public health system.

Consumer and producer moral hazard may not necessarily imply general under-provision. More likely it implies that resources are allocated inefficiently, with some worthwhile treatments not being carried out while others that are not beneficial are being carried out. The asymmetry of information may mean that providers do not compete in terms of price because purchasers (consumers and insurers) will not recognize if the price represents good value or not. Instead they compete by providing indicators of quality that the purchasers will recognize. These indicators include high technology equipment, high-quality hotel services and highly esteemed clinicians. All of these indicators will represent a large cost to providers of health care. The tendency will be for demand and prices to rise to much higher levels than if consumers of health care were fully informed. High-cost services will be over-provided. On the other hand, low-cost treatment will be under-provided such that less well-off people will not be able to obtain treatment, even though it is cost-effective for them.

The economies of scale in the health insurance industry represent a market failure for another reason. Some of the costs incurred by insurers are *transaction costs*. Transaction costs are the costs of engaging in trade, as opposed to the costs of production and distribution. According to Parkin *et al.* (2003) they are: 'the costs arising from finding someone with whom to do business, of reaching an agreement about the price and the other aspects of exchange, and of ensuring that the terms of the agreement are fulfilled'. If the transaction costs are particularly large then it may be that a single supplier is a more efficient allocation mechanism. This is because, in the absence of competition, many transaction costs may be avoided. Although it has not yet been made explicit, the absence of transaction costs can be considered another condition of perfect competition.

The problem with having only one supplier is that it is likely to exploit its monopoly power. In contrast, a social insurance or a tax-financed health system may be more efficient than a competitive private insurance system. This is because the former systems can exploit economies of scale fully and they can avoid certain transaction costs. For example, in the UK, administration constitutes only 2.6 per cent of NHS costs compared with 26 per cent for private hospitals in the USA (Audit Commission for England and Wales 1995; Woolhandler and Himmelstein 1997).

Moral hazard is tackled by providing appropriate incentives to consumers and providers of health care. Consumer moral hazard is countered by making consumers pay part of their bill. These payments are called *co-payments* if they are a proportion of the total payout, or *deductibles* if they are a fixed amount. Often insurers also put an upper limit on the payout. In publicly-funded health systems, user charges may be applied. The patient therefore has an incentive to look after their health just as if they were having to pay for part of their treatment.

Alternatively, insurers can try to reduce their payouts by providing health care providers with appropriate incentives. Insurers can negotiate contracts where they pay the providers in advance. This prospective payment forces the risk on to the providers. The providers now have a fixed budget to work from and they therefore have an incentive to provide all necessary care to an insured population. Alternatively, the insurer could build protocols into their contracts with providers. This would mean that providers can only charge the insurer for services rendered if certain (clinical) criteria have been met.

There will be two groups of people who are uninsured. First, those who consider themselves to be of low risk but cannot find an insurance policy that reflects this low risk. This will happen if the insurer is not independently informed of this low risk. This constitutes a market failure (adverse selection) because a premium acceptable to both insurer and insured could be found if the asymmetry of information did not exist.

The other group who are likely to remain uninsured are those at high risk who cannot afford to pay an actuarially fair premium. This is not a market failure but might be seen as unjust, in which case it may receive a large amount of political attention. Government intervention for reasons of justice is examined in Chapter 12. Even in the USA, which spends more money per capita on health care than any other country, there are an estimated 42 million people with no health insurance cover at all (Schroeder 2001). It seems that many of these people may have a higher than average health risk. A compulsory social insurance system might be justified on both efficiency and equity grounds. Such a system was the basis of the health reforms that were proposed by President Clinton but rejected by the US Congress in the early 1990s. The idea of compulsory insurance is looked on critically in the USA where freedom of choice is seen as a high ideal.

Health care externalities

External benefits arise from infectious disease control and, it is argued, from health care generally because people value the health of others. It is largely for this reason that there are many health-related charities. Given such support, could health care be funded entirely in this way? Historical examples, such as the voluntary hospital movement in nineteenth century England, suggest not because there are substantial transaction costs. First, there is the cost of searching for a worthwhile cause. Second, charities have administrative costs such that only a proportion of the money donated reaches the needy. There may be a free-rider effect as well. Although people do get benefit from seeing other people healthy, they may be happier letting other people's donations achieve this goal. Therefore some government action may be necessary to reduce the transaction costs and increase health care output to the social optimum.

External benefits from programmes to control communicable diseases mean that these services will be under-provided by private markets. There is a good case for government intervention in this area to increase production. Caring externalities would imply that health services in general are under-provided by private markets. This suggests a need to subsidize health care or subsidize incomes so that people can afford to buy more health care.

The first strategy may be very costly, in terms of the tax revenue required, because you are subsidizing everyone including the people who were able to pay in the first place. As was noted in Chapter 6, the more responsive the quantity demanded is to price, the more cost-effective is the subsidy. Of course, if the subsidy is taking place as part of a social insurance system then there will be efficiency savings from reduced transaction costs as well as from internalizing externalities.

The second strategy of giving cash benefits to the needy may be cheaper but there are a couple of difficulties associated with it:

- First, there is the problem of identifying who is needy. There may be considerable administrative costs involved. If there are costs to the applicant as well then many needy people may be discouraged from applying.
- The second problem is that people might spend their benefits on things other than health. Just as the effectiveness of a price subsidy is dependent on the price elasticity, so the effectiveness of an income subsidy is dependent on income elasticity. One way of getting around this is to give to the needy 'health vouchers' which can be spent only on health care. However, such systems have higher administrative costs than cash benefit systems.

Health care market failures

A major difficulty with subsidizing health care, whatever the method, concerns the existence of asymmetry of information. Purchasers of health care are not fully informed about the effectiveness of treatments. Therefore, you cannot be sure that injecting more money into the system will definitely lead to more socially beneficial treatment.

There may be a role for government in the evaluation of different treatments to assess their cost-effectiveness. The government could use these evaluations to decide which treatments should be provided out of the fixed budget and which ones are not beneficial enough. The government could also collect and disseminate evidence on the effectiveness of different interventions and different providers to try to reduce the asymmetry of information between providers and consumers.

Activity 11.3

From your reading so far and your own experience and understanding, try and answer the following questions:

1 Licensing of doctors and other health care professionals is necessary and inevitable. Why might it be inefficient though?
2 It has been observed that health systems with fee-for-service payment systems (i.e. providers are paid for the care they decide to provide) have higher utilization rates. What might explain this observation?
3 In a system with third-party payers (such as social insurance), there are theoretically three asymmetries of information. One is the doctor–patient relationship, which may lead to supplier-induced demand. What might be the other two?

Feedback

1 It was noted earlier that the existence of licensing is a barrier to entry into the health care market. As such it provides a potential for the exploitation of market power. In most countries there is a large number of doctors so we would expect the health care market to be competitive, but there are several reasons why this might not be the case:

a) Because doctors are much better informed than the purchasers of their services, they may be able to act as if they were a monopoly even though they are not. They can influence price because purchasers are uninformed about the relative quality of different providers. Patients who are uninformed about the effectiveness of services may, on the advice of their doctor, buy them at a price that is higher than the benefit they receive. This is called *supplier-induced demand*. Doctors will only have an incentive to do this if the financial reward for giving the service is relatively high.

b) Organizations that represent the interests of particular professions may have considerable power in a health service. It is important that these bodies do not have a role in setting fees for services. This would mean that doctors had control over both output and price in the health care market. If the fee was set relatively high then doctors would have incentives to increase provision beyond the allocatively efficient level (supplier-induced demand). You may recall that it was argued in Chapter 10 that there were efficiency gains in the US health care system after the powers of professional bodies were limited.

c) Specialist doctors may find that they really do have a monopoly on the services that they supply. They will be able to supply their services to patients or employers at a very high price.

2 Doctors have the ability to induce or reduce the demand of their patients for various services. This is because they are more informed than their patients about the

effectiveness of these services. If they receive a fee and the fee level is set relatively high then doctors have an incentive to encourage the patient to accept relatively ineffective tests or treatments. (The observation that health systems with fee-for-service payments have higher utilization rates has been cited as evidence of this. However, there are other interpretations of this evidence.) Doctors will only have an incentive to do this if the financial reward for giving the service is relatively high. Furthermore, if the fee levels are relatively low then they have an incentive to provide a less than optimal level of service. Another interpretation of the evidence is that the doctors in fee-for-service systems are providing optimal service levels but that the other systems are providing below the social optimum. It is also possible that there are differences in the quality of services between the different systems. Anecdotal evidence suggests that the non-medical aspects of care (e.g. accommodation) may be better where there is fee-for-service although not necessarily the effectiveness of treatment.

One role of government in the area of health care could be to control fee levels for doctors' services. The government would try to set fees at the allocatively efficient level. This would be the level that would be set by the market if patients were perfectly informed.

3 Table 11.1 outlines the possible asymmetries.

Table 11.1 Relationships with asymmetric information

Informed party	Uninformed party	Market failure
Doctor	Patient	Imperfect agency
Doctor	Payer*	Provider moral hazard (supplier-induced demand)
Patient	Payer*	1 Consumer moral hazard
		2 Adverse selection

* Payers may be private insurers, the social insurance system, or the government

You have read about the different types of inefficiency that occur in the health care market. In the next chapter you will look at the other major economic objective, equity, and you will see how this concept relates to health and health care.

Summary

You have learned about the role of government, according to economic theory, and the four situations in which governments can and should get involved: protecting public goods; controlling monopoly power; considering externalities; and coping with information asymmetries. You went on to learn about the particular features of health care markets.

References

Audit Commission for England and Wales (1995) *A price on their heads: measuring management costs in NHS trusts*. London: HMSO.
Mills A and Gilson L (1988) *Health economics for developing countries: a survival kit*. London: London School of Hygiene & Tropical Medicine.

Parkin M, Powell M and Mathews K (2003) *Economics* (5th edn). Harlow: Addison-Wesley.

Schroeder SA (2001) Prospects for expanding health insurance coverage. *New England Journal of Medicine* 344:847–52.

Woolhandler S and Himmelstein DU (1997) Costs of care and administration at for-profit and other hospitals in the United States. *New England Journal of Medicine* 336:769–74.

12 Equity

Overview

Chapters 10 and 11 have been concerned entirely with promoting efficiency in health systems – that is, getting the largest possible health gain from available resources. However, economics is concerned not only with the amount of benefit produced but also with the distribution of this benefit across the population. In this chapter you will look at equity issues in health and health care. You will try to answer the question 'what is a fair health system?' Finally, you will review the role of government in the health sector of the economy. You will also consider why government intervention offers only an imperfect solution to the inefficiencies and inequities of the health sector.

Learning objectives

After working through this chapter, you will be able to:

- **describe the relationship between equality and equity**
- **explain why there might be a conflict between efficiency and equity objectives**
- **evaluate different equity objectives for providers of health care**
- **summarize the advantages of government intervention**
- **describe the drawbacks of government intervention**

Key terms

End-state equity A situation where there is an equal distribution of income (or utility, or health, etc.).

Horizontal equity The equal treatment of individuals or groups in the same circumstances.

Process equity A situation where people have the same opportunities even if the outcomes are unequal.

Vertical equity The principle that individuals who are unequal should be treated differently according to their level of need.

Ideas about fairness

Mortality and morbidity are not distributed equally across socioeconomic groups, not even in high income countries. The following are potential explanations of the observed socioeconomic inequalities in health:

- *inequalities are an artefact*: there are no real differences between the health of social classes; any apparent difference is due to statistical errors such as missing data;
- *health status affects social status*: people with poorer health have low paid jobs or are unemployed and as a result are in lower social classes;
- *behavioural differences between social classes lead to health differences*: people in lower social classes take more risks with their health such as smoking, a poor diet and drug abuse;
- *material inequalities lead to health inequalities*: people in lower socioeconomic groups are exposed to health risks such as poor housing, dangerous jobs and worse environmental pollution.

The last two are probably the most convincing explanations. The health production model, introduced in Chapter 7, also explained health inequality through material inequality and behavioural differences. The behavioural differences were expressed in terms of preferences and education levels.

Many health systems are concerned not only with the maximization of welfare (efficiency) but also with the fair distribution of welfare (equity) – recall the study on cigarette taxation in Chapter 6. But what exactly is a 'fair distribution'? What makes a health system fair? Is there any single definition of justice that should be applied to health systems? Furthermore, does this objective conflict with the need to make health systems efficient? The following extract by Michael Parkin and colleagues (2003) considers the different philosophical approaches to equity that have been proposed.

 Activity 12.1

When you have finished, answer the following questions as they apply to health and health care:

1 What different equity objectives are identified?
2 Why might there be conflict between different equity definitions?
3 Why is there a trade-off between efficiency and equity?
4 In your culture, which is considered more important, end-state equity or process equity?

 Is the competitive market fair?

To think about fairness, think of economic life as a game – a serious game. All ideas about fairness can be divided into two broad groups. They are:

It's not fair if the *result* isn't fair.

It's not fair if the *rules* aren't fair.

It's not fair if the *result* isn't fair

The earliest efforts to establish a principle of fairness were based on the view that the result is what matters. And the general idea was that it is unfair if people's incomes are too unequal. It is unfair that bank directors earn millions of pounds a year, while bank tellers earn only thousands of pounds a year. It is unfair that a shop owner enjoys a larger profit and her customers pay higher prices in the aftermath of a winter storm.

There was a lot of excitement during the nineteenth century when economists thought they had made the incredible discovery that efficiency requires equality of incomes. To make the economic pie as large as possible, it must be cut into equal pieces, one for each person. This idea turns out to be wrong, but there is a lesson in the reason that it is wrong. So this nineteenth century idea is worth a closer look.

The nineteenth century idea that only equality brings efficiency is called utilitarianism. Utilitarianism is a principle that states that we should strive to achieve 'the greatest happiness for the greatest number'. The people who developed this idea were known as utilitarians. They included the most eminent minds such as David Hume, Adam Smith, Jeremy Bentham and John Stuart Mill.

Utilitarianism

Utilitarianism argues that to achieve 'the greatest happiness for the greatest number', income must be transferred from the rich to the poor up to the point of complete equality – to the point that there are no rich and no poor.

They reasoned in the following way: first, everyone has the same basic wants and are similar in their capacity to enjoy life. Second, the greater a person's income, the smaller is the marginal benefit of a pound. The millionth pound spent by a rich person brings a smaller marginal benefit to that person than the marginal benefit of the thousandth pound spent by a poorer person. So by transferring a pound from the millionaire to the poorer person, more is gained than is lost and the two people added together are better off.

The big trade-off

One big problem with the utilitarian ideal of complete equality is that it ignores the costs of making income transfers. The economist, Arthur Okun, in his book *Equality and Efficiency: The Big Trade-off*, described the process of redistributing income as like trying to transfer water from one barrel to another with a leaky bucket. The more we try to increase equity by redistributing income, the more we reduce efficiency. Recognizing the cost of making income transfers leads to what is called 'the big trade-off' – a trade-off between efficiency and fairness.

The big trade-off is based on the following facts. Income can be transferred from people with high incomes to people with low incomes only by taxing incomes. Taxing people's income from employment makes them work less. It results in the quantity of labour being less than the efficient quantity. Taxing people's income from capital makes them save less. It results in the quantity of capital being less than the efficient quantity. With smaller quantities of both labour and capital the quantity of goods and services produced is less than the efficient quantity. The economic cake shrinks.

The trade-off is between the size of the economic cake and the degree of equality with which it is shared. The greater the amount of income redistribution through income taxes, the greater is the inefficiency – the smaller is the economic cake.

There is a second source of inefficiency. A pound taken from a rich person does not end up as a pound in the hands of a poorer person. Some of it is spent on administration of the tax and transfer system. The cost of tax-collecting agencies, such as the European Community, and welfare-administering agencies, such as the British Child Benefit Agency, as well as regional government welfare departments, must be paid with some of the taxes collected.

Also, taxpayers hire accountants, tax specialists and legal experts to help them ensure that they pay the correct amount of tax. These activities use skilled labour and capital resources that could otherwise be used to produce goods and services that people value.

You can see that when all these costs are taken into account, transferring a pound from a rich person does not give a pound to a poor person. It is even possible that with high taxes, those with low incomes end up being worse off. Suppose, for example, that highly taxed entrepreneurs decide to work less hard and shut down some of their businesses. Low-income workers get fired and must seek other, perhaps even lower-paid work.

Because of the big trade-off, those who say that fairness is equality propose a modified version of utilitarianism.

Rawlsianism

A Harvard philosopher, John Rawls, proposed a modified version of utilitarianism in a classic book entitled *A Theory of Justice*, published in 1971. Rawls says that, taking all the costs of income transfers into account, the fair distribution of the economic pie is the one that makes the poorest person as well off as possible. The incomes of rich people should be taxed and, after paying the costs of administering the tax and transfer system, what is left should be transferred to the poor. But the taxes must not be so high that they make the economic pie shrink to the point that the poorest person ends up with a smaller piece. A bigger share of a smaller cake can be a smaller piece than a smaller share of a bigger cake. The goal is to make the piece enjoyed by the poorest person as big as possible. Most likely this piece will not be an equal share.

The 'fair results' ideas require a change in the results after the game is over. Some economists say these changes are themselves unfair and propose a different way of thinking about fairness.

It's not fair if the *rules* aren't fair

The idea that it's not fair if the rules aren't fair is based on a fundamental principle that seems to be hard wired into the human brain. It is the *symmetry principle*. The symmetry principle is the requirement that people in similar situations be treated similarly. It is the moral principle that lies at the centre of all the big religions. It says, in some form or other, 'behave towards other people in the way you expect them to behave towards you'.

In economic life, this principle translates into *equality of opportunity*. But equality of opportunity to do what? This question is answered by another philosopher, Robert Nozick, in a book *Anarchy, State, and Utopia*, published in 1974. Nozick argues that the idea of fairness as an outcome or result cannot work and that fairness must be based on the fairness of the rules. He suggests that fairness obeys two rules. They are:

> The state must enforce laws that establish and protect private property.

> Private property may be transferred from one person to another only by voluntary exchange.

The first rule says that everything that is valuable must be owned by individuals and that the state must ensure that theft is prevented. The second rule says that the only legitimate way a person can acquire property is to buy it in exchange for something else that the person owns. If these rules, which are the only fair rules, are followed the result is fair. It doesn't matter how unequally the economic pie is shared provided it is baked by people each one of whom voluntarily provides services in exchange for the share of the pie offered in compensation.

These rules satisfy the symmetry principle. And if these rules are not followed, the symmetry principle is broken. You can see these facts by imagining a world in which the laws are not followed.

First, suppose that some resources or goods are not owned. They are common property. Then everyone is free to participate in a grab to use these resources or goods. The strongest will prevail. But when the strongest prevails, the strongest effectively *owns* the resources or goods in question and prevents others from enjoying them.

Second, suppose that we do not insist on voluntary exchange for transferring ownership of resources from one person to another. The alternative is *involuntary* transfer. In simple language, the alternative is theft.

Both of these situations violate the symmetry principle. Only the strong get to acquire what they want. The weak end up with only the resources and goods that the strong don't want.

In contrast, if the two rules of fairness are followed, everyone, strong and weak, is treated in a similar way. Everyone is free to use their resources and human skills to create things that are valued by themselves and others and to exchange the fruits of their efforts with each other. This is the only set of arrangements that obeys the symmetry principle.

 Feedback

1 Parkin and colleagues identified two objectives of equity:

   a) The distribution of outcome or end-state (health) is fair.
   b) People have the same opportunities even if the outcomes are unequal. This allows differences in tastes, differences in skills, and differences in diligence to influence outcomes.

2 The latter view implies that it is fair for someone to smoke and to be less healthy than someone who does not because their behaviour suggests that the smoker places less value on good health. It also holds that it is fair that someone on a higher income is healthier. Their extra income is seen as a reward for their skill and effort and having extra health is considered part of the reward. These definitions of fairness are clearly in conflict with an egalitarian view, which holds that people's health should be equal regardless of their preferences, behaviour or genes.

3 Okun's 'big trade-off' exists because removing money or wealth from people creates disincentives and administrative costs. If income is taxed then people will have a smaller incentive to work long hours; therefore production will be smaller than without taxation and consequently there is a smaller 'pie' to redistribute from. Similarly, taxing interest or profits means that people have a smaller incentive to invest in business. If the tax is levied on sales of a good then the producers will have a smaller incentive to produce and sell that good. The implication is that by imposing tax we reduce the benefits of engaging in productive activities and therefore fewer of these activities are carried out. The extent of this inefficiency is debated though. For one thing, consumer theory shows that a fall in income could make some people work more, not less.

4 In the USA there appears to be a strong association with equality of opportunity (process equity). After all, it has been long billed as the 'land of opportunity' and government intervention has always been looked on with scepticism. End-stage equity was an explicit policy goal in socialist countries, many of which experienced dramatic changes in their social policies in the 1980s and 1990s. In the few surviving socialist countries, such as Cuba, and in the social democratic countries of Europe, there is far more emphasis on end-state equality. Equality is often an explicit policy objective and these countries often have a long history of welfarism.

Would you say that your country has ideological leanings towards the USA, towards the European system or something else?

Equity and health care

Now that you have considered some different perspectives on fairness, you can see what work has been done in applying these theories to health care. First, you need to consider whether end-stage equity (equality of health) is a practical health care objective.

 Activity 12.2

Why might equity of outcome (health) be impossible to achieve?

 Feedback

There are several reasons you may have suggested:

• many factors influence health in addition to health care
• genetic differences between people mean that complete equality of health simply is not possible
• there is no precise definition of 'good health'
• equalizing health might be seen as elitist or paternalistic because it does not allow for individual preferences
• equalizing health will be inefficient and may mean that average health levels are lower

Given these difficulties, perhaps process equity should be the goal of health systems. There are several ways in which process equity can be defined:

• equal access to health care for equal need
• equal use of health care for equal need
• equal health care expenditure for equal need

All of these refer to equity between people with the same health care needs. This is known as *horizontal equity*. It is also important to recognise the corollary, that people with different or unequal needs should receive different or unequal health care. This is known as *vertical equity*. Note that the difficulties involved with measuring equality of *access* mean that equality of *use* is usually used as a proxy when equity is being assessed.

Activity 12.3

What assumption lies behind the interpretation of use of health care being the same as access to health care?

 Feedback

It assumes that everyone expresses the same preference or choice when they feel unwell or fall ill. But as you know, some people are more inclined to use formal health services than others. At one extreme there are hypochondriacs and at the other extreme stoics. In addition, some people have more social support and material resources than others and may not perceive their need to be as great as others who are less fortunate. And finally, some may prefer to seek care from other medical systems such as acupuncture or homoeopathy. All these factors affect a person's illness behaviour.

Equality of access requires that, for different communities:

• travel distance to facilities is equal
• transport and communication services are equal
• waiting times are equal
• patients are equally informed about the availability and effectiveness of treatments
• charges are equal (with equal ability to pay)

Even though it is more feasible than equality of health, equality of access clearly poses quite a challenge to health planners.

The ability to achieve an equitable health care system will be tempered by the need to be efficient. That is, it is not possible to both maximize health and equalize access to health care.

Arguments against government intervention

Equality of health may or may not be a major societal goal. If it is, then it may best be approached through public health interventions (health education, environmental control etc.) and by redistributing income and wealth. However, fairer access to health care will also influence health inequality. It has been advocated by some that people should be charged for health care according to their ability to pay. The obvious way of doing this is by funding health care from a progressive taxation system or through a social insurance system.

There are several reasons why government intervention is imperfect:

1 Financing government programmes requires diverting money (resources) from other areas of the economy. This is usually done by levying taxes on people's incomes or on the sales of goods and services. Taxes cause substitution and change within markets. Prices are raised and output is reduced and there is a

deadweight loss to society – a loss of consumer surplus and producer surplus. If the loss is very large then the intervention may not be justified.

2 Besides programme costs, there are administration costs involved in every government action. For example, there is no such thing as a cost-free transfer. If you want to take money from one group of people and give it to another group then you have to pay the following people:

- the lawyers who draft the law;
- the civil servants who administer the transfer;
- the police and lawyers who enforce the law.

This means that the gaining group will gain a smaller amount of money than the amount that is taken away from the losing group.

3 You ought to assume that politicians and civil servants act in their own interests in the same way that patients and doctors are each assumed to act in their own interests. This means that due to an asymmetry of information between the general public and civil servants the latter will not always do as the former would like. For one thing, some civil servants try to expand their own department because this increases their power and prestige. They will press for this even if it is not beneficial to society, although civil servants may have an ethical code that constrains their actions just as doctors do.

4 As for the provision of services, it may be difficult to replace the coordinating powers of market forces with a large number of independent decisions made by a group of civil servants. It may be even harder without the added incentive of the profit maximizing motive.

All four of these complications are examples of inefficiency of government intervention.

The case for government provision

The scale of market failure in the area of health care would seem to imply that some government financing of health care is inevitable. However, as you have just read, government intervention has its own inherent inefficiencies, and therefore should only be advised when the extent of market failure is so large that it outweighs the costs associated with the intervention.

The coordination and incentive problems associated with bureaucracy mean that the case for government provision of services is not as persuasive as the need for government finance. It might be better to retain private provision of services but regulate them and create appropriate incentive structures for providers.

In perfectly competitive market systems, commodities will be produced at an efficient output level – they are produced up to the point where marginal benefit is no longer greater than marginal cost. In health care, because of asymmetric information and other failures, markets will not operate efficiently. Therefore, it is the role of governments (and insurance companies and providers) to decide which services should be provided and in what amounts. This is done by weighing up the costs and benefits. The systematic measurement of costs and benefits is called economic evaluation.

Summary

You have learned about two objectives for equity: equality of health (end-stage) and equality of opportunity (processes such as access and use). You saw how equity and efficiency are involved in a trade-off and how governments can intervene to promote equity but often at the cost of efficiency. Finally you saw that to be effective, purchasers need information on the costs and benefits of health care. This can be obtained through economic evaluation, the subject of Chapters 16–20.

Reference

Parkin M, Powell M and Mathews K (2003) *Economics* (5th edn). Harlow: Addison-Wesley.

SECTION 4

Health financing

13 The changing world of health care finance

Overview

This chapter introduces the question of where funding for health services comes from and how it is used. After an introduction to the historical development of various countries' provision of health care, it looks at third-party arrangements and out of pocket payments, the distinction between public and private agents in the finance and provision of health services, and the question of the extent to which governments take responsibility for organizing health services.

Learning objectives

By the end of this chapter, you should be able to:

- **distinguish between the principal ways of funding health services and paying providers**
- **identify historical and cultural factors that have influenced the evolution of health finance**
- **identify factors which have determined the growth of health care spending**
- **distinguish between the different options of private–public mix in the finance and provision of health services**

Key terms

Capitation payments A prospective means of paying health care staff based on the number of people they provide care for.

Community financing Collective action of local communities to finance health services through pooling out-of-pocket payments and ensuring services are accountable to the community.

Co-payments (user fees) Direct payments made by users of health services as a contribution to their cost (e.g. prescription charges).

Financial intermediary An agency collecting money to pay providers on behalf of patients.

Out-of-pocket (direct) payment Payment made by a patient directly to a provider.

Over the counter (OTC) drugs Non-prescription drugs purchased from pharmacists and retailers.

Regulation Government intervention enforcing rules and standards.

Universal coverage Extension of health services to the whole population.

Unofficial payments Spending in excess of official fees, also called 'under the table' or 'envelope' payments.

Out-of-pocket and third-party payment

In a most basic way, health care financing represents a flow of funds from patients to health care providers in exchange for services. As Figure 13.1 shows, there are two ways of paying for health services:

*   *Out-of-pocket payments*: this is the simplest and earliest form of transaction between patient and provider. Access to care depends on ability to pay.
*   *Third-party payments*: the uncertainty of need and the great costs of health care mean that people choose to finance health services through payments to a third party, an insurance company or a government. These third parties are involved in the economic transaction between patients and providers.

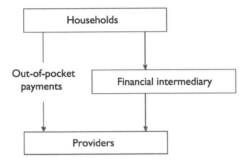

Figure 13.1 The flow of funds in health care provision

Much of this chapter focuses on the principal type of financing, through third parties. Beforehand it is appropriate to think more about out-of-pocket payments, which are a significant source of health care finance.

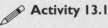

Activity 13.1

1   For which health services do you need to pay out-of-pocket in your country?
2   Which expenses are unlikely to be covered out-of-pocket?
3   Do you think that out-of-pocket spending has increased during the past few years?

Feedback

1   In many countries out-of-pocket payments for health care play an important role. From low income countries there is evidence that people who are not covered by insurance pay high amounts for health care in relation to their income. In Africa, more than 50 per cent of health care expenses come from directly paid private sources (Bennet *et al.* 1997). Types of out-of-pocket expenditure include:

- Private consultations with doctors
- Over the counter (OTC) drugs

- Co-payments and user fees: where third-party payment is prevalent, cost sharing in the form of co-payments plays an important role. Co-payments may apply to prescribed drugs, hospital care, outpatient care and emergency transport.
- Unofficial fees: besides official fees, unofficial payments to health workers are common in many countries. Additional payments to staff to get access to hospital care are common in some Asian countries. In a range of countries in central and eastern Europe, doctors used to expect unofficial payments as a supplement to their income.
- Services not covered by insurance: transport costs, traditional or complementary medicine and luxury services such as cosmetic surgery.

2 These are expenses that are high in relation to income. For example, expensive therapies are unlikely to be paid out of pocket, as people would need to spend a large proportion of their income or wealth on health care. Usually, individuals seek insurance to protect themselves against such potentially catastrophic losses. You may also think of services with characteristics of a public good which are financed publicly because they are not provided by private markets. Remember the example of pond cleaning to control malaria in Chapter 8. Or think of preventive services, such as health education, which the individual consumer may not value as beneficial and so be unwilling to purchase privately.

3 Overall out-of-pocket spending on health care is increasing. This is due to the growing proportion of OTC drugs and increasing cost sharing.

The evolution of health service finance

International comparison shows that countries use different ways of paying for health services. For example, France and Sweden have developed distinctly different practices to fund hospitals and to pay for doctors. Latin American countries have social insurance systems whereas in many African countries government funding is common.

To a large extent, these differences are due to historical factors. Analysing the historical context will make you aware that health finance today has been shaped by cultural and political factors from the past. It will explain why the approach to health finance differs between countries. And this will help you to make more meaningful comparisons between countries and enable you to understand the strengths and weaknesses of your own country's health system.

From private to social health insurance

Early in the history of health care, *government* or *charities* financed services for groups of the population for whom they perceived a duty of care. For example, hospitals for the poor existed in India, China, Arabia and medieval Europe (Abel-Smith and Campling 1994).

For the more affluent, *private* (or *voluntary*) *health insurance* was pioneered in Europe as early as the eighteenth century. In the nineteenth century, private insurance was developed throughout Europe and spread to North and South America.

Meanwhile, *social* (or *compulsory*) *insurance* was introduced in Germany for industrial workers in 1883, building on the existing voluntary precedents. Coverage was extended later to family members, other employees and pensioners. Payroll-based social insurance systems developed steadily in Europe, and later in Latin America and Asia.

Achieving universal health care coverage

Countries have used different means of making health care available to all: *universal coverage* is achieved either through the extension of social insurance or government provision to the whole population.

The Soviet Union extended coverage through government provision in 1938, and that example was followed by the countries of the Soviet bloc after World War II. The UK extended coverage to all in 1948. The British NHS was established as a major part of the social reforms recommended by William Beveridge with the aim of providing health services for the whole population.

In the USA, private insurance has assumed a larger role than in Europe. However, even in the USA, publicly funded health care pays a large role for the elderly (Medicare), the poor (Medicaid), and past and present armed services personnel.

The health finance systems of low income countries have been strongly influenced by their colonial past. In British colonies, government funded services for the armed forces and civil services provided the basis for further extension of health care, whereas in French colonies the model was provided by larger firms, which were required to provide services for their employees. To a variable extent, charitable organizations and missions also played a role in financing hospitals. In the post-colonial era these countries made efforts to extend services 'as far as economic growth and available resources allowed' (Abel-Smith and Campling 1994).

Two models of health care finance for achieving universal coverage

Two models that are often referred to in connection with attempts to ensure universal health care coverage are the Bismarck model, which is based on compulsory (social) health insurance, and the Beveridge model, based on tax funded services:

* *Otto von Bismarck (1815–98)*: Prusso-German statesman and founder of social insurance in Germany. Bismarck introduced in 1883 a plan based on compulsory insurance protecting workers against accidents, sickness and invalidity.
* *William Beveridge (1879–1963)*: British economist and architect of the British welfare state. The Beveridge Report proposed a tax funded plan to provide 'full preventive and curative treatment' to every citizen of the UK, leading to the foundation of the NHS in 1948.

Activity 13.2

This activity gives you an opportunity to identify the current basis of the health finance system in your country.

1 What is the main way of financing health services in your country (out of pocket payment, private insurance, social insurance or taxation)? What were the precedents of the current funding system?
2 Approximately what proportion of the population is covered by each source of funding?

Feedback

1 The health finance systems in most countries can be traced back to one of the several means of funding which had evolved by the end of the nineteenth century. The earliest form of finance is by direct payment from those using the service to health care providers. Later, services funded by government or charities evolved, followed by private and social insurance. Precedents in many low income countries are services for the armed forces and civil service, and mission hospitals. In many countries, voluntary schemes prevailed before social insurance or tax funded systems were introduced.

2 Having a large single source of funding doesn't necessarily mean that the whole population is covered. Most countries rely on several sources of funding, as they often retain some elements of previous arrangements when a new means of finance is introduced.

Developing methods to pay providers

Methods of paying health care providers have evolved along with the development of funding systems. Finding the optimal means of providing payment has been a constant source of political debate. Strategies used by doctors to gain favourable conditions have included boycotts and takeovers as well as the foundation of their own insurance organizations (Abel-Smith and Campling 1994). Conflicts between the medical profession and financing agents are related to issues of whether:

- doctors should be employed or act as independent contractors;
- payments should be based on a *salary*, on the number of patients cared for (*capitation*), on the items of care provided (*fee-for-service* – FFS), on the quality of their performance or on a combination of these options;
- patients should pay health care providers directly and then claim reimbursement from government or insurance companies or payments should be made directly to the providers by the funders.

Activity 13.3

Patients, trade unions, employers and doctors are important interest groups which have shaped the development of health care finance. For example, failure of the USA to achieve universal coverage has been related, among other reasons, to the influence of a medical profession with 'the power to use a political system, which responded to strong lobbies' (Abel-Smith and Campling 1994). To what extent has the medical profession influenced the way health services are paid for in your country? Think of the employment status of providers of health care and methods for paying them.

 Feedback

You should be aware that many of the current ways of paying providers reflect political conflicts from the past. Along with the development of health financing, doctors have employed strategies to achieve an independent status from the financial agent and more favourable payment conditions. This was less successful in countries where strong consumer and government interests shaped the organization of health care, such as in the Nordic countries, where employed doctors are common. In the USA, the dominance of private insurance companies has supported the trend towards independent practitioners who are paid by FFS. Many countries have mixed systems for paying doctors, for instance salaried doctors in hospitals and independent contractors in primary care.

The changing world of health services finance

The means of paying for health care is an issue of concern in most countries. Governments are worried about the economic and political consequences of the increasing cost of providing health services and try to limit spending through tighter controls. There is a large body of literature to suggest that many countries are dissatisfied with the existing methods of finance and delivery of health services. During the last decade, governments have introduced a series of reforms. Though the motives and types of reform may differ, there have been some common themes:

- Separation of purchaser and provider responsibilities. This concept refers to the separation of responsibility for purchasing and providing health care between two different organizations. In general, funders (government and insurance companies) have two options: to run their own hospitals or to act as purchasers and buy services from providers, including the private sector. The underlying idea is that purchasers contract with those providers offering best value for money and that this increases efficiency of service delivery.
- Redefinition of the role of the state in responsibility for health care.
- Encouragement of the private sector.
- Encouragement of competition between providers.
- Alternative sources of funding: economic crises have exacerbated the problems of financing the health sector and governments have sought alternative ways of mobilizing resources.

When considering the last of these it is helpful to distinguish between *macro-level* and *micro-level* changes. Macro-level changes involve a change in the basic principle of funding, such as the move from social insurance towards a system mainly based on taxation in Italy and Spain. Probably the most radical recent changes have occurred in the former Soviet Union and eastern Europe. A large number of former communist countries have undergone a change from government funded services to social insurance. Eleven countries passed social insurance laws between 1991 and 1996 (Ensor and Thompson 1997).

Radical changes have also been taking place in some low income countries where greater use of community financing and patient charges have been pursued. The term 'community financing' doesn't refer to a special finance mechanism; it is related to the way fundraising is organized by local communities. The collective effort of rural communities often has other targets than health, such as crop insurance or credit financing. Community funding for health care is more likely to develop where there are no free government services.

In contrast, micro-level changes don't affect the basic method of funding. Such changes include introduction of co-payments and changes in the way providers are paid.

Increasing health care costs

Why are health services getting more expensive? There are several answers to this question: an ageing population, increased population coverage, technological advance and growing expectations. Some authors (Relman 1988; Hurst 1992) have put forward a three-stage model to explain how health systems have changed during the last 60 years:

1 During the first stage, policies removed the existing financial barriers to health care. New funding arrangements increased population coverage and triggered the *expansion* of health services.
2 The subsequent increase in demand led to a rapid growth of health care expenditure. Often spending grew faster than the gross domestic product (GDP) and policy efforts were focused on *cost control*.
3 From the experience of ever-rising costs, it was realized that cost control alone is not effective. Policies of the third stage aim to *improve efficiency* of service delivery and use.

You need to be aware of microeconomic and political considerations when analysing changes in health care costs. A brief overview of a range of potential factors is presented below.

Demographic factors

You need to distinguish between *absolute population growth* and *relative changes within a population* towards groups with higher health care needs (the elderly, the very young, displaced populations). Both mechanisms may influence health care costs.

Economic factors

Economic growth is associated with rising costs for health services. Economic recession has opposite effects. But you need to be aware that unemployment and poverty are related to ill health and put additional strain on health services. When assessing cost escalation, you need to consider relative prices by taking account of the inflation rate. Supply factors also exert important pressures – for example, increasing numbers of doctors and hospitals or payment increases for health workers.

Health technology advances

At the beginning of the twentieth century, health services had only a few effective treatments. Since then, the number of effective interventions has steadily expanded – for example, antibiotics (1938), open heart surgery (1954), haemo-dialysis (1960) and computerized tomography (1973).

Disease patterns

Why does the change of disease patterns, which has been observed in many low income countries, affect health care costs? First, new diseases like HIV/AIDS increase the level of ill health in the population. Second, the relative increase in chronic diseases and long-term illness is related to higher treatment costs.

With economic development, countries are likely to experience higher health care costs, as deaths among infants from communicable diseases decrease relative to adult deaths from chronic diseases. This trend has been described as the epidemiological (or health) transition. Note that in 1990 56 per cent of all deaths in the world were from non-communicable diseases. But these figures are unevenly distributed among social classes: non-communicable diseases were responsible for only 34 per cent of the deaths among the poorest 20 per cent of the world as compared to 85 per cent among the richest. This indicates that inexpensive, effective interventions against communicable disease still have a high priority in improving the health of the poor (Christopher *et al.* 1996).

Political factors

Health budgets are inevitably based on political judgement. There may be additional 'cash injections' before elections or deviations from planned growth rates because of other priorities. Health funds may be diverted officially to support other purposes. Concerns about equity may improve access to services and increase costs. On the other hand, corruption of politicians, civil servants or health care providers may lead to substantial economic losses.

Some popular fallacies of the current debate

Be cautious with estimates of the effect of ageing on health care costs. Recent research has shown that the highest costs occur during the last year of life, irrespective of age. Very old people may even tend to consume fewer resources than younger ones (Hamel *et al.* 1996). In high income countries, the increasingly high costs of dying seem to be a more important factor than the steadily increasing proportion of the elderly.

You should be aware that, contrary to popular belief, *prevention and early treatment* can lead to increased costs in the long run. For example, lifetime health care costs are lower among smokers than among non-smokers, suggesting that early death from smoking prevents paying extra costs of treating other diseases (Barendregt *et al.* 1997). In addition, earlier death reduces the cost of paying retirement pensions.

Another fallacy is related to the effect of *new health care technologies*. New equipment may be expensive initially but may ultimately be more cost-effective than the older technologies it replaces. As you will see in Chapter 19, new technologies can only be justified if they lower costs or improve services. It is important to be aware that it is not technological advance *per se* that escalates costs, rather the failure to implement the rules of economic evaluation (Normand 1991).

The public–private distinction

A common feature of all health systems is the distinction between public and private health care. This distinction refers to both the finance and the provision of health services. The concept of *ownership* is used to distinguish whether an organization belongs to the private or public sector.

The notion of a public agency refers not only to government organizations but also to public bodies with statutory responsibilities like social insurance companies. The private sector can be divided into *for profit* and *not for profit* organizations. The former include the drugs industry and private hospitals or clinics in which some (sometimes most) of any financial surplus goes out of the organization to the shareholders. Not for profit organizations reinvest any financial surplus in their organization by developing facilities and training staff. The distinction from for profit isn't so clear-cut as some surplus in not for profit organizations can also go out of the organization in the form of enhanced salaries and bonuses.

The following extract from Donaldson and Gerard's (2005) book gives a framework for analysing the private–public relationship.

 Activity 13.4

Focus on the different options for organizing health care and compare the examples given in the text to the situation in your country. Consider where on Figure 13.2 the following services in your country would fit in terms of their finance and provision:

1 Primary care.
2 Hospital care.
3 Traditional/complementary medicine.

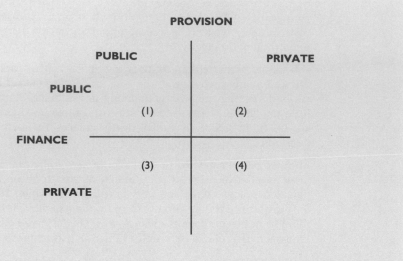

(1) Public finance and public provision   (3) Private finance and public provision
(2) Public finance and private provision   (4) Private finance and private provision

Figure 13.2 Public–private mix in health care financing and provision

Source: Donaldson and Gerard (2005)

Public–private mix in finance and provision

The organisation of financial intermediaries may be on a monopolistic, oligopolistic or competitive basis. In a monopolistic system, the financial intermediary is usually a public agency such as a government, a quango or a health corporation. In an oligopolistic system (i.e. one in which there are a small number of large intermediaries) finance can be controlled by public agencies or private agencies, such as insurance companies, or a combination of these. In a competitive system, a large number of small private intermediaries would exist . . .

The provision of services, however, does not necessarily have to match the financial organisation. For instance, hospital care in many European countries represents a large, vertically integrated health system, in which finance and provision are combined within one organisation. Thus, both finance and provision are public as in the case of quadrant (1) in Figure 13.2. In many countries, general practice would fall into quadrant (2), such care being provided by self-employed doctors who, nevertheless, happen to receive almost all of their income from the public purse . . . Also, it is important to recognise that systems do not have to be vertically integrated in these ways: a third-party private payer, such as an insurance company, could also fit into segments (3) and (4). The basic point is that public finance does not have to match public provision, nor private finance private provision. Public provision could be financed by private arrangements (private insurance, direct charges, etc.) and private provision by public finance (e.g. prospective payments made by government agencies directly to private hospitals).

. . . [There is] a stronger case for government intervention in *financing* rather than in *providing* health care. Control of financial arrangements permits governmental bodies more direction of the health care system in the pursuit of societal objectives: as the collective purchaser of care on the community's behalf, a public body can dictate terms of provision with equal power to both public and private providers. Simply providing public services does not guarantee use by those groups for whom they are intended, because less ill, rich or privately insured patients may be more 'attractive customers' for such hospitals than those more in need of care.

Feedback

You have probably discovered that both provision and finance can have a private and a public dimension. Sometimes it may be difficult to draw a clear dividing line between public and private. For example, in Germany, general medical practitioners are privately set up but they need to be members of a public body if they want to take part in social insurance work. In many countries it is not uncommon for publicly employed doctors to engage in private practice and use – to a varying extent – government facilities. Under options (1) and (4) in Figure 13.2 the situation is straightforward, with both finance and provision being either public or private: for example, a government-owned hospital funded from social insurance (1) or a traditional healer paid by private fees (4). Category (2) applies to doctors who are self-employed but paid from public funds. Category (3), private finance and public provision, is not unusual: pay beds in a public hospital.

Governments can organize finance, act as purchaser, provide services and regulate health services. In many low income countries, governments have historically had the major role in the provision of health care. Governments see it as the most efficient and equitable method of providing services. Though the private sector may play an increasing role, socioeconomic conditions are such that private care will not totally replace public services. In particular, primary health care in low income countries is reliant on the public sector.

Activity 13.5

Contrast this view with the opinion presented by Donaldson and Gerard that there is a 'stronger case for government intervention in *financing* rather than in *providing* health care'.

Feedback

Donaldson and Gerard argue that simply providing government services does not ensure equity and efficiency. They favour the separation of responsibilities between purchasers and providers of care. As a purchaser of care, 'a public body can dictate terms of provision with equal power to both public and private providers'. Later in this book you will explore the options for state intervention in health care in more depth.

Summary

In this chapter you have learned about the different ways of funding health services, and how and why different systems have evolved in different countries. The reasons for increasing health care costs have been explored. Finally the possible combinations of public and private funding and provision have been explored. In the next two chapters, two of the main methods of funding health care, private and social health insurance, are considered in more depth.

References

Abel-Smith B and Campling J (1994) The history of the organization and financing of services, in *An introduction to health policy, planning and financing*. London: Longman.

Barendregt JJ, Bonneux L and Van der Maas J (1997) The health care costs of smoking. *New England Journal of Medicine* 337:1052–7.

Bennet S, McPake B and Mills A (1997) *Private health providers: serving the public interest*. London: Zed Books.

Christopher JL, Murray CJL and Lopez AD (eds) (1996) *The global burden of disease: a comprehensive assessment of mortality and disability from diseases, injuries and risk factors in 1990 and projected to 2020*. Cambridge, MA: Harvard School of Public Health.

Donaldson C and Gerard K (2005) *Economics of health care financing. The visible hand* (2nd edn). Basingstoke: Palgrave Macmillan.

Ensor T and Thompson R (1997) *Health insurance as a catalyst to change in former communist countries*. Annual HEU conference, MOH, Dhaka.

Hamel MB *et al.* (1996) Seriously ill hospitalized adults: do we spend less on older patients? *Journal of American Geriatrics Society* 44:1043–8.

Hurst J (1992) *The reform of health care: a comparative analysis of seven OECD countries*. Paris: OECD.

Normand C (1991) Economics, health and the economics of health. *British Medical Journal* 303:1572–7.

Relman AS (1988) Assessment and accountability: the third revolution in medical care. *New England Journal of Medicine* 319:1220–2.

14 Private health insurance

Overview

Having examined sources and uses of health care finance in Chapter 13, you will now explore the strengths and weaknesses of private insurance. The essential criteria you will apply are equity and efficiency, which were discussed in previous chapters, and a further important criterion, the viability of funding – for example, whether a new finance arrangement is sustainable and affordable.

Learning objectives

By the end of this chapter, you should be able to:

- explain the economic rationale for insurance and how insurance works in health care
- give examples of how insurance companies try to counteract moral hazard and adverse selection
- distinguish between the main types of managed care organizations
- suggest reasons why private insurance fails to provide equity and efficiency

Key terms

Actuarial (experience) rating Premium based on an individual's risk of illness.

Community rating Insurance premium based on pooled risk of a defined group of people.

Diagnosis related group (DRG) Classification system that assigns patients to categories on the basis of the likely cost of their episode of hospital care. Used as a basis for determining the level of prospective payment by the purchaser.

Health maintenance organization (HMO) Organization that provides comprehensive health care for a fixed, periodic per capita payment.

Preferred provider organization (PPO) Private insurance that restricts choice to approved providers.

Private insurance in context

This chapter gives an overview of the various products of private health insurance markets and examines measures for counteracting the risks of moral hazard and adverse selection. You will begin by revising the theoretical principles you studied previously and then look more closely at how insurance and managed markets work in practice. First though, Figure 14.1 puts private financing of health care in context.

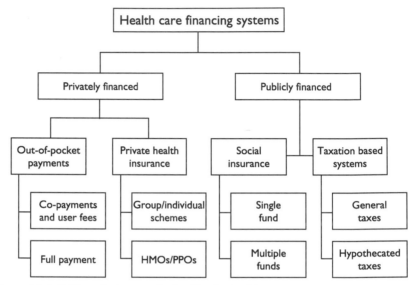

Figure 14.1 Public and private methods of funding health care

Though private insurance is of limited significance in most countries, it is important to study the methods which try to reduce the inefficiencies of this source of finance. This chapter helps you understand why most countries use more efficient and equitable ways of funding health care.

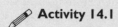 **Activity 14.1**

This activity gives you an opportunity to revise your understanding of how insurance works. Suppose you are part of a community with an annual risk of 1 in 100 of needing hospital treatment and the average cost per case is £1500 plus £5 for administration.

1   What is your annual actuarially fair premium?
2   What conditions need to be met for insurance to be offered at this premium?

Feedback

1 The premium P would be: $P = p \times c + a$ where p is the probability of the insured event, c the cost to cover the loss, and a the administration costs. Inserting the above values results in: $(0.01 \times £1500) + £5 = £20$, thus the premium would be £20 per year. (Note that unlike the definition in Chapter 7, this definition includes the cost of administration.)

2 This formula is valid only under certain conditions:

   a) There needs to be a large number of subscribers to pool the risks. The larger the number of pooled events the less likely unexpected costs per case will occur.
   b) The insured risks need to be independent. This means that the risk of falling ill is not caused by a single event which affects equally all insured individuals. This explains the difficulty of insuring risks due to wars or transmissible disease in regions where large populations are at risk.
   c) The probability of the insured event must be less than 1. It is therefore difficult to insure pre-existing conditions which will inevitably produce illness.
   d) People should not be able to influence their risk (moral hazard) and there should be no adverse selection.

The significance of private insurance

The USA is one of the few countries which depend on private insurance as a major funding mechanism for health care. The following extract by Donaldson and Gerard (2005) raises the key concerns about private insurance. (Note they refer to social insurance as public insurance.)

 Activity 14.2

As you read, make notes on the main sources of failure in private insurance markets.

 Private health care insurance

Moral hazard exists in private insurance-based health care systems. With a third party (i.e. the insurance company) paying health care bills on a full reimbursement basis and employers contributing heavily to premiums, neither the consumer nor the provider has an incentive to be cost-conscious. The consumer faced with free or low cost health care at the point of consumption has little or no financial incentive to restrain demands on the service. Likewise, doctors have no financial incentive to moderate such demands. Indeed if reward is on a FFS (fee-for-service) basis, as is often the case, they may have an incentive to generate demand for their services (the phenomenon of supplier-induced demand). If insurance is accompanied by retrospective cost reimbursement of providers (such as hospitals) by insurance companies, as used to be common in the US, moral hazard will be further exacerbated. Such a method gives no incentive to be cost-conscious.

To combat the problem of moral hazard, cost-sharing or co-payment schemes have been introduced by many intermediaries in private systems. Essentially the aim of these schemes is to place some financial burden on the consumer to eliminate or at least reduce 'unnecessary' use of health care. Individual schemes differ according to the nature of the financial arrangement but take four main forms: a flat rate charge for each unit of service; co-insurance (the insured individual has to pay a certain proportion of each unit of health care consumed); a deductible akin to the 'excess' in some motor vehicle insurance policies (the individual pays 100 per cent of all bills in a given period up to some maximum amount beyond which insurance benefits are paid in full); or a combination of the last two.

Depending on the level of charges for health care, people in low-income groups or high-utilisation groups may be excluded from consumption as a result of lack of ability to pay. Thus, further government intervention may be required. There is also likely to be some anxiety about the effect on individuals' health if they are deterred from 'non-trivial' utilisation.

Another, more recent, method of combatting consumer moral hazard has been the intro-duction of medical savings accounts (MSAs). These have two essential features: first, and individual- (or household-) specific account with balances earmarked for health care expenses; and, second, a high-deductible, catastrophic insurance plan to cover expenses above the deductible. Advocates would claim that these accounts, through encouraging greater personal responsibility on the part of consumers, enhance system efficiency. How-ever, they are likely to suffer from many of the challenges faced by cost-sharing.

Cost-sharing need not, however, reduce the overall impact of supplier induced demand. Doctors may, for example, switch their demand-inducing abilities from lower-income groups to those more able to pay. With the presence of supplier-induced demand, cost containment does not seem so obviously achievable through cost sharing. Even worse, serious health problems may be left untreated as more minor (but able-to-pay) cases replace more serious (not-able-to-pay) cases. The end result could be that the same amount is spent on health care but to less effect in terms of improvement or maintenance of the community's health.

Of course, some advocates of charges claim that doctors could discriminate between groups on the basis of ability to pay, so that everyone would be able to afford the charge. However, this argument does not make sense. If everyone can afford the charge, there will still be much strain on the health care system. Again, the incentive for doctors, in such a situation, would be to concentrate on those more able to pay. Service use would remain the same, but more would be spent on health care because charges would be higher, and care would be going to those less in need.

In addition . . . the billing of patients and the collection of payments under cost-sharing schemes, checking against fraud and so on, are likely to be administratively expensive.

To combat moral hazard in the hospital sector, DRGs are now used (or are being con-sidered for use) in many countries as a means of controlling costs. For instance, since October 1984, US Federal Government payments for hospitalised patients over the age of 65 in the Medicare programme have been changed to fixed amounts of money by type of case which are set prospectively, rather than all 'reasonable' expenses being reimbursed retrospectively. This has changed the incentives for non-government hospitals, to which they have responded. Hospitals are experiencing some decline in utilisation. However, patients may have increased their use of other services not covered by the DRG system, for example ambulatory visits to doctors' surgeries. Government-financed programmes in a primarily private market can also realise some of the gains from 'countervailing power' obtainable in more thoroughly collectivist systems, particularly by 'squeezing' doctors and hospitals in the way the USA DRG system has done.

 Feedback

Moral hazard relates to potential changes in attitude of both consumers and providers under insurance arrangements, which may result in excess demand for health care. With full reimbursement of bills through insurance, neither the consumer nor the provider has an incentive to contain costs.

Adverse selection arises from consumers having more complete information than insurers on their own health status, which may result in selecting plans that give them the greatest benefit. On the other hand, insurers can profit by excluding high-risk individuals.

Along with diseconomies of small-scale operations, these are the three main sources of failure in private insurance markets.

 Activity 14.3

What proportion of the population in your country is covered by private insurance and who is likely to subscribe?

 Feedback

In most countries private insurance is a secondary source of finance, covering for example 13 per cent of the population in the UK in 2002 (Laing and Buisson 2003) and less than 2 per cent in most low income countries. In these countries it attracts only the affluent members of the population, as enrolment is based on ability to pay, and thus contributes little to total health expenditure despite the growth of the private sector and increased competition between insurance agencies (Hsiao 1995).

Regulation of private insurance markets

Private insurance involves high transaction costs, related to marketing, claims processing, handling of reimbursements and fraud detection. In unregulated markets, administration costs plus profits may account for up to 35–45 per cent of the premiums (Griffin 1992).

To protect consumers and increase coverage, governments may regulate premiums, benefit packages and profits of insurance companies or offer tax relief to firms who enrol their employees in private insurance. However, following the recent trend towards economic liberalization (less state control and regulation), many low and middle income countries have deregulated their private insurance markets. In Sri Lanka, for example, this has increased the number of insurance companies without substantially increasing coverage of the population.

Managed care

In the USA, the private insurance sector has developed (or rediscovered) several methods of enhancing the quality and cost-effectiveness of care, which are subsumed under the term *managed care* (Smith 1997). Two particular schemes, health maintenance organizations (HMOs) and preferred provider organizations (PPOs) are described by Donaldson and Gerard (2005) in the following extract.

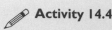

Activity 14.4

As you read, consider what the advantages and the disadvantages to patients of HMOs and PPOs might be.

Health maintenance organizations and preferred provider organizations

Health maintenance organisations (HMOs) are a product of private insurance systems. They represent one of the most prominent health care reforms and have had an influence in publicly-funded systems beyond the US. HMOs provide (or arrange and pay for) comprehensive health care for a fixed, periodic per-capita payment (or premium) which is paid by the consumer (usually with a subsidy from employers or social security). Consumers do not usually pay charges at the point of use. The premium is set in advance and is independent of the volume of services provided to the individual during the period. Providers can be salaried or paid by FFS.

Adverse selection and experience-rating will inevitably arise if, as is likely, competition develops. Doctor demand inducement [supplier induced demand] is not likely to be very prevalent, because not only do doctors compete for custom, usually on an annual basis, but also the annual HMO budget is fixed in advance. Doctors, therefore, will be cost conscious, with the residual between the budget and expenditure accruing to the HMO and, thereby, to the doctors. High spending doctors will then be financially penalised.

Organisationally, HMOs can be of one of four types: a staff model, in which all doctors are employed and/or contracted directly by the HMO; a group model, in which the HMO contracts with an independent group practice to provide services; a network model, in which more than one independent group is contracted to provide services; and an independent practice association in which the HMO contracts several doctors in independent practice. Thus, there are many financial and organisational variations on the basic HMO model.

Consumers select the health care plan of their choice on an annual basis. Therefore more choice is thought to exist. Because consumers usually receive only a fixed subsidy towards payment (or a fixed percentage of the premium), they too have an incentive to be cost-conscious. Additionally, some HMOs do have user charges, particularly for drugs.

. . . Preferred provider organisations (PPOs) have arisen in the US as a result of attempts by insurance companies to enter into competition with HMOs. Premiums are paid either by employers or are shared between employer and employee. Price at the point of use of services is zero. Insurers contract selectively with providers (e.g. primary care doctors and hospitals who provide care below a certain cost per case). The contract is on the basis of both a negotiated fee schedule which the preferred providers accept as payment in full and acceptance of utilisation review. User charges and deductibles tend to be lower in PPOs than under previous private insurance arrangements.

Once more, adverse selection and experience rating will almost inevitably develop within a care system based on PPOs, leaving the more costly groups without cover for health care unless they are subsidised. There is also no financial risk to primary care providers with respect to the volume of services provided. With FFS as the basis for payment the doctor can, to some extent, still manipulate utilisation. However, this has a limit for, if cost per case rises above a certain limit, then the doctor may not be selected as the preferred provider at the next review. The incentive for hospitals to keep costs down arises because a set of prices has been agreed in advance.

Patients can choose between a limited set of providers or choose another provider on less favourable terms, so incentives also exist on the demand side. One specific advantage of PPOs is that they have enabled employers in the US to move quickly to control health care costs for employees who are already under FFS schemes. Companies either organise schemes themselves or persuade insurance companies to do it. Insurance companies co-operate because this provides a means of competing with HMOs.

Feedback

The main advantages of HMOs and PPOs are there is no limit to the amount of health care a patient can use, there are no (or few) user (out of pocket) expenses and no incentive for providers to over-investigate and over-treat.

The disadvantages are adverse selection, a limited choice of providers and fear of being insufficiently investigated and treated.

Adverse selection, in which a private insurer selects the healthier members of society in an attempt to minimize the health care use they will have to fund, is also referred to as 'cream skimming'. Although in theory it can be outlawed by governments, insurers can find ingenious ways round the law. For example, if the office for joining a private insurance scheme is based on the second floor of a building with no lift (elevator), it will be impossible for people with mobility problems to gain access.

Activity 14.5

1 Which groups of the population are likely not to be covered by community-rated private health insurance?
2 What are the likely consequences?

Feedback

1 If insurance in a competitive market sets a community-rated premium, those who perceive their risk as lower will opt out and take experience-rated insurance.

2 This will increase the average risk and as a result the premium for the remaining clients

will go up and further low-risk individuals will drop out. This self-reinforcing mechanism will leave the chronically ill, the elderly and the poor without (affordable) insurance.

In response, governments have several options available:

- prohibit experience rating
- extend social insurance
- provide tax funded services for the elderly and the poor
- regulate premiums, profits, or benefit packages or implement tax relief

 **Activity 14.6**

This activity lets you apply your knowledge of private insurance to analyse patterns of private and public spending in the USA. Take your calculator and turn to the national health account of the USA, Table 14.1, and compare private and public expenditure.

Table 14.1 National health expenditures in the USA by source of funds and type of expenditure ($billion 2002)

	Private consumer				Public			Total
	Private insurance	Out-of-pocket	Other	Sub-total	State and local	Federal	Sub-total	
Hospital care	165.0	14.7	20.3	200.1	56.5	229.9	286.4	**486.5**
Professional services	218.9	78.2	31.3	328.4	43.4	129.7	173.2	**501.5**
Home health care	6.7	6.5	1.1	14.3	5.7	16.2	21.9	**36.1**
Nursing home care	7.7	25.9	3.5	37.1	20.5	45.5	66.1	**103.2**
Retail sales of medical products	81.0	87.2	–	168.2	15.6	29.1	44.7	**212.9**
Government administration and net cost of private insurance	70.2	–	1.4	71.7	14.3	19.0	33.3	**105.0**
Government public health	–	–	–	–	44.1	7.0	51.2	**51.2**
Research	–	–	2.7	2.7	4.2	27.4	31.6	**34.3**
Construction	–	–	17.1	17.1	4.4	0.8	5.2	**22.4**
Total	**549.6**	**212.5**	**77.5**	**839.6**	**208.7**	**504.7**	**713.4**	**1 553.0**

Source: Centers for Medicare & Medicaid Services

1 For which categories does public expenditure exceed total consumer expenditure? Suggest reasons to explain this.
2 Compare private insurance expenditure with out of pocket payments. For which categories do the latter exceed those financed through insurance? Discuss possible explanations.
3 Calculate programme administration costs as a percentage of total expenditure for public and for private insurance spending, and compare the figures.

Feedback

1 Public spending exceeds spending through private health insurance for hospital care, home care and nursing home care. Elderly people who use these services are mainly covered by Medicare. Note that government finances exclusively public health activities and bears the major part of research expenditure.

2 Out of pocket payments exceed insurance payments for nursing home care and retail outlet sales of medical products. Private insurance plans usually fail to insure against the risk of long-term care. Many plans exclude cover for common risks which are considered predictable, including products available in retail outlets.

3 Administration costs make up 13 per cent of private insurance (70.2/549.6) and 4.5 per cent of government spending (33.3/713.4). These figures demonstrate the high transactions cost of private health insurance.

Summary

Private insurance companies relate the personal premium to the actuarial risk of the individual. Under retrospective payment neither consumer nor provider has incentives to contain costs. Various methods of cost sharing are used to discourage excess demand. Private insurance involves high transaction costs and is not an efficient method of mobilizing funds for the health sector. To improve efficiency, the industry has developed a variety of schemes which are based on prospective payment. In general, private insurance has inherent limitations in providing coverage for high-risk individuals and the poor. Government intervention is required to provide these groups with access to care.

References

Donaldson C and Gerard K (2005). *Economics of health care financing. The visible hand* (2nd edn). Basingstoke: Palgrave Macmillan.

Griffin CC (1992) *Health care in Asia: a comparative study of cost and financing*. Washington, DC: World Bank.

Hsiao WC (1995) Abnormal economics in the health sector, in Berman P (ed) *Health sector reform in developing countries*. Cambridge, MA: Harvard School of Public Health.

Laing W and Buisson W (2003) *Private medical insurance: UK market report 2003*. London: Laing & Buisson.

Smith MB (1997) Trends in health care coverage and financing and their implications for policy. *New England Journal of Medicine* 337:1000–3.

15

Social health insurance

Overview

In the previous chapter you saw that private insurance is an inadequate method of financing health services for the entire population. You will now assess the viability of social health insurance as a means of mobilizing resources for the health sector and providing services efficiently and equitably.

Learning objectives

By the end of this chapter, you should be able to:

- **define the principles of social insurance and contrast it with private insurance**
- **describe advantages and disadvantages of social insurance**
- **discuss the impact of a payroll-based insurance system on wages, the labour market and employer behaviour**
- **describe the significance of pre-payment schemes for health insurance in low income countries**

Key terms

Formal labour Employment with taxable income.

Payroll deduction Contribution raised as part of wages.

Redistribution A government intervention to transfer income and wealth between groups of the population.

Principles of social insurance

Social health insurance is insurance operated by a public agency. Conventionally, the premium takes the form of compulsory contributions which are deducted from the payroll as part of earnings. The characteristics of social insurance systems are:

- compulsory membership;
- payroll deduction of contributions;
- run by public bodies, either single or multiple organizations;
- redistributional policies;

- clearly defined earmarked resources;
- complex administration, relatively high costs;
- can mobilize additional resources for the health sector.

As you have seen in earlier chapters, redistribution is based on the notion of equity and seeks to transfer income or wealth from the rich to the poor. Social insurance is based on redistributional policies to equalize the financial burden of health care and to ensure access to care on the basis of need and not on ability to pay. The main difference between social and private insurance is the extent of the redistributional intention of the former. Social insurance aims at four means of cross-subsidization:

1 *from the healthy to the ill*: contributions regardless of individual risk;
2 *from the young to the old*: smaller contributions from the elderly;
3 *from the rich to the poor*: contributions are a fixed percentage of earnings;
4 *from singles to families*: equal contributions regardless of the number of dependants.

Note that private insurance offers risk sharing only between the healthy and the acutely ill. The extent of additional cross-subsidization may vary between social insurance schemes and there is also variation in a number of other aspects, such as:

- *Coverage*: social insurance may either cover part of the population (Latin America) or the whole population (Canada). High earners may be allowed to insure privately if their earnings are above a defined income (Germany).
- *Subsidies:* governments may subsidize social insurance funds to keep contributions affordable for the poor.
- *Number of funds*: social insurance systems may consist of several funds or a single fund for the whole population.
- *Contributions:* usually compulsory, payroll deducted, progressive with income, but voluntary contributions and flat rates are also possible.
- *Ownership of health care facilities* by social insurance agencies is uncommon though agencies in Latin America act as providers as well as purchasers of health care.
- *Benefit package*: may vary between basic and comprehensive health care and include benefits in cash and kind.

 **Activity 15.1**

Focus on the advantages of social insurance and answer the following questions:

1 What do you think might be the advantages of a large *single* insurance fund (rather than lots of small ones) when contracting with providers?
2 How might adverse selection or cream skimming (avoiding accepting unhealthy, high risk people) be counteracted in social insurance systems?
3 Imagine a country with several social insurance funds which are subject to government regulation. What provisions would government need to take to avoid adverse selection?

Feedback

1 Large social insurance funds can (in theory) exert their monopsony of buying power and thus determine what services are provided, reducing the risk of supplier induced demand.

2 By having a single, monopolist fund. As only one organization has the obligation to cover the entire population, there is no opportunity to exclude bad risks.

3 Regulation needs to ensure that all social insurance funds take on all applicants and offer the same benefit package. They should be encouraged to contract jointly with providers. For example, Germany's 500 social insurance (or sickness) funds are regulated in this way and, additionally, money is transferred from funds with good risks to funds with bad risks, to equalize the distribution of available resources.

 Activity 15.2

This activity lets you assess the differences between private and social insurance by using an example from the German health care system. In that country 90 per cent of the population are covered by social insurance and only those above an annually determined income level can insure privately (Schulenburg 1994). Table 15.1 compares the terms of social and private insurance.

Table 15.1 Contract terms of social and private health insurance

Terms of contract	Social health insurance	Private health insurance
1 Enrolment	Compulsory	Voluntary
2 Right of insurer to refuse insurance	No	Yes
3 Coverage of pre-existing conditions	Yes	No
4 Waiting times	Not applicable	3 months in general, 8 months for pregnancy and dental prostheses
5 Co-payments	Drugs, hospital care, dental care	Dental care
6 Contributions/premium	A fixed proportion of income	Varying with age, sex, health status and benefits scheme
7 Insurance of family members	Covered	Not covered, additional policies required
8 Elderly	Lower contributions	Increasing premiums with age
9 Home care, rehabilitation	Covered	Not covered
10 Sick payment	Covered	Additional policy required
11 Private care	Not covered	Covered

Source: Schulenberg (1994)

1   Study Table 15.1 and identify those terms of contract that are controlling for moral hazard and adverse selection.
2   Assess differences between the schemes with regard to redistributional policies.
3   What differences can you identify between services included in the social insurance benefit package and those offered by private insurance?

 Feedback

1 Numbers 1–4 relate to terms controlling for adverse selection. Unlike private insurance, social insurance cannot refuse to take on bad risks. With private insurance, waiting times apply before a subscriber is entitled to benefits. Co-payments are used under both schemes to reduce moral hazard.

2 Social insurance subsidizes services for low earners, families and elderly people.

3 Social insurance also covers non-medical benefits like home care, rehabilitation and sick payment whereas private insurance includes private consultations and additional hotel services in hospitals.

Payroll deduction

Payroll deductions are a common way of raising contributions. Payroll contributions depend on formal labour. If the informal sector is relatively large, as is the case in many low income countries, social insurance may be impractical to implement.

Similarly, where the income tax system is not reliable, it may be difficult to assess contribution levels for the self-employed. Particularly difficult, but not impossible, is providing insurance for the agricultural sector. A number of successful rural health insurance schemes have been launched in low income countries using annual flat fees.

From the point of view of employers, contributions increase labour costs. It is a form of employment tax. A reason for having employer contributions is that it may encourage them to keep costs down. On the other hand, there is an ongoing debate as to whether high payroll charges may increase unemployment and negatively affect the competitiveness of an industry or of a nation as a whole.

In many high income countries, the gross domestic product (GDP) proportion of income from labour has been declining as compared to corporate income from capital. But as labour income falls, it is expected to finance growing health care costs. Additional corporate contributions have been suggested to balance the financial burden.

 Activity 15.3

Suppose a country with health services financed and provided by government considers introducing social insurance. This scenario has been common in central and eastern Europe and in low income countries, which want to mobilize additional resources for the health sector and improve quality of care. The following extract from

Normand and Weber (1994) focuses on the advantages and disadvantages of social insurance and the reasons why it might not be feasible. Answer the following questions when you have finished reading:

1 What benefits might social insurance have as regards provider performance?
2 Introduction of social insurance needs careful consideration. What conditions need to be met to support its successful implementation with regard to:

   a) the labour market?
   b) health services infrastructure?
   c) administration and management?

3 What are the main disadvantages of social insurance?
4 What are potential effects on equity if social insurance is introduced for only part of the population?

 ## The desirability and feasibility of social insurance

It is necessary to identify the administrative needs of an insurance system and decide whether they can be met. Insurance arrangements tend to be more complex (and often more expensive to administer) than tax funding, and certainly require considerable administrative skills . . .

Payroll deductions

Social health insurance is normally provided through a system of payroll contributions to a health fund. It is typical (although not essential) for the total contribution to be calculated as a percentage of income. This amount is normally split between employer and employee: for example, if the total social health insurance contribution for a worker is 12% of the wage, this may be made up by contributions of 8% from the employer and 4% from the employee.

The distinction between employee and employer contributions may not be important. For the employer, the decision to employ a worker depends on the overall cost of wages and other payroll costs. For the employee, the main areas of interest are take-home pay and other benefits. If contributions to the insurance fund are tax-free, there is little analytical difference between employer and employee contributions, although there may be important psychological differences. One reason for having employer contributions is that they encourage employers to seek cost containment, since the employer benefits from any savings in resources.

One important question is whether payroll contributions are the best source of funds for health care. In most countries, the payroll is already a major source of taxation – income tax, pension contributions, unemployment insurance and sometimes insurance against loss of earnings due to ill-health. If the deduction rate is already high (i.e. the proportion of total payroll costs taken out in compulsory deductions is high) then it is not advisable to use this source for additional deductions. The effect of further payroll charges is likely to be to discourage employers from retaining or taking on staff, with the consequence of higher unemployment . . .

Labour market structure

Social insurance for health is funded by a percentage deduction from incomes (or salaries), and this depends on there being an agreed measure of income. Social health insurance therefore works best in the context of a relatively large formal sector, with a large proportion of the population working as employees, so that there is little scope for doubt about their incomes.

Although it is difficult to assess contributions for any self-employed person, there are particular problems with people working in agriculture. Farmers have the additional problem that incomes are very uneven over the year. A large proportion of their income may be realized in a few weeks (e.g. at harvest time) and so they will have real difficulty in paying regular weekly or monthly contributions.

Of course it is possible to operate social health insurance for self-employed people, and there are many examples of ingenious ways of assessing the level of contributions. If incomes are consistently understated, it is possible to charge a higher rate for self-employed people, or to insist on a higher level of copayments.

Social health insurance and national infrastructure

Social health insurance requires some additional administrative arrangements for collecting contributions and providing access to care, and it can only be effectively developed if these arrangements can be put in place. The overall level of education within the country can be important in this respect. Adequate standards of literacy and numeracy in the general population may be important to the extent that self-assessment is an element in the determination of insurance contributions. Thus education in general, as well as the educational level of the administrative staff, can be significant.

Some countries have an established system for collecting income tax through payroll deductions. Under these conditions, it may be possible to introduce social health insurance contributions using the same basic procedures, but paying the money into different funds. This can simplify the operation of social health insurance and reduce costs . . .

Social health insurance and health care infrastructure

Health insurance gives the insured population an entitlement to health services. It is therefore important to ensure that the health infrastructure exists to provide those services and that there is some incentive to comply with the insurance. It is important that an individual should have better access to care if he/she pays the contributions due and obtains insurance. This is true even if the insurance is compulsory, since it helps to ensure that contributions are paid.

In principle, insurance does not require a system of hospital-based secondary and tertiary health services, although such provision is typically popular with the population, and thus with the insured population. The important thing is to ensure that the health services to which insured people are entitled can be delivered.

When social health insurance is introduced, it is often difficult to offer advantages to members in the form of better access to care. Most countries have a system of access to some emergency care, regardless of ability to pay or insurance status. There is considerable disquiet when people in serious medical need are refused treatment because of their inability to pay or lack of insurance. There is therefore a potential conflict between the desire to protect the population, regardless of people's insurance status, and the need for insurance to offer significant advantages to the insured population. This problem is particularly severe when insurance is proposed in a country with an existing system of state-funded, free or heavily subsidized health services (however poor these services may be). People will question the advantages and resist the introduction of additional and highly visible insurance contributions unless they bring demonstrable additional benefits.

Several mechanisms can be used to resolve these difficulties. It is sometimes possible to give immediate access to emergency care for everyone who needs it, and to recover the money later from those who can afford to pay. Alternatively, the incentive to be a member may be better access to non-emergency care.

↻ Feedback

1 a) Improved productivity. In government-run services, a provider unit – such as a hospital – is financed through a budget allocation, whereas under social insurance the provider is paid for specified services rendered to specific patients. This means that 'money follows the patient'.
   b) Improved quality of care. Paying contributions creates a specific *entitlement* to services, which is considered to give patients more explicit rights to demand high quality services.

2 a) Social insurance is easier to implement where the formal sector is large in relation to the informal sector. Provisions need to be in place to collect contributions.
   b) The health services need to be prepared to offer the services to which the subscribers are entitled. This means that facilities, staff and equipment need to be available to meet the increased demand. An unprepared infrastructure may turn entitlements into 'paper rights'. New schemes need to offer advantages to subscribers, such as better access to care, otherwise there would be no incentive to join.
   c) Administration of social insurance is more complex than government funding and involves higher costs. Administrative structures for collecting contributions, claims handling and paying providers, management staff and a legal framework are essential.

3 Disadvantages include high administrative costs, problems of cost containment and problems of ensuring coverage for workers in agriculture and the informal sector. Cost escalation is salient where insurers fail to control providers, as experiences in the 1990s in China, South Korea and Brazil demonstrate (Kutzin and Barnum 1992).

4 Moving part of the population from government to insurance finance may free government resources for priority services. But increased demand from the insured could worsen access for the uninsured. Partial coverage can exacerbate equity problems, as the insured tend to have higher incomes and better access to care. If government extends insurance, it needs to ensure services for the uninsured.

A variety of rural risk-sharing schemes, which are based on the idea of mutual support, operate successfully in low income countries (Shaw and Griffin 1995). The schemes are organized by local communities, government or non-governmental organizations. The premium takes the form of a flat amount per adult or per household and covers the most essential services for the subscribers and their dependants. Premiums also need to cover commissions for enrolment agents, administration and incentives for people to join the scheme. The following extract by Per Eklund and Knut Stavem (1995) describes their main conclusions from evaluating a community insurance scheme in 18 villages in Guinea-Bissau in west Africa.

Activity 15.4

As you read the extract, consider the following questions:

1 How do the schemes of the 18 villages vary in relation to the degree of cross-subsidization between adults and dependants?
2 How do rural pre-payment schemes control for moral hazard and adverse selection?
3 What has been the reported effect on drug availability and quality of care?

Community health insurance through pre-payment schemes in Guinea-Bissau

The village health post (USB) system is based on community participation and involves a significant amount of local resource mobilization. A contract between the village leaders and the Ministry of Public Health (MINSAP) defines responsibilities as the following.

i.   The village decides on the fee levels for the prepayment scheme, whether payment is based per capita, per adult or per household, and the timing of payments.

ii.   The village must collect funds under the prepayment system to ensure that initial drug supplies are continually replenished. Drugs are sold to USBs with substantial subsidies, set at the central level and equal across regions.

iii. Some villages create special health sub-committees to oversee USB operations, but in the smaller villages, the responsibilities are performed by the political committee.

iv.   The village provides the labor and most construction materials for building the health post. MINSAP provides materials for windows, doors, and hinges.

iv.   The government supplies simple equipment, including a metal cupboard for storing drugs, a bed, stretcher, four chairs, one obstetrical stethoscope, one lantern, a kit of posters and other teaching aids, and an initial stock of drugs estimated to last for six months (for the population of each village).

v.   The village selects one or more of its residents to be trained as VHWs (village health workers) and midwives.

Funds are collected at USBs by the village committee treasurer or one of the health staff and a record of the contribution is kept in each village. The funds are then transferred through the regional health directorate to Bissau, where they are deposited into a special account earmarked for the purchase of drugs at the central drug depository.

The prepayment scheme in Guinea-Bissau is an example of a simple scheme that pools risks for basic primary health care services (particularly drugs), while simplifying management demands. Once prepayment levels have been determined by the village, the prepayments are collected all at once and forwarded up through the health system. This system is easier for illiterate villagers to manage than one of user fees for consultations and drugs. The latter would require an accounting of fee revenues for each use of the various services by different categories of clients and finding a way to safeguard the funds. The USB prepayment scheme is also much easier to manage than most insurance schemes. Since there is no billing necessary, providers are not being reimbursed for services used and it is not necessary to assess prepayment rates based on risk. The services provided by USBs are limited to prenatal care and treatment of a few basic ailments with essential drugs.

. . . Adverse selection is prevented by almost universal membership within each village participating. Moral hazard is avoided through the vigilance of village health workers and midwives, who dispense drugs only as needed, based on diagnosis, and by the pressure of the local community.

Although the level of cost recovery . . . is low, this understates the total amount of resource mobilization. Villagers provide construction materials for the USB and the labor of village health workers and midwives for implementation and management of the scheme – none of which is reflected in cost recovery figures. Further, respondents indicated their willingness to prepay greater amounts, provided that drugs could be made available on a timely basis. Drugs are heavily subsidized to the USBs, however, and their price is not regularly increased, to reflect inflation and devaluation. The degree of subsidization of USB drug supplies is thus increasing over time.

The survey found that the level of satisfaction with the village health posts was high, despite evidence that drug stocks are rapidly depleted. Respondents' willingness to prepay was often linked to improvements in the quality of service, including greater availability of drugs and better training for village midwives. Yet, the quality of service that can be provided at village health posts depends critically on the extent of support from the rest of the health care system. Even when villagers prepay, drugs are not available immediately because of more general problems of finance and procurement in the health system. The health posts also rely on supervision, training and referral services from health centers.

 Feedback

1 Most schemes are based on fixed rates per adult or per household, which also cover children. Contributions are flat rates regardless of income, but the poor are exempt from payments.

2 Moral hazard is easier to control in small communities where villagers know each other and health workers know the needs of their patients. Adverse selection is prevented through nearly universal membership.

3 Although the availability of drugs continues to be uneven, the quality of care overall was perceived to be higher after the introduction of insurance.

 Activity 15.5

By way of revision, given what you have learned about social insurance, what do you think are its advantages and its disadvantages compared with the alternative of tax-based funding?

Feedback

The principal advantages are:

- funds for health care are clearly identified and do not have to compete with other demands on government such as defence, housing and social security
- people may be happier paying social insurance knowing that it will be spent on health care than paying taxes which may not be used for health care
- employee contributions mean that people may behave as better, more responsible consumers of health care, reducing the risk of moral hazard, and may be more likely to demand high quality services from providers
- employer contributions mean that they have an incentive to ensure premiums are as low as possible, thus encouraging health care providers to be as efficient as possible

The disadvantages are:

- social insurance is a form of employment tax (i.e. it is paid by those in employment) and this may prove to be a disincentive for employers to create new jobs
- the amount raised will vary with the number of people employed so the health care system has no guaranteed income
- the cost of collecting funds from employees and employers (extra costs that don't arise with tax-based systems)
- if there is more than one social insurance fund, there is the risk of adverse selection of enrollees

Summary

You have learned about the characteristics of social health insurance and its advantages and disadvantages. You have seen how moral hazard and adverse selection can be handled, and how even in rural areas with little formal employment, prepayment social insurance can be successfully implemented. That completes your consideration of the principal methods of funding health care: taxation, social insurance, private insurance and out of pocket expenditure. You will now go on to the final section of this book on economic evaluation.

References

Eklund P and Stavem K (1995) Community health insurance through prepayment schemes in Guinea-Bissau, in Shaw RP and Ainsworth M (eds) *Financing health services through user fees and insurance*. Washington, DC: World Bank.

Kutzin J and Barnum H (1992) *Health insurance affects the delivery of health care in developing countries*. Working paper. Washington, DC: World Bank.

Normand C and Weber A (1994) The desirability of social health insurance, in *Social Health Insurance: A Guidebook for Planning*. Geneva: WHO.

Schulenburg JMG (1994) The German health care system at the crossroads. *Health Economics* 3:301–3.

Shaw RP and Griffin CC (1995) *Health care in Sub-Saharan Africa through user fees and insurance*. Washington, DC: World Bank.

SECTION 5

Economic evaluation

16

What is economic evaluation?

Overview

This chapter presents key concepts frequently used in economic evaluations. You will encounter these concepts throughout the following four chapters so it is essential that you understand them – they will also be used to build a framework for economic evaluation.

Learning objectives

After completing this chapter, you will be able to:

- **define and give examples of disease burden**
- **define and give examples of outcome**
- **define economic evaluation**
- **list the two major types of economic evaluation and how they differ from one another**
- **define and give examples of perspectives**

Key terms

Burden of disease A measure of the physical, emotional, social and financial impact that a particular disease has on the health and functioning of the population.

Cost The value of resources usually expressed in monetary terms.

Cost–benefit analysis An economic evaluation technique in which outcomes are expressed in monetary terms.

Cost-effectiveness analysis Economic evaluation with outcomes measured in health units.

Cost–utility analysis Economic evaluations where the outcomes are measured in health units which capture not just the quantitative but also the qualitative aspects of the outcome, such as quality of life.

Economic evaluation The systematic assessment and interpretation of the value of a health care intervention. It is done by systematically examining the relationship between their costs and outcomes.

> **Health care intervention** A programme, activity or technology designed to reduce a health problem. Interventions include prevention, control, screening, diagnostic tests and treatment.
>
> **Outcomes** Change in status as a result of the system processes (in the health services context, the change in health status as a result of care).
>
> **Time frame** The period of time from the intervention to assessing the outcome.

A day in the life of a minister of health

A minister of health once remarked that 'the only thing a minister of health is ever destined to discuss with the medical profession is money'. There never seems to be enough money to do everything worth doing and Ministries of Health frequently encounter situations where each request for additional funding may be legitimate in that it will improve health but the budget often cannot cover all of the requests.

For example, suppose a minister of health receives requests from two different programmes, one from the Tuberculosis Programme (TB) and the other from the Expanded Programme on Immunization (EPI). The TB Programme wants additional funding for 'Directly Observed Therapy – Short Course' or DOTS. The EPI wants to add hepatitis B vaccine (HBV) to its routine programme. Without an increase in the overall budget, the new programmes could not be covered unless some other programmes are cut.

The question, then, is how can the minister decide which of the requests should be supported? Giving support for one, or possibly both, means that something else should be cut back – which programme should it be? Which interventions are 'worthwhile'?

The burden of disease

People naturally want to live long and healthy lives. One of our great preoccupations has been to alleviate health problems: disease, injury or a risk factor for one of these. The burden of such health problems can be manifested in different ways – physical disability, morbidity and mortality, emotional distress, social difficulties and isolation, and financial and economic losses. Each manifestation can be seen at the level of the individual, the family and household, the local community, and the rest of society. The burden of disease can be measured as:

- the number of cases;
- the number of deaths;
- the amount of disability, pain or suffering;
- the number of people with a risk factor;
- the amount of money spent on the health problem;
- the amount of lost income due to a health problem.

For example, the death during childbirth of a mother who already has two children and who is the only schoolteacher in the village can be measured in various ways, such as:

- a 'case' of maternal mortality;
- the number of years of life she has lost by dying prematurely;
- the amount of her wages that her family will no longer receive;
- the loss of her wages, particularly on her school-age children who can't be educated because the money for school fees is no longer available;
- the loss to her husband who misses her company and her skills as a housekeeper and part-time farmer;
- the loss of her guidance and training for her young children;
- the loss of the investment her own parents made in training and educating her to be a teacher;
- the loss to the school system which now has to hire or train new teachers to replace her.

So, in economic evaluation the burden of disease can be assessed using a variety of health measures (such as the number of cases of illness, the number of deaths due to illness or the number of potential years of life lost due to illness) or in monetary terms as the *cost of health problems* – the monetary value of resources spent or lost because of the health problem.

Resources needed for an intervention

You know in advance that you will never have enough money to do everything you would like – so knowing all the possible interventions available for a health problem is not enough. You also need to know what the interventions cost. Determining the cost of an intervention can sometimes be complicated. A first step is to know what specific resources are used to implement the interventions.

Resources are the ingredients of health interventions. They are also referred to as *inputs* or *resource inputs*. A useful approach is to divide the resources into seven categories:

- personnel;
- buildings and space;
- equipment;
- supplies and pharmaceuticals;
- transportation;
- training;
- social mobilization and publicity including information, education and communication.

Activity 16.1

Look at the photograph (Figure 16.1) of a growth monitoring session in a low income country. What resources are being used in the health intervention depicted? (Don't forget to note the 'invisible' resources which are needed to make the intervention happen.)

Figure 16.1 A health intervention in a developing country
Source: Global Samaritans

 Feedback

In the photo your attention was probably first drawn to the equipment, such as the stationery and other equipment, in particular the weighing scale. Then you will have noticed the staff – the person who is writing down the weights of the babies. She has been trained to carry out this activity. You may have forgotten the vehicle and driver (not in the picture) who would have transported the staff to the village. Other costs would include the maintenance of vehicles and equipment, the training of staff, the supervision by higher levels of staff at a health centre or wherever they are based. Another resource to keep in mind is the time of the mothers – they could be doing other activities instead of waiting for their babies to be weighed. And how did the mothers know that there would be a growth monitoring session in this place at this time? Resources have gone into informing and motivating the mothers to bring their babies.

Having identified the resources, you need to measure how much of each resource is used. Finally you need to establish the value of each so that you can calculate the cost of the intervention. The most straightforward way to value resources is to use money as the measure. Some costs will not be easy to determine – think of the time of the women who brought their children for the growth monitoring session. How would you estimate its value in money terms? This will form the subject of Chapter 18. For the moment it is enough that you begin to be aware that costing is not always a simple matter of collecting price information – it may require skill and judgement on the part of the economist.

Outcomes

The goal of an intervention is to reduce the burden of the health problem. For economic evaluations, you need to measure how much the burden is reduced. To figure out if the intervention has done enough good to justify its cost, you need to know how the health problem changes after the intervention. Specifically, you need to know what occurs *as a result of* the intervention, in other words, the outcome of the intervention.

You can assess this change by measuring the difference in the health problem in one of two ways. You can either measure the burden of the health problem:

- before and after the intervention; or
- with and without the intervention.

Since the burden is assessed using either health measures (number of deaths, number of cases, etc.) or their monetary equivalent, and since outcome is merely the difference in burden, the units used to measure outcome are identical to the units used to measure burden. Outcomes which use monetary indicators are often referred to as (monetary) 'benefits'.

Take the example of the use of impregnated bed-nets to prevent malaria. If you wanted to determine their impact, you could calculate the number of deaths in children aged 6 months to 5 years in a village where the nets were impregnated and compare this to the number of malaria deaths in villages of similar size and characteristics where the bed-nets were not impregnated. Suppose that the results showed that:

- villages which did not receive the intervention had 73 deaths from malaria;
- villages where bed-nets were impregnated (with the intervention) had 16 deaths from malaria.

As a result of the intervention, you could conclude that there were 57 fewer deaths from malaria. The *outcome* of the new malaria intervention is therefore a reduction of 57 deaths.

While health care's goal is to achieve as much reduction in burden as possible, your health care budget often won't allow you to implement all desirable interventions. This is exactly the same dilemma faced by the minister of health at the beginning of this chapter. He or she still faces the challenge of comparing the request for funding by the TB Programme for DOTS with the request for funding from the EPI programme to introduce HBV vaccination. Some decision must be made as regards the relative value of the interventions. This is how economics as a discipline can assist.

Economic evaluation

Economic evaluation with the outcome measured in health units is called cost-effectiveness analysis (CEA). You can calculate the 'cost per unit of outcome', such as the cost per reduction in cases of illness.

There is a subset of cost-effectiveness analysis (CEA) called cost–utility analysis (CUA) where the outcomes are measured in health units, which capture not just extension to the length of life but also changes in the quality of life. The most commonly used measure is the Quality Adjusted Life Year, or QALY. Cost-effectiveness analysis and cost–utility analysis are discussed in Chapter 19.

When outcomes are expressed in monetary terms, the technique is called cost–benefit analysis (CBA). This will be discussed in Chapter 18.

 Activity 16.2

Consider a programme of providing impregnated bed-nets to some villages to prevent malaria. Suppose that 57 deaths from malaria were prevented and the cost of the programme was $17,955. Since outome is measured in terms of deaths, you could use cost-effectiveness analysis for the economic evaluation.

The cost-effectiveness ratio (CER) is a meaningful way of comparing the costs and the outcomes. For the bed-net programme, calculate the cost-effectiveness ratio (costs/health outcomes).

 Feedback

The CER would be $17,955/57 deaths = $315 to prevent one death.

This can then be used to compare the bed-net programme to other programmes that also prevent deaths.

Framing an economic evaluation

There are three steps in undertaking an economic evaluation:

- framing the evaluation;
- identifying, quantifying and valuing the resources needed;
- identifying, quantifying and valuing the health consequences.

You will learn about the second step in the next chapter and the third step in Chapters 18 and 19. Framing the evaluation should include clear statements about the purpose, time frame and perspective.

Purpose

It's important to be very clear about *why* you are carrying out the economic evaluation. The statement of purpose should include the following information:

- the intervention;
- the health problem addressed by the intervention;
- the reason for conducting the evaluation and its importance;
- the units of analysis.

You want your analysis to have an impact on policy. Therefore it's important that results should be easy to communicate in terms that are both useful and understandable to the target audience. People want to know what they are getting for their money and this is most easily communicated when costs and outcomes are simplified to units that people can understand. For example, for an intervention such as a vaccination programme, it may be helpful to present the results in terms of cost per child immunized. However, although easy to measure, it is not generally regarded as very helpful.

Time frame

Interventions often have different time patterns for their costs and outcomes; costs and outcomes are usually spread out over time (often a number of years) and, frequently, costs and outcomes change over time. It is quite common that the costs of the intervention are incurred at the beginning, while the benefits occur far in the future – an example would be an immunization programme for hepatitis B. A cost analysis must therefore consider the time course of interventions and outcomes separately and adjust for changes over time.

To understand how and why the costs of intervention vary, you divide the intervention into start-up costs (those needed to set up the intervention) and maintenance costs (those needed to keep it going). If you do the cost analysis when beginning the intervention, it would be a mistake to assume the start-up costs (such as building a new clinic) are representative of the costs you will incur in later years. Conversely, if you begin the cost analysis after the intervention has begun, you cannot assume that everything put in place at the beginning of the project no longer has to be paid for and therefore has a value of zero.

Perspectives: whose costs and whose outcomes?

It is important to realize that health interventions frequently have costs and outcomes that affect different parts of a society. The party that pays for the intervention may not necessarily be the party that receives the benefit and the relative value of costs and outcomes may depend on the *perspective* from which the analysis is done. The perspective should be chosen on the basis of who is going to use the results of the evaluation.

Correctly thinking through the perspective can save large amounts of time and effort in performing the analysis because, depending on the perspective taken, some hard to measure costs and outcomes may not have to be considered.

The simplest example is the expenditure for a prescription drug. If the patient must pay 100 per cent of the cost of the drug, then the cost might not be important to the health service. On the other hand, if the health system must bear all of the costs of the drug, then this will directly reduce the funds available for other interventions and the health system might be very concerned with the drug costs – as the example below will show.

Should expensive drugs be provided free?

Consider a disease for which there is a drug treatment but the drugs are very expensive (e.g. they cost $10,000 to $12,000 per year for each patient). Citizens' groups representing those affected by the disease are requesting that the Ministry of Health provide this medication free of charge to everyone with the disease. Now consider two contrasting perspectives: that of the Ministry of Health and that of a group of citizens.

From the perspective of the Ministry, providing this drug will indeed help patients with the disease but the opportunity cost of these drugs is significant in terms of what could be provided for other patients. The budget is limited – what is the best use of available resources?

In contrast, the citizens' group will focus on the impact on people with the disease who will be able to lead more normal lives, of higher quality, be able to perform their household duties and will remain productive members of society. Their need to use the health services over any given period of time will be reduced. However, if they do not get the drug their responsibilities will have to be shifted onto their families and friends. Because they cannot work, the patients will not be able to support themselves financially. So supplying the drug will lessen the burden on the family.

You can see from the above example that the perspective you choose will dictate how you look at costs and outcomes. Commonly used perspectives include those of:

- *society* – takes into account all the costs and all the outcomes of a health intervention, regardless of who incurs them or who gains from them;
- *government* – includes the costs borne and the outcomes received by the health sector (and other government agencies or sectors).

 Activity 16.3

As a quick review of terms in this chapter, write down the word being defined by the following:

1 The value of resources usually expressed in monetary terms.
2 Changes in health problems that occur as a result of an intervention. These can be measured either in health units or monetary units.
3 The ingredients of a health care programme. These are the components or building blocks needed to make a health programme work.
4 A programme, activity or technology to reduce a health problem, including prevention, control, screening, diagnosis and treatment.

 Feedback

The answers are as follows:

1 Costs.

2 Outcomes.

3 Resources.

4 Intervention.

Summary

You have learned about the many ways the burden of a disease may be measured and the classification of interventions in terms of primary, secondary and tertiary prevention. The costing of interventions requires the identification, quantification and valuation of the resources needed. The costs of interventions can be related either to health outcomes in a cost-effectiveness (or cost–utility) analysis or to monetary outcomes in a cost–benefit analysis. Finally the importance of the perspective adopted was considered. The next step is to learn more about costing, the subject of the next chapter.

Reference

Creese A and Parker D (eds) (1994) *Cost analysis in primary health care: a training manual for programme managers*. Geneva: WHO.

Overview

It is important to know the cost of things you buy in the health sector. Every time a decision is made to implement one intervention instead of another, it is the same as making a purchase. The cost of the intervention becomes a very important part of the decision to use one intervention rather than another. But figuring out the cost of an intervention is often not easy. In this chapter you will learn about estimating, calculating and comparing costs, known as cost analysis. In particular, you will learn about marginal costs – the cost of providing one additional unit of service.

Learning objectives

After completing this chapter, you will be able to:

- **define and set up a cost analysis**
- **define and give examples of each of the following types of costs: financial and economic costs; direct, indirect and intangible costs; capital and recurrent costs; fixed and variable costs**
- **calculate the following as they relate to an intervention: total costs; annual and annualized costs; average costs; and marginal costs**
- **explain why discounting may be necessary**

Key terms

Annual cost The cost of an intervention, calculated on a yearly basis, including all the annually payable capital costs as well as the yearly recurrent costs.

Annualized costs The annual share of the initial cost of capital equipment or investments, spread over the life of the project – usually modified to take account of depreciation.

Average cost Total cost divided by quantity.

Capital cost The value of capital resources which have useful lives greater than one year.

Direct cost Resources used in the design, implementation, receipt and continuation of a health care intervention.

Discount rate The rate at which future costs and outcomes are discounted to account for time preference.

Di... s and outcomes which occur in different
tin... resent.

Fi... ood or service usually representing the
ori... portunity cost.

Inc... its and their carers to enable individuals
to r...

Int...
Mar... onal unit of output is produced.

Ove... providing patient care but are
nece... nel funtions).

Recu... ful lives of less than one year that have
to be...

Time... r use of resources) now rather than
later... the same consumption in the
futur...

Total... vention or health problem.

Costing

ree steps in determining the cost of an
rces needed; quantification of the
each resource. In this chapter you will
sources and ways of relating costs to

On the surface, costing sounds easy; many types of resource have a readily obtainable price. But think of the resource which is most scarce for some people in the busy world – their time. How can you value the time of individuals? Frequently, the price of a resource is not easily obtainable. It may be that there are no records about what was paid, the purchase was made long ago and the resources have declined in value or the people who have information are not willing to share it.

And even when the price is available, it may not reflect the true value of the resource to society. And if a resource is donated, the price may be zero but the value of the equipment is not zero. Price paid also does not reflect the value of the resources when the resources are subsidized or taxed.

Economists are always on the lookout for goods or services, the price of which does not reflect their true value to society – and that is the major difference between finance and economics. A financial analysis will be concerned strictly with the market price of goods and services, whereas an economic analysis will be concerned with the cost of the goods or services to society, and in some cases the economist will make a decision to value a resource differently from the market price.

Schemes for classifying costs

There are five commonly used schemes for thinking about or classifying costs. They are not mutually exclusive – you may need to use more than one to ensure all relevant costs are included. Considering each will help to ensure you include everything necessary.

You have already learned in Chapter 16 about one scheme, functional costs, in which resources are classified according to their use or function within the intervention such as buildings, personnel and equipment. The other four are: financial and economic costs; direct, indirect and intangible costs; capital and revenue costs; and fixed and variable costs. You will consider each in turn.

Financial and economic costs

Financial costs are defined as the actual money spent on the resources. Such costs appear on a programme's financial statements and in a budget. Examples of financial costs usually include costs of supplies, maintenance, personnel, electricity and rent. Financial costs are also known as budgetary costs. Financial costs are important in programme planning and budgeting as revenues must be generated to cover for these actual financial outlays for the programme to be sustained.

The financial cost of resources may not reflect their real value to society. They include donated goods and services; legally-set minimum wages, which may overstate the value of the output of the person; and foreign exchange. Even though some resources do not require an actual financial expenditure, their value is not zero. Inclusion of the costs of all resources, regardless of their financial cost is known as the *economic cost*.

The economic cost of a resource depends on its *opportunity cost*, or the value of the next best alternative foregone as a result of using the resource. This can be, but need not be, the same as its financial cost.

The following activity will give you an idea of why the distinction between financial and economic costs might be important.

✐ Activity 17.1

You are costing a primary health care project and have been asking around for the prices of resources. From a well-informed local source, you find out that the official prices of some resources do not seem to reflect their real value. Specifically, you are given the following information (Creese and Parker 1994):

* annual wages paid in the private sector for nurses and nurse assistants are US$1350 and US$1050, respectively
* the driver is paid the national minimum wage, but in the informal sector, drivers are paid only US$300
* there is always a shortage of fuel on the official markets and in the black market the price is four times the official price

- the official exchange rate is 50 shillings = US$1 but on the black market the average rate is 250 shillings
- space which is given free would rent for US$300 on the private market
- some community women have volunteered their time – most of them are housewives and earn extra money by cooking for the market for which they would normally earn about US$300 in a month

Now recalculate the cost of the inputs using the *economic costs*, entering them in the economic costs column in Table 17.1. What is their total? And which are the 'big ticket' items? Which resources are undervalued in terms of their financial costs, and which are overvalued?

Table 17.1 Financial costs of an identified primary health care project

Resource	Financial cost (US$)	Economic cost (US$)
Staff:		
• nurse	900	
• nurse assistant	700	
• driver	600	
• volunteer helpers	0	
Vaccine	5 000	
Vehicle fuel	3 000	
Building space	0	
Total cost		

Source: Creese and Parker (1994)

 Feedback

Check the economic costs you calculated by comparing them with those shown in Table 17.2.

Table 17.2 Financial and economic costs of an identified primary health care project (solution)

Resource	Financial cost (US$)	Economic cost (US$)
Staff:		
• nurse	900	1 350
• nurse assistant	700	1 050
• driver	600	300
• volunteer helpers	0	300
Vaccine	5 000	25 000
Vehicle fuel	3 000	12 000
Building space	0	300
Total cost	**10 200**	**40 300**

Source: Creese and Parker (1994)

You can see that the actual value to the economy and society of many of these resources is greater than their financial price – especially in the case of nursing staff, who are paid relatively poorly compared to the private sector. The driver, by contrast, is overpaid. The fuel and vaccines are also undervalued by comparison with their scarcity value in the economy.

Direct, indirect and intangible costs

Direct costs are resources used in the design, implementation, receipt and continuation of the health intervention. The division of direct costs into health care costs and non-health care costs is useful because it helps you to remember costs which are health-sector related and those which are not.

1 Direct health care costs are resources which are essential to the implementation, receipt or continuation of the intervention. Either a patient or the health sector can incur direct health care costs. Unless the study perspectives dictate otherwise, costs incurred by the patient and those incurred by the health sector should be included. The most commonly used classification of direct health care costs is the classification by function.
2 Direct non-health care costs are resources used in connection with an intervention but which are not exclusively resources from the health sector. Most direct non-health care costs are costs from the patient's perspective such as the cost of transport to and from health care facilities.

 **Activity 17.2**

Imagine that the minister of health has proposed that seven primary health care centres (PHCs) be built to decrease demands on a regional hospital. In Table 17.3 you will see a list of the resources identified as necessary for this project. Consider the resources listed and, in the right-hand column, write down whether each is a health care or a non-health care cost.

Table 17.3 Resources used to establish and run seven new PHCs

Resource	Type of cost
Building the 7 PHCs	
Child care costs while mother is in hospital	
Education of parents on how to prevent exacerbation of asthma	
Laboratory equipment for PHCs	
Lunch while waiting at PHCs	
PHC health education to prevent smoking	
Salaries of intervention personnel	
Soap for hand washing in PHCs	
Training PHC teams	
Transportation to PHCs	
Vehicles to carry vaccines for PHCs	

Feedback

The classification of costs would probably be as shown in Table 17.4.

Table 17.4 Cost classification of resources used in setting up and running seven new PHCs

Resource	Type of cost
Building the 7 PHCs	Direct health care
Child care costs while mother is in hospital	Direct non-health care
Education of parents on how to prevent exacerbation of asthma	Direct health care
Laboratory equipment for PHCs	Direct health care
Lunch while waiting at PHCs	Direct non-health care
PHC health education to prevent smoking	Direct health care
Salaries of intervention personnel	Direct health care
Soap for hand washing in PHCs	Direct health care
Training PHC teams	Direct health care
Transportation to PHCs	Direct health care
Vehicles to carry vaccines for PHCs	Direct health care

In order to use an intervention, a patient may have to take time away from work to travel to and from a clinic, wait for examinations or buy medications. Similarly, other family members may also have to change their work schedules to take over some of the jobs that would have been done by the patient, or to accompany the patient to receive care. The resources thus given up or forgone are termed *indirect costs* – productivity changes which happen as a result of the intervention or health problem. Indirect costs are usually measured using wages and earnings lost. If wages and earnings are not available or the person is not working, the opportunity cost questions could be used to find the value of time. What is the value of the activities that would have been assumed by this patient if he or she had not spent time receiving the intervention?

Some interventions may themselves cause pain and suffering. The value of pain and suffering is termed *intangible costs*. Because measuring intangible costs is a formidable task, most economic evaluations do not value these costs. However, you should bear in mind that intangible costs could be major factors affecting the patient's and society's decision regarding treatment options.

Activity 17.3

Consider the following aspects of the problems posed by polio in a society. Classify the items in Table 17.5 as direct health care, direct non-health care, indirect and intangible costs of health problem or intervention, noting your classification in the right-hand column.

Table 17.5 The costs of polio

Resource	Type of cost
Polio vaccine	
Salary of physical therapist who treats polio victims	
Loss of wages due to polio	
Loss of wages due to vaccine-induced polio	
Bus fare for family members visiting child at hospital	
Pain and suffering following a case of polio	
Cost of care of siblings to enable mother to take ill child for rehabilitation	
Time lost taking child to clinic for immunization	
Salary of nurse who runs immunization clinic	
Hospital cost for child with vaccine side-effects	

↻ Feedback

The classification of the resources devoted to the problem of polio could be described as shown in Table 17.6.

Table 17.6 The costs of polio classified

Resource	Type of cost
Polio vaccine	Direct health care
Salary of physical therapist who treats polio victims	Direct health care
Loss of wages due to polio	Indirect
Loss of wages due to vaccine-induced polio	Indirect
Bus fare for family members visiting child at hospital	Direct non-health care
Pain and suffering following a case of polio	Intangible
Cost of care of siblings to enable mother to take ill child for rehabilitation	Direct non-health care
Time lost taking child to clinic for immunization	Indirect
Salary of nurse who runs immunization clinic	Direct health care
Hospital cost for child with vaccine side-effects	Direct health care

Capital and recurrent costs

An important way to further classify direct costs, especially those borne by the health sector, is to classify direct costs as either capital or recurrent costs. *Capital costs* include the cost of equipment, vehicles, buildings and one-time training programmes. Capital costs are often equated with start-up costs because they are paid for at the beginning of the programme but the capital resources are defined on the basis of the useful life of the resource, not when they are purchased.

When you obtain a loan from a bank, you spread a one-time cost over years. The yearly payment is a recurrent cost. Similarly, in an economic evaluation, capital costs should be spread out over time. There are two methods to do this.

The simplest method is straight-line depreciation, which simply divides the initial cost by the number of years of useful life. For example, a $10,000 X-ray machine which has a useful life of ten years has an *annualized cost* of $1000 per year.

Most economists prefer a slightly more complex method that takes account of the opportunity cost of money – the interest that would be earned if it were invested in the bank. This is called the annualization method. Banks calculate payment schedules by the annualization method.

 Activity 17.4

Suppose you were calculating the annual costs of a family planning clinic. Calculate the annual cost of the resources in this example, using straight-line depreciation. The expected useful lives of the different resources are shown in Table 17.7.

Table 17.7 The cost and lives of resources for a family planning clinic

Resource	Useful life (years)	Total cost ($)	Annual cost ($)
Equipment	5	8 650	
Buildings	30	54 080	
Land	50	31 150	
Vehicles	5	8 165	
Initial training (nurses and midwives)	30	48 321	

 Feedback

The annual costs of these items, using straight-line depreciation are shown in the right-hand column in Table 17.8.

Table 17.8 The annual cost of resources for a family planning clinic (solution)

Resource	Useful life (years)	Total cost ($)	Annual cost ($)
Equipment	5	8 650	1 730
Buildings	30	54 080	1 803
Land	50	31 150	623
Vehicles	5	8 165	1 633
Initial training (nurses and midwives)	30	48 321	1 611

Recurrent resources are those with useful lives of less than one year and have to be purchased at least once a year – yearly, monthly, weekly, daily or irregularly but frequently. *Recurrent costs* are the value of recurrent resources. The sustainability of a health service depends heavily on whether funds are available to cover these recurrent costs.

Any given capital investment will require some recurrent funds to keep it running. The recurrent cost coefficient (r-coefficient) is used to estimate the approximate amount a given capital investment will require to run adequately. Typically r-coefficients in the health field run from about 0.25 for a basic clinic to 0.33 for a more high-technology referral hospital.

In many situations, a resource will be used for a number of purposes. This is particularly true for so-called overhead costs. For example, a hospital administrator works on all the different activities of the hospital. One aspect of a cost analysis will be to determine a fair allocation of shared resources among the different activities which use the resource. One method is to attribute to a specific intervention the percentage of the resource which is used by the intervention. Typically, the following are used for calculations:

*   *buildings* – the percentage of floor space or square footage (or metres) used for activities related to the intervention
*   *staff* – the percentage of their time that staff spend on the intervention
*   *equipment* – the percentage of time the item of equipment is used for the intervention
*   *utilities (water, electricity, gas)* – the percentage of floor space used by the intervention
*   *maintenance* – the percentage of floor space used by the intervention

However, using the percentage of floor space may be misleading. A storeroom and an operating theatre in a hospital may occupy the same floor area but the latter would consume much more in the way of utilities and maintenance. An alternative is to use the number of staff as a proxy for the percentage use – in this case it would be eight times greater for the theatre. This would be a more realistic reflection of the resources used in the theatre.

Obtaining estimates of personnel time may be difficult. In some cases it is possible for an administrator to make a list of who works where and for how many hours per week. In other cases, staff can easily keep a log of where they work. If estimates of personnel time are not available, you could perform time and motion studies, which entail the use of a trained observer to determine the amount of time personnel actually spend performing tasks related to the intervention.

 Activity 17.5

A new roof at a hospital costs $1 million and is expected to last 20 years. The TB ward occupies one floor in this ten-storey hospital. What is the share of the total cost of the roof which should be attributed to the TB ward?

 Feedback

First, the total cost of the roof of $1 million should be annualized. With straight-line depreciation, the annual cost is $50,000 ($1 million/20 years = $50,000). There are ten floors, so the percentage use of the shared input (the roof overhead) for the TB ward is 10 per cent – only 10 per cent of the annualized cost of the roof should be attributed to the TB programme. So $5000 is the annualized cost of roof for the TB programme ($50,000 × 10% = $5000).

Fixed and variable costs

The final cost classification scheme you have already learned about in Chapter 8 – fixed and variable costs.

Some items have both a fixed and a variable cost component. These are termed *semi-variable costs*. A good example is the telephone. You'll have to pay the monthly line rental whether or not anyone makes any calls – this part is fixed. A variable amount is payable depending on the amount it is used.

Calculating costs

So far you have learned about framing the study and making an inventory of the costs. Finally you have reached the last of the three main steps – calculating the costs.

 Activity 17.6

You learned in Chapter 8 about four commonly used measures of costs:

1 Total cost.
2 Annual cost.
3 Average cost.
4 Marginal cost.

Explain what each one means.

 Feedback

1 Total cost is the sum of all costs. This gives an indication as to how much the intervention costs overall – taking account of the value of all the resources used.

2 Annual cost is the cost of the intervention calculated on a yearly basis – including all the annualized costs of capital expenditures as well as the yearly recurrent costs. Annual costs will vary from one year to another – in the first year, the start-up costs will be greater whereas after the intervention has been in operation for a while, the recurrent costs may form a higher part of the annual cost.

3 Average cost is the total cost divided by the total units of activity or outcome. Average cost gives an indication of how efficiently, on average, different providers are functioning.

4 Marginal cost is the change in the total cost if one extra unit of output is produced. Marginal cost can also be used to calculate how much would be saved by contracting a service. In practice you can see that often it is more than a change of only one unit of output which is of concern but rather a group of 10 or 100 extra units. In this case the correct term for the cost of the change is *incremental cost*. The difference between incremental and marginal cost was discussed in Chapter 2. You may see some applications where the term incremental cost is used, rather than marginal cost.

The following activity is drawn from a real-life situation and shows an application of the incremental cost (and incremental benefit) concept to decision making.

 **Activity 17.7**

An evaluation of a sexually transmitted disease (STD) clinic found that while the service was much appreciated by the clients who were using it, quite a few people with STDs were not able to come during its opening hours, from 9.00 a.m. to 5.30 p.m, because they worked or were in school. A decision was made, therefore, to extend the opening hours to 7.30 p.m. on Monday and Thursday nights on a trial basis. This meant that staff would have to be paid more for the overtime and the managers were interested to know what the impact would be on the overall attendances at the clinic. The costs per week of the clinic *before* the extension of the hours are shown in Table 17.9.

Table 17.9 Costs per week of the clinic before the extension of the hours

Cost	$
Rental of premises	200
Staff:	
• receptionist	300
• practice nurse	385
• doctor	595
Medicines etc.	270
Electricity, gas etc.	55
Other operating costs	580
Total	2 385

The number of clients seen on average each week was 20 per day, or 100 per week.

1 What was the average cost per patient seen in the clinic?

Option 1: evening hours

After opening for an extra two hours on Monday and Thursday evenings each week, the following additional costs were incurred: staff $115, medicines $80, electricity $25 and other items $130.

During the trial period, the clinic was very busy in the evenings, and an additional 15 patients were seen on Monday evenings and 12 on Thursdays.

2 What was the incremental (or marginal) cost per patient seen in the evenings?
3 What was the new average cost per patient of the clinic?
4 What recommendation would you make to the health authority about whether to maintain these new evening opening hours of the clinic?

Option 2: Saturday hours

The clinic management held a meeting and decided that perhaps it would be good to open on Saturday mornings from 8.00 a.m. to 12 noon as well, to serve especially young people who come from outlying areas. The additional costs of opening on Saturdays were $250 for staff, $27 for medicines and $120 for other costs. The clinic was not as popular as predicted, with only 5 people coming on average on Saturdays.

5   What was the total incremental cost of this option?
6   What was the incremental cost per client of this additional group of clients?
7   What was the overall average cost per client (with Options 1 and 2)?
8   Overall, with the information you now have about the opening hours (Options 1 and 2) what recommendation would you make to the management regarding the best combination of opening hours of the clinic?
9   Now consider this: if the costs of opening on Saturday afternoons are the same as Saturday morning ($397), how many patients would you estimate are needed to make it worthwhile?

 Feedback

1   The average cost per patient at the beginning of the period was $23.85.

2   The incremental cost of the patients seen in the evening was $12.96 ($350 marginal costs/27 extra patients).

3   The total costs now (including evening hours, Option 1) are $2735 ($2385 + $350), the number of patients now attending is 127, so the new average cost is $21.54 ($2735/127).

4   The evening hours seem to be a success – the incremental cost is below the average cost so the costs are still going down. Keep the new hours.

5   The new incremental costs of Saturday opening (Option 2) are $397.

6   The new incremental cost per patient is $79.40 ($397/5 patients).

7   The new total cost of the original clinic hours plus Options 1 and 2 is $3132, and the new average cost per patient is $23.72 ($3132/132 total patients).

8   Evening hours were a success but the incremental costs of $79.40 per Saturday patient are high. Either give up on Saturdays altogether – or try Saturday afternoons!

9   It seems unlikely that the same incremental cost could be obtained for the Saturday hours as for the evening hours. The evening hours cost only around $13 per patient so ideally Saturday hours would give the same result – this would require about 30 patients ($397/13). If the average cost per patient could be kept at or near the average with Option 1, this would mean that the clinic was still operating efficiently and therefore 17 patients would make this worthwhile ($397/23.72 = 16.7). This seems attainable if the clinic is well situated, user-friendly and the Saturday opening hours are made known to the teenage target group.

Some practical considerations

Until now the discussion has assumed that you are doing 'bottom-up' costing – starting from scratch and building up the costs, in the same way as you build up a budget. But sometimes you are faced with a situation of retrospective costing, whereby you have information on total expenditures by line item and most of the costs are joint costs – used by several activities. If it is not possible to go back to get the information on individual units of resources that were used or the costs of those resources, you can use the aggregated information you have, broken down by activity or 'cost centre'.

By now you may be wondering where you will find all the information you need for your cost analysis and which costs to use. There are a number of sources, depending on what exactly you are trying to cost.

Health services costs

If you are costing the activities of a health facility such as a hospital, there is probably an accountant or financial officer who can provide much of the information you need. Information on personnel allocation can often be obtained from the nursing manager or sister, from the medical director and from the administrator who is responsible for the non-medical and non-nursing staff of the facility. Information on supplies and drugs can be found either on invoices or from catalogues of equipment and drugs; if the drugs for example were donated, you will probably need to refer to an international source of information to find out the international market price. Vehicles and vehicle costs can often be obtained from the person responsible for managing the fleet of vehicles.

A handy hint in doing costing is to concentrate on the more expensive items and those which constitute the biggest fraction of the total – the 'big ticket' items – usually vehicles and vehicle running costs, personnel, drugs and supplies. Often half or more of the total cost will be spent on personnel, so getting good information on the wages and benefits and the allocation of staff will be a good start in getting an overall cost. Vehicles and drugs may be another major expenditure category, and time spent getting precise measures here may enhance the accuracy of your overall estimates.

Don't spend too much time chasing a detailed piece of information when the decision will not be affected by it. It is unlikely that time spent getting precise estimates of the allocation of electricity and cleaning supplies, for example, will make much of a difference in the overall total. If time is limited (as it almost always is) you would probably be better off spending it on refining your estimates of expenditures on the 'big ticket' items.

Patient and family costs

There are a number of ways to estimate these costs. The best way is probably to carry out a survey of the patients to find out:

- what they have spent getting to the service;
- how many hours they have spent in activities other than the ones they would normally be doing, in order for them or their household member to be able to use the service.

However, you may not have enough time to carry out a full survey, and if this is the case you could ask a small sample of patients and make some estimates of their expenditure and the time they have spent, and of their lost wages.

Calculating the value of wages lost can prove problematic – should you use the minimum wage, the average wage or some estimate of the wage of the actual patients? There is also seasonal variation in the value of time in many agricultural areas – should you take account of that in your analysis? Again, it depends on the purpose of your analysis. The important thing is to include patient costs if appropriate – too often the difficulty of calculating the patients' costs has meant that they have simply been left out of the analysis altogether and this clearly leads to a misleading result – effectively costing the patients' costs as zero.

Which cost should you use?

One issue which you may face is which cost to use – say, for example, you are costing a project which used a vehicle. If the vehicle was purchased five years ago and cost $10,000 but a new one now costs $15,000, which cost should you use? Or should you use the annualized straight-line depreciation cost? This depends on the purpose of your analysis. Here are three possibilities.

1 If you are looking 'for historical purposes' at the past cost of an intervention which will not be repeated, you could safely use the original cost of $10,000.
2 If you wanted to know the annual cost of running the programme for the past five years, you would use the annualized cost of the original expenditure, $2000 per year.
3 But if you wanted to know the cost of replicating the programme in another place, you should use the present replacement cost of $15,000. The annual cost of running the project in the future would use the annualized cost of $3000 per year, if you expect it to last five years.

Time preference and discounting

Costs and outcomes often occur at different times. Many people place a different value on costs and outcomes that occur in the future compared with those which occur sooner. Other things being equal, you'd probably rather receive health outcomes (save money, and decrease morbidity and mortality) now and pay for the interventions later. Unfortunately, especially when it comes to preventing disease, the opposite is usually true. We often have to pay for the interventions now and receive the benefits later. The example of hepatitis B vaccine illustrates this – you have to pay for the vaccination now but receive the outcomes much later (fewer cases of hepatitis, chronic liver disease and liver cancer).

In conducting economic evaluations, this observation presents a dilemma. Because people do not place equal value on costs or outcomes that occur this year and those that occur in later years, economic evaluation must also value these costs and outcomes differently. While there are theoretical and practical problems, many economic evaluations are performed using some sort of adjustment for the occurrence over time, or discounting, both for costs and for outcomes.

Discounting is a way to adjust future costs (and outcomes) to today's equivalent costs (and outcomes) – termed the present value. The discount rate is the rate at which future costs and outcomes are discounted to account for time preference. The discount rate used is usually between 3 per cent and 5 per cent, after controlling for inflation (a 'real' discount rate). In some countries, the central government imposes a specific real discount rate when economic evaluations are performed for publicly funded projects. In other countries where no specific rate is imposed, the economists frequently choose one rate and then perform sensitivity analysis to ensure the conclusions are stable with respect to the assumption about discount rates.

However, discounting is controversial. Drummond *et al.* (1997) give an example of a comparison of two ways to reduce deaths from heart disease. One is an expansion of funding for coronary artery bypass grafting (CABG) and the other is a health education campaign to influence diet and lifestyle which would not yield benefits for some time to come. So if discounting is applied, CABG will look more attractive than the preventive campaign.

Discounting is a concept not accepted by all economists. While the majority agree that time preference exists empirically, the theoretical foundation of time preference, especially as regards health, is not very well established. In terms of costs, most economists agree that future and present costs are interchangeable with the use of money interest rates which reflect the opportunity cost of using funds today rather than in the distant future. However, controversies surface when discounting is applied to health outcomes because they are not as interchangeable as money. For instance, do people really as a general rule place a lesser value on future health outcomes? This implies that we really care less about future generations.

Summary

You have learned why costing is often not straightforward and simple. You went on to learn about four classification schemes to help ensure all relevant costs are included: financial and economic cost; direct, indirect and intangible costs; capital and recurrent costs; and fixed and variable costs. Finally some of the practical difficulties were discussed: obtaining data, estimating costs and people's time preferences.

References

Creese A and Parker D (eds) (1994) *Cost analysis in primary health care: a training manual for programme managers*. Geneva: WHO.

Drummond MF, O'Brien B, Stoddart GL and Torrance GW (1997) *Methods for the economic evaluation of health care programmes* (2nd edn). Oxford: Oxford University Press.

18 Cost–benefit analysis

Overview

In this chapter you will be able to bring together what you have learned in the previous two chapters and to see how that information can be used to guide decisions about resource allocation for health.

Learning objectives

After completing this chapter, you will be able to:

- **define and give examples of health outcomes in monetary terms**
- **explain cost–benefit analysis**
- **describe three ways of expressing the results of a cost–benefit analysis**

Key terms

Benefit–cost ratio (BCR) A way of presenting the results of a cost–benefit analysis, this is simply the benefits divided by the costs.

Human capital approach An approach that uses wages to measure the value of productivity lost through illness.

Net benefit The benefits of an intervention minus its costs.

Willingness to pay (WTP) A method of measuring the value an individual places on reducing the risk of developing a health problem or gaining an improvement in health.

What is cost–benefit analysis?

Cost–benefit analysis (CBA) is a method of economic evaluation where the monetary value of the resources consumed by a health intervention (costs) is compared with the monetary value of the outcomes (benefits) achieved by the intervention. While the lay meaning of 'benefit' is 'something good', in CBA it means the 'monetary value of the outcomes' achieved by an intervention.

You will first examine how to compare costs and benefits. You will then look at how results from such a comparison can be interpreted and finally, at how to measure benefits in monetary terms.

How to compare costs and benefits

The prime concern of economic evaluation is to determine whether outcomes are worth their costs. There are two ways to express the results from comparing costs and benefits:

- *net benefit* – this result is expressed as a single number with monetary units;
- *benefit–cost ratio (BCR)* – this result is expressed as a ratio of benefits to costs.

Net benefits

Net benefits are calculated by subtracting the cost of an intervention from its benefits. When the benefit is bigger than the cost, the net benefit will be greater than zero. This says that the value of the outcomes is worth more than the value of resources used up by the intervention, so the intervention is worthwhile. A simple example will illustrate this.

Assume that an illness costs a patient £800 per year (perhaps from reduced working capacity). With an intervention the cost of the illness is reduced to £300 per year – the benefit is £500. Now suppose the intervention costs £100 per year. The net benefit is £500 – £100 = £400, suggesting the intervention is worthwhile.

Benefit–cost ratio (BCR)

The other main way to compare cost and benefit is the BCR. This is simply the benefits *divided by* the costs. In the example above, the benefits are £500 and the costs are £100, so the BCR is 5:1. (A BCR of 5:1 is a very respectable BCR by the way – more often the BCR is closer to 2 or 3.) The higher the BCR, the better the intervention – and some interventions can actually be cost-saving, in other words, implementing them can save money for health services or for society as a whole. A good example of this is the eradication of smallpox – the costs were incurred in the late 1970s and the benefits should be forever – they are infinite!

 Activity 18.1

Suppose you were the manager of a vaccination programme. An evaluation of the programme has just revealed that it was suffering because it took too much time to track children using a paper-based charts and record system, and many children were being lost to follow-up and were not completely immunized. One of the recommendations of the study was that you might improve your immunization coverage by buying a computer and hiring a programmer to replace the papers and filing clerks in your main office.

The problem in this case is the 'inability to do paperwork efficiently and fast enough' to run a heavy volume immunization programme. The intervention is computerization and the cost of intervention includes:

• the costs of purchasing the computer hardware, of hiring the programmer to write the program and of retraining your staff in computer data entry (capital cost)
plus
• the cost of maintaining the computer system and of electricity to run the machine (recurrent cost)

What are some of the possible effects of such a change?

↻ Feedback

The following are some of the effects you are likely to have identified:

1 Lower costs. Once the computer is installed, costs should go down because of lower personnel costs (salaries for clerical personnel to file records) and reduction in purchase of paper forms. The amount of space your programme requires might even go down as you replace the paper records with computerized ones. Or you could use the free space to set aside a space for a coffee machine. The difference between your business expenses before and after the purchase of the computer is your saving. (Of course it is possible that you might have to hire more highly skilled workers to run the computer, and your costs might increase.)

2 More immunizations (process measures) given due to increased efficiency. There may be fewer missed immunizations because your records are better or your staff have more time to attend to the patients (rather than their records). This translates to reduced numbers of children with vaccine preventable diseases and ultimately may save lives because of the disease reduction.

The reduced number of diseases and deaths translates into:

• reduced future health care costs (health care savings)
plus
• increased productivity of the parents as well as their children when grown (productivity gains)
plus
• the reduction in pain and suffering when people know that they're protected from the threat of these diseases

The difference between all those costs associated with the vaccine preventable diseases before and after the intervention (computerization) is your net benefit.

Interpretation of cost–benefit analysis results

From a societal perspective, as long as net benefits are greater than zero, or benefits exceed costs (the BCR is greater than 1), the intervention should be implemented – or at least considered seriously.

Policy makers want to know whether, for a given amount of investment, one health intervention gives more benefits back (returns). Sometimes, they are also interested in knowing whether investing in a health intervention would give better returns than investing in an educational or an industrial project. These questions are most readily answered by using the BCR. Benefit divided by cost is the same as 'return' divided by 'investment', and the ratio tells what return is possible given a particular investment.

Measuring benefits in monetary terms

You learned in the previous chapter how to calculate the cost of an intervention. But how do you calculate the burden of illness and any change in the burden that occurs as a result of the intervention, in monetary terms? There are two main ways of measuring these monetary outcomes:

*   changes in the cost of illness;
*   willingness to pay (WTP) surveys.

You will learn about willingness to pay surveys later in this chapter. First, you will consider using cost of illness to measure the magnitude of a health problem. You need to consider direct, indirect and intangible costs. Benefits are then calculated as changes in the cost of illness with the intervention compared with the cost of illness without the intervention. They are a measure of how the cost of the health problem has changed due to the health intervention. In the simplest terms, benefits are the value of cost reductions.

Calculating direct costs and benefits

Direct costs of illness were covered in Chapter 17 and will not be reviewed here. It is essential that the perspective of the analysis be considered in determining which direct costs are to be included in the analysis. Direct benefit is merely the reduction in direct costs due to the intervention.

Calculating indirect costs and benefits: the human capital approach

You will remember from Chapter 17 that indirect costs are a measure of the value of time. Time is a proxy for productivity because people fill up their time each day with all kinds of 'productive' work – work in the market to earn a wage, work in the household to fulfil domestic duties and work at leisure to 'fully enjoy ourselves'. It is possible to value the time spent in each of these activities.

One simple way to value time lost due to an illness is to look at the wage rate of those affected by the health problem. In general, the wage rate reflects the value (and therefore the costs) of people's time. The value of productivity lost is then equated to the wage multiplied by the time missed. When the value of lost productivity is measured by wages, the approach is known as the *human capital measure*. The following examples show how to calculate indirect costs using the human capital approach.

A bicycle rickshaw driver

Suppose an illness required a bicycle rickshaw driver to rest frequently and reduced his working capacity from 40 hours per week to only 20. Normally he was able to earn an average of $0.40 an hour. What is the value of the lost productivity over the period of a week?

The cost would be: 20 hours × $0.40/hour = $8 per week. If the illness is chronic and lasts one year, what is the indirect cost of illness for a year, assuming 45 weeks of work per year? The cost would be $360 for a year – half his previous expected earnings of $720.

A coal miner

Consider a different situation. A man used to be a coal miner, a physically demanding and difficult job but which paid a respectable wage of $10 per hour. But now due to a respiratory illness he has been given a job making tea in the office – a less demanding job but which pays only $4 per hour. Assuming again that the period of analysis is a year and the year contains 45 working weeks, what is the indirect cost of illness for that person?

The indirect costs would be the value of the wages the miner has lost as a result of the illness. Before his illness this person worked 40 hours for $10 per hour, for 45 weeks: $400 × 45 = $18,000. But now, since the illness, he is only earning $4 per hour: 40 hours × $4 × 45 weeks, or $7200. The loss is $18,000 – $7200, or $10,800.

There are three reservations about the use of the human capital measure as a proxy for indirect costs and benefits you should be aware of.

Objection 1: is it equitable?

High-wage workers will be deemed to have higher indirect benefit than low-wage workers, even if the intervention affects both groups' productive hours by the same amount. This will favour the rich in all cost–benefit results and will be inequitable.

Objection 2: the value of non-market time

The human capital measure undervalues the work of housewives and retired people because they do not earn a wage to be used in the indirect benefit calculation, yet their time is also valuable – to them and their families.

Some economists use proxies for these people's value such as using the wage of domestic workers as a proxy for the time of housewives. Alternatively, analysts have used the amount someone could earn if they were in paid employment. But this still leaves the question of how to assess retired people's value of time. There is also an ongoing debate as to whether leisure time is valued the same as working time.

Activity 18.3

Compared to the time at your job that you are paid for, how do you value your own leisure time? How much of your leisure time would you give up, for pay, if your employer paid you:

1   50 per cent of your usual wage per hour?
2   100 per cent of your usual wage per hour?
3   150 per cent of your usual wage per hour?

 Feedback

You might not want to give up any additional time for half pay. For your usual wage you might consider some additional hours. For 1.5 times your wage, often called 'time and a half', you might be tempted to work quite a lot of extra hours – and for 200 per cent, or 'double time', the temptation would indeed be great.

Objection 3: intangible costs not included

Most studies on cost of illness exclude intangible costs but doing so may do severe injustice to people who suffer and their families and friends. Excluding the psychological cost of pain and suffering may actually leave out a significant component of the costs associated with an illness. You should bear this in mind when interpreting the findings of such studies.

Calculating indirect costs and benefits: using willingness to pay surveys

An alternative method of calculating indirect costs and benefits uses an approach called willingness to pay (WTP). It is a method of measuring the value that an individual places on reducing their risk of developing or of treating a health problem.

If a person must bear all the costs associated with an illness, then the monetary equivalent of all the direct, indirect and intangible costs of illness is what they lose because of the illness – the full cost of illness.

Suppose that the full cost of illness is $1000 and that an intervention can reduce the illness from a serious one to a mild one. Suppose further that *other than the cost of the intervention* the patient is responsible for all the costs of the illness after the intervention ($300). The patient will, therefore, be burdened with $700 less in the cost of illness after the intervention.

Think for a moment about the cost of illness before and after the intervention. Because of the intervention, the monetary burden on the person will probably end up less. In other words, if the individual is responsible for paying for everything related to an illness and the intervention reduces the illness, the individual pays less. So, given this situation, what is the *maximum* amount of money the individual is willing to pay for the intervention? In theory, the individual would be willing to pay up to $700.

You can see that actually measuring the costs before and after an intervention is not possible in most situations. Luckily there is another way to measure the change in cost of illness. This is by doing a WTP survey. Such surveys ask a representative sample of the population how much they would be willing to pay to gain something. This type of survey can be used for both health and non-health interventions.

For example, suppose you want to find out how much people living near a landfill site would value its removal. You can go to the community and survey the residents by asking 'what is the *maximum* amount of money you're willing to pay to get rid of the dump?' You can then sum up the total amount people are willing to pay, which is a measure of how much people would benefit if the dump disappeared.

As another example, WTP can be used to see how much people would value a new HIV vaccine. Suppose a representative population of 10,000 is surveyed and asked how much they would be willing to pay to see that such a vaccine becomes available. The survey would describe the outcomes before and after the vaccine so that the respondents are clear as to what the benefits of a reduction in HIV transmission would be. The important morbidity and mortality aspects of HIV would be described, and the likely reduction of morbidity and mortality after the vaccine would also be presented. If after this explanation, on average each respondent says they would be willing to pay $20 for such a vaccine, then the total sum of WTP from the representative sample would be 10,000 × $20, or $200,000 in this population. This is an estimate of how much the population would potentially benefit if HIV vaccines were marketed.

You may be wondering how representative the people who respond to WTP surveys are. They tend to be better educated (Thomas *et al.* 2000) so may not reflect the views of the whole population.

WTP surveys are especially helpful if a market had not previously existed for an intervention but one needs to know whether the cost of the intervention is justifiable when compared with the value of the outcomes. Although your first reaction may be that the HIV vaccine is 'worthwhile' at whatever cost 'because it will save lives', by now you know that for each dollar spent on the HIV vaccine, one dollar less could be spent on, for example, measles vaccination.

Another example will highlight both the strengths and weaknesses of the WTP approach. Suppose you want to introduce a new water container to reduce morbidity from diarrhoea but find it difficult to measure the benefits of the programme. Haddix *et al.* (1996) asked 100 households in a village about their WTP to avoid diarrhoea – the villagers understand that the trade-off is between buying the container and coping with diarrhoea in the household. The results of the survey are shown in Table 18.1.

Table 18.1 Water vessels for diarrhoea prevention – WTP survey

Number of households	WTP ($)	Total 'benefit' ($)	Cumulative percentage of group (coverage)
5	25	125	5
10	20	200	15
50	15	750	65
15	10	150	80
15	5	75	95
5	0	0	100

Source: Haddix *et al.* (1996)

In other words, if you charge $25 for the water container, only 5 per cent of households will buy it (these five between them value the benefit as $125). However, at $15 half the people would buy it and at $10, 80 per cent coverage would be achieved. If it was decided to supply the containers at $10 each, the total cost to the village will be $800 (80 households × $10). The benefits are $1225 ($125 + $200 + $750 + $150). So the value (benefits – costs) is $425 ($1225 – $800).

The above example raises a number of issues. First, the WTP will be affected by the level of education and understanding about the causes of diarrhoea and by how important a health problem it is believed to be. Secondly, where a third party pays for health care, the respondents may not have an accurate idea of what illness costs. And thirdly, the estimates are based on what people *say* they will do – not what they actually do. It is possible they give answers to try to please the interviewer or that they don't want to reveal how poor they are and so give an estimate which is higher than what they actually *could* pay.

Valuing benefits resulting from reduction in mortality

Reduction in premature mortality may be an important aspect of the outcome of an intervention. Monetarizing this reduction in mortality becomes tricky when using the 'change in cost of illness' approach. Because outcomes of interventions frequently entail saving of lives, the valuing of lives saved poses a dilemma for the analyst trying to ascertain the benefits of the intervention. Many people are unwilling and often feel it is impossible to value lives; they frequently place an infinite value on life when responding to surveys. If this is the case, then all interventions which save lives will have infinite benefits which will invariably exceed their costs and will therefore be worthwhile according to the survey respondents. However, you know that because it is not possible to fund all interventions, some allocation scheme must be devised. On the other hand, putting no monetary value on mortality reduction would undervalue the benefits of the intervention.

For indirect benefits, one could assume that the reduction in mortality is equivalent to lengthening of productive life and attach a value to it. Sometimes analysts use the average payout of accident insurance companies to relatives of fatal casualties to put a monetary value on human life. However, for intangible benefits such as a reduction in pain and suffering, it is difficult to find a similar proxy.

This is where WTP surveys come in handy, as the individual cost reductions do not have to be calculated separately. Pain and suffering reductions could be valued together with all the other attributes from the outcome of an intervention. However, the inability or unwillingness of survey respondents to attach a value to reduced mortality has become an obstacle to the widespread use of cost–benefit analysis in health care decision making.

Summary

In this chapter you have seen that the 'benefit' is the monetary value of the outcomes of the intervention. In cost–benefit analysis, you compare monetary costs with monetary outcomes, or costs of intervention with benefits of intervention. As long as the benefit is bigger than the cost, you can prove that you've done something 'worth' the money spent. The results of a cost–benefit analysis are usually expressed as net benefits or benefit–cost ratios.

To circumvent the dilemma of placing value on lives, health economists have devised economic evaluation methods which do not require the direct valuation of lives. This leads naturally to cost-effectiveness and cost–utility analysis, where the outcomes are not expressed in terms of monetary value but, rather, remain as health outcomes – and these are the subject of the next chapter.

References

Haddix AC, Teutsch SM, Shaffer PA and Dunet DO (1996) *Prevention effectiveness – a guide to decision analysis and economic evaluation*. Oxford: Oxford University Press.

Thomas R, Donaldson C and Torgerson D (2000) Who answers 'willingness to pay' questions? *Journal of Health Services Research & Policy* 5:7–11.

Cost-effectiveness analysis

Overview

In the previous chapter you learned how to compare costs of interventions with their monetary outcomes by performing a cost–benefit analysis. You also saw some of the problems associated with trying to establish a monetary value for many health outcomes – many of us are reluctant to place a value on human life. This chapter will focus on how to compare costs and health outcomes without establishing a monetary value of the outcomes. This type of economic evaluation can help to determine whether the value of the resources spent on the intervention is worthwhile. Cost-effectiveness analysis is the most widely used and most useful technique of economic evaluation.

Learning objectives

After completing this chapter, you should be able to:

- **compare final and intermediate health outcomes and process measures**
- **define cost-effectiveness ratio, the costs included in the ratio and the outcomes included in the ratio**
- **describe the process of allocation of a health care budget using cost-effectiveness league tables**

Key terms

Cost-effectiveness league tables A ranking of interventions according to cost per unit of health outcomes.

Disability Adjusted Life Years (DALYs) A measure of health based not only on the length of a person's life but also their level of ability (or disability).

Incremental cost-effectiveness ratio (ICER) The ratio of the difference in costs between two alternatives to the difference in effectiveness between the same two alternatives.

Intermediate health outcome A short-term measure of outcome known to be associated with a long-term outcome.

Process measures Measures of the activities carried out by health care providers such as admission rates and length of hospital stay.

Quality Adjusted Life Years (QALYs) A year of life adjusted for its quality or its value. A year in perfect health is considered equal to 1.0 QALY.

What is cost-effectiveness analysis?

Cost-effectiveness analysis (CEA) is a method of economic evaluation where the value of the resources spent on an intervention is compared with the quantity of health gained as a result. A very simple example will illustrate this – imagine a vaccination programme which cost $100,000 and saved 200 lives. The cost-effectiveness of this programme would be $500 per life saved.

You can see from this simple example that unlike cost–benefit analysis (CBA) which compares monetary costs with monetary outcomes, CEA compares the cost of an intervention with the intervention's *health outcomes*. It is expressed as a ratio of costs divided by health outcomes. The *cost-effectiveness ratio* of one intervention can then be compared with that of another.

Suppose there are two interventions, A and B, and you want to know which intervention is the better buy. Intervention A, the vaccination programme above, saves 200 lives at a cost of $500 each. Intervention B costs $150,000 but saves 500 lives at a cost of $300 each and, therefore, looks like the better option. While you can't say if intervention B is worthwhile in itself, you can say it is *more* worthwhile than intervention A.

In CBA, as long as the benefit–cost ratio (BCR) is greater than 1, you know that the intervention is worthwhile. In CEA, because you haven't monetarized the benefit, you don't know if its value is greater than that of the cost.

 Activity 19.1

As you saw in Chapter 16, there are three steps in conducting an economic evaluation. What are they?

 Feedback

Framing the evaluation; identifying, quantifying and valuing the resources needed; and identifying, quantifying and valuing the health consequences.

In this chapter you will first consider which health consequences to include, then which resources (or costs) to include and finally the ways in which the results of CEA have been used in decision making in health care.

What measures of health consequences are available?

The most commonly used measures are:

- *health outcomes* – such as mortality or disability;
- *intermediate health outcomes* – such as a change in the risk of ill-health;
- *process measures* – such as length of hospital stay;
- *Quality Adjusted Life Years (QALYs)* – that combine quantity of survival with quality of life;

- *Disability Adjusted Life Years (DALYs)* – that combine quantity of survival with level of disability.

Health outcomes

Reduction in mortality and improvement in health status are perhaps the most important aspects of many interventions. Health outcomes can be used to compare interventions for the same health problem or interventions for different health problems, as long as mortality reduction and improvements in health status are important aims of both interventions.

Intermediate health outcomes

Intermediate health outcomes are changes in the risk of illness a patient faces. For example, if you wanted to determine the effectiveness of a drug for high blood pressure, you would have to wait many years to judge it in terms of health outcome (i.e. reductions in the incidence of strokes or deaths). Instead, you could measure the effect the drug has on reducing patients' blood pressure, an intermediate outcome.

Process measures

Process measures refer to activities which, it is known or believed, have a direct bearing on the outcomes achieved by the intervention. For example, it is known that people suffering a heart attack should be given thrombolytic drugs as soon as possible to improve their health outcome. The proportion of such patients given the drug would be a useful process measure. You can probably see that process measures are useful only when comparing interventions for the same health problem.

When you use process measures, you assume that the change in process measure correlates with the change in the health problem. This is often difficult to prove. For example, in a condom social marketing programme, how certain can you be that the condoms sold are used properly? And therefore what contribution would these condom sales make to the reduction of cases of HIV infection?

 Activity 19.2

What process measures might you use as an indication of the success of a programme to control malaria? What characteristics would they need to have?

 Feedback

You might have suggested the rate of use of impregnated bed-nets or the prescribing of anti-malarial medicine. You would asume that the interventions were properly used and that both were known to be associated with an improvement in health outcome.

Quality as well as quantity of life

By now you have probably noticed that measures of health outcome rarely capture all the nuances of effectiveness achievable with an intervention. This is because interventions may have an impact not only on the *quantity* of life but also the *quality*, and the measures discussed so far do not capture both. For instance, improvement in survival rates provides no clue as to the quality of survival – ten years of life with full function represents a much higher quality of life than ten years in a coma.

To capture both quantitative and qualitative aspects, measures which combine the two have been devised. The two most common measures in use are the Quality Adjusted Life Year (QALY) and The Disability Adjusted Life Year (DALY).

The Quality Adjusted Life Year (QALY)

The Quality Adjusted Life Year, or QALY, has been in use since the 1970s. The quality of life measurement is done using a variety of different measures. One commonly used is the EQ-5D, which attempts to measure the ability of a person to function in five different dimensions (see Table 19.1). For each dimension, a person is classified as having no problem, some problems or major problems. This means there are 243 possible combinations or health states to which are added 'unconscious' and 'dead' to make 245.

Table 19.1 EQ-5D

MOBILITY
I have no problems in walking about
I have some problems in walking about
I am confined to bed

SELF-CARE
I have no problems with self-care
I have some problems washing or dressing myself
I am unable to wash or dress myself

USUAL ACTIVITIES (e.g. work, study, housework, family or leisure activities)
I have no problems with performing my usual activities
I have some problems with performing my usual activities
I am unable to perform my usual activities

PAIN/DISCOMFORT
I have no pain or discomfort
I have moderate pain or discomfort
I have extreme pain or discomfort

ANXIETY/DEPRESSION
I am not anxious or depressed
I am moderately anxious or depressed
I am extremely anxious or depressed

Each health state is then valued on a scale from 0 to 1. If someone is dead their quality of life is valued as 0, if in perfect health they are rated as 1. Some health states are valued as worse than death and these can be given a negative value (i.e. less than 0). Several methods have been used to value health states, in particular standard gamble and time trade-off. One problem raised by the QALY is the difficulty of establishing the value of someone else's life. It can be argued that health care workers are not necessarily the best people to do this.

Clearly, who decides on health state values is critical to the method. Research has shown that doctors consistently give different ratings for particular conditions than nurses. Patients with that condition might give yet again different ratings. Nevertheless, the QALY remains the best available measure. Studies that use the QALY are sometimes referred to as cost–utility analysis (CUA) – a subset of CEA.

The Disability Adjusted Life Year (DALY)

Rather than taking account of the *quality* of a person's life, the DALY takes account of their level of *disability*. Similar to determining QALYs, levels of disability have been rated by international panels of health care workers who were asked to rank the severity of 22 conditions. This weighting then produced seven categories, ranging from mild (class 1) to very severe (class 7) as shown in Table 19.2.

Table 19.2 The categories included in the DALY

Disability class	Indicator conditions
1	Vitiligo on face, weight for height less than 2 standard deviations
2	Watery diarrhoea, severe sore throat, severe anaemia
3	Radius fracture in a stiff cast, infertility, erectile dysfunction, rheumatoid arthritis, angina
4	Below-the-knee amputation, deafness
5	Rectovaginal fistula, mild mental retardation, Down's syndrome
6	Unipolar major depression, blindness, paraplegia
7	Active psychosis, dementia, severe migraine, quadriplegia

Source: Murray and Lopez (1996)

The DALY incorporates two additional value judgements – those of age weighting and discounting. One of the problems with the DALY is that it involves a systematic bias against individuals with permanent disabilities. An intervention which extends the life of a person in a wheelchair another year (without altering their disability) prevents fewer DALYs than the same treatment given to an otherwise perfectly healthy person. This is because, given the existing disability of the person in a wheelchair, weighted at 0.5 for example, extending their life by a year will only result in half the number of DALYs as extending the life of an able-bodied person.

Another important value judgement which is implicit in the DALY is that of discounting. The DALY incorporates a discount rate of 3 per cent. However, the rate chosen affects the cost-effectiveness of any given intervention and reduces the comparative value of interventions, especially preventive measures which pay off in the future – hepatitis B vaccination being a prime example. At the 3 per cent discount rate, one life saved today will be worth more than five lives saved in 55 years' time.

Anand and Hanson (1998) have argued that DALYs are:

> an inequitable measure of aggregate ill-health and an inequitable criterion for resource allocation. Through age weighting and discounting, they place a different value on years lived at different ages and at different points in time. They value a year saved more for the able-bodied than the disabled, more for those in middle age-groups than the young or the elderly, and more for individuals who are ill today compared with those who will be ill in the future.

The debate surrounding the use of the DALY will continue for some time – and later in this chapter you will see one controversial application to which it has been put.

Which measure of health consequence to use?

Choice will depend on whether you are comparing different interventions for the same health problem or for different health problems.

Different interventions for the same health problem

When the goal of the analysis is to compare different health interventions that address the same health problem, a number of different common outcomes can usually be employed.

Suppose you are trying to decide how to spend some funds on preventing HIV transmission. Two interventions you are considering are screening blood transfusions for HIV and improving syndromic management of sexually-transmitted diseases (STDs). Both interventions have been shown to reduce HIV transmission: the former by reducing the risk of transmission through blood transfusion and the latter by reducing the transmission through lesions caused by (non-HIV) STDs. You have the results of two studies – one was carried out in Monze, Zambia (Foster and Buvé 1995) and the other in Mwanza, Tanzania (Gilson et al. 1997). Suppose the measure of outcome chosen is HIV infections prevented (see Table 19.3).

Table 19.3 Two interventions to prevent HIV transmission

Intervention	Incremental intervention cost ($)	HIV infections prevented	Cost/HIV infection prevented ($)
Monze, Zambia: blood transfusion screening	4 745	150	31.63
Mwanza, Tanzania: STD treatment	54 839	252	217.62

Sources: Foster and Buvé (1995); Gilson et al. (1997)

There are a number of problems in comparing these studies because they were done in different, although comparable settings. Both compare the addition of a service to an existing service – in the Monze case, blood will be transfused whether or not it is screened for HIV, and in Tanzania, a routine STD treatment service was offered in the clinics. The intervention involved additional training of health workers and provision of highly effective drugs plus monitoring of drug resistance to ensure that drugs remained effective. But for Activity 19.3, assume that they can be fairly compared.

Activity 19.3

Suppose you have just received word that a donor has promised $1 million a year for the next five years for HIV prevention. You want to allocate it between blood transfusion screening at district hospitals and improved STD treatment at clinics.

Answer the following questions, using the figures given in Table 19.3.

1 Monze district hospital is one of approximately 50 district hospitals in Zambia. Assuming the cost of screening would be the same for all 50, what would be the cost of HIV screening of transfusions for all the district hospitals of the country?

2 If you had $1 million to spend on HIV prevention, given these figures, how would you allocate the resources between these two interventions?

3 How many infections would each prevent, and what would be the total number of infections you could prevent using this $1 million?

 Feedback

1 The cost of HIV screening for all hospitals would be $237,250 (50 × $4745).

2 Since HIV screening of the blood is more cost-effective than STD treatment, one way to proceed would be first to implement HIV screening of the blood as widely as possible, and then to spend any remaining funds on STD treatment. So after screening all the blood at district hospitals, that would leave you $762,750. For this amount of money, you could prevent an additional 3505 sexually transmitted HIV infections ($762,750/$217.62 = 3505).

3 The number prevented by blood transfusion screening would be 50 × 150 or 7500. So for your $1 million you could prevent an estimated 11,005 HIV infections – good work! Later in the chapter you will get a chance to try to allocate a budget over a number of different interventions which produce different outcomes.

Different interventions for different health problems

Often the comparison is not between different interventions for the same health problem, but rather a more general question – what is the best way to spend money to improve health?

When you want to compare interventions that treat different illnesses, it is essential to use a measure that reflects the outcomes common to both health problems. The most likely choice of outcomes will be deaths prevented, QALYs or DALYs. These measures are comparable across different health interventions. Later in the chapter you will see some tables which compare different interventions in terms of the QALYs or DALYs they produce.

Which costs should be included in a CEA?

Which costs ought to be included depends on the perspective of the analysis. The most common perspective that requires the use of CEA is that of the health sector planner. The task of health sector planners is to maximize health gain by selecting a package of health interventions that fit the budget or by deciding whether a new intervention is better than the existing interventions. So which costs should be included from the health planner's point of view?

1 Clearly, the *direct cost of the intervention* comes out of the health budget. Direct costs of side-effects are also included if the Ministry or health services will have to pay for these.
2 The budget may also save some money as a result of the intervention, so *health care savings* should also be included and subtracted from costs.
3 Intangible benefits from reduction in costs of pain and suffering, of course, also do not translate into savings for the health sector. These usually do not get included although they may have an overwhelming influence on the decision made.

What about *indirect costs of productivity gain or loss*? The health care budget is not directly affected by any change in a patient's productivity since such changes in indirect costs or benefits are not part of the health care budget. However, society is interested in any changes in productivity and a health service which is centrally funded from tax revenues has an interest in seeing that people are well and productive. This is because their earnings are fed back into tax support for the health services, whereas if they are in poor health the government will incur expenditures in supporting them. The decision to fund a programme may have been at least in part justified on the basis of its impact on productivity.

Applications of CEA

One major use of CEA is to improve programme efficiency. It helps to identify the most economical strategy among interventions that produce a common outcome. Existing resources can then be reallocated to achieve even greater health outcomes.

Because economic analyses compare outcomes and costs of alternative interventions for treating patients, a number of possible combinations of results can occur. An intervention that is both better for patients and results in lower cost is referred to as 'dominant'. However, many interventions will result in a better outcome but at greater cost. The incremental cost per unit of incremental health outcome is a measure of the relative economic attractiveness of an intervention. A high incremental cost-effectiveness ratio (ICER) means a better outcome will require considerable extra expenditure and will therefore be less attractive than an intervention with a low ICER.

ICERs can be used to set spending priorities. Comparison of incremental ratios gives an indication of the economic consequences of investing in different interventions or programmes. Such comparisons can extend to creating 'league tables' which rank interventions in terms of their ICER.

QALY league tables and the planning process

The QALY has been used, and misused, for planning purposes. QALY league tables are controversial and their use for planning and allocation of resources raises many questions. In addition to problems with the quality of life measurement within the QALY, such league tables raise issues with regard to the costing information on which they are based and the epidemiological data. Table 19.4 has been extracted from a QALY league table which was published in 1991. The table ranks interventions by their incremental cost per QALY gained.

Table 19.4 Extract from a QALY league table

Intervention	Cost/QALY (1990 £)
Cholesterol testing and diet therapy	220
Neurological intervention for head injury	240
GP advice to stop smoking	270
Hip replacement	1 180
CABG (coronary artery bypass graft), left main vessel disease, severe angina	2 090
Kidney transplant	4 710
Breast cancer screening	5 780
Heart transplantation	7 840
Home haemodialysis	17 260
Hospital haemodialysis	21 790
Neurosurgical intervention for malignant intracranial tumours	107 780

Source: Maynard (1991) cited in Drummond et al. (1997)

Such league tables raise many issues. These figures are the result of many different studies, but how comparable are they? They use different discount rates, different methods for estimating health state preferences (such as the EQ-5D above), and consider different ranges of costs and consequences.

A DALY league table

Table 19.5 is adapted from a longer table of cost-effectiveness of health interventions included in 'the minimum package of health services' for low income countries, proposed in the 1993 *World Development Report* (World Bank 1993).

This table provides a brief description of what is proposed for inclusion in a 'minimum package' of health services for low income countries, estimated to cost about $12 per person – of which one third would be for public health and preventive services, and two thirds for essential clinical services. It represents the cost of treating all those in a given country with the condition – not just those who are currently under treatment. These services would be provided at district level assuming one hospital bed per 1000 population, one doctor and two to four nurses per 10,000.

Table 19.5 Cost-effectiveness of health interventions

	Cost per beneficiary	Cost per capita	DALYs potentially gained per 1000 population	Effectiveness (a)	Cost per DALY ($)
1 Public health					
AIDS prevention programme	112.2	1.7	35	0.58	3–5
EPI plus (b)	14.6	0.5	45	0.77	12–17
School health programme	3.6	0.3	4	0.58	20–25
Tobacco and alcohol control programme	0.3	0.3	12	0.14	35–55
Other public health interventions	2.4	1.4	–	–	–
2 Clinical services					
STD treatment	11	0.2	26	0.42	1–3
TB treatment	500	0.6	34	0.51	3–5
Family planning	12	0.9	7	0.70	20–30
Integrated management of the sick child	9	1.6	184	0.25	30–50
Prenatal and delivery care	90	3.8	57	0.42	30–50
Limited care (c)	6	0.7	–	0.03	200–300
Subtotal, clinical services	–	7.8	–	–	–
Total	–	12	–	–	–

(a) Calculated by multiplying efficacy, diagnostic accuracy (when applicable) and compliance
(b) EPI plus hepatitis B vaccination and vitamin A supplementation
(c) Includes treatment of infection and minor trauma; for more complicated conditions, includes diagnosis, advice and pain relief, and treatment as resources permit.

Source: adapted from Bobadilla *et al.* (1994)

A similar package for middle income countries includes the same interventions but at different costs per DALY – due to the different costs of labour, the different epidemiological profile and magnitude of the burden of disease and, therefore, the different effectiveness of interventions.

 Activity 19.4

Suppose you were given information about a variety of interventions, as shown in Table 19.6, and asked to construct a programme to maximize the health gain from a fixed budget of $10 million. Suppose the health interventions are independent of one another, meaning that the costs and outcomes of one programme do not depend on whether another programme is implemented or not. For instance, A might be a cardiovascular programme, B a genitourinary programme, C an orthopaedic programme, D a labour and delivery programme, and so on. Which programmes should be funded?

Table 19.6 Cost-effectiveness data for possible interventions

Programme	Years of life saved	Cost ($)	C/E ratio
A	500	1 000 000	2 000
B	500	2 000 000	4 000
C	200	1 200 000	6 000
D	250	2 000 000	8 000
E	100	1 200 000	12 000
F	50	800 000	16 000
G	100	1 800 000	18 000
H	100	2 200 000	22 000
I	150	4 500 000	30 000
J	100	5 000 000	50 000

Feedback

Choice based on ranking according to the number of lives saved would include A, B, D, C, I and would cost about $10,700,000 and save 1600 years of life.

However, choice based on ranking the cost-effectiveness of interventions would include A, B, C, D, E, F, G and would cost $10,000,000 and save 1700 years of life. Programmes H, I, and J are not implemented. This option would be within budget and save more years of life than would be the case without the cost-effectiveness information.

Incremental CEA

Most of the examples of cost-effectiveness ratios in this chapter have in fact been ICERs: the ratio of the difference in costs between two alternatives to the difference in effectiveness between the same two alternatives.

The rules for allocating a fixed budget between health interventions are fairly simple:

1 Rank programmes by ICER from lowest (the most efficient) to highest.
2 Allocate the budget by the ranking until the budget is exhausted.

In order to compare ICERs, you first arrange the interventions in order of increasing effectiveness. The ICER is the additional costs of any option over another, divided by the differences in the health outcome produced by the options. An example will help to illustrate this.

Remember (from Chapter 17) the STD clinic which was considering different opening hours? Assume that the health consequence of interest is the number of STD cases treated (a process measure). The costs and number of patients visiting are set out in Table 19.7. The table shows that the evening hours are cost-effective but that Saturday hours are much less cost-effective. Because resources are scarce, the

Table 19.7 STD clinic – costs and patients visiting

	Base case (A)	Total with evening hours (B)	Increment of evening hours (B – A)	Total with evening and Saturday hours (C)	Increment of Saturday hours (C)
Total costs ($)	2 385	2 735	350	3 132	397
Cases treated	100	127	27	132	5
Average cost per STD treated ($)	23.85	21.55		23.72	
Incremental CE ratio	23.85		12.96		79.40

money might be better spent on other interventions that give a greater health gain per dollar spent.

Another example of the use of ICERs was shown by the work of Ettling *et al.* (1991), who were comparing different combinations of three types of malaria clinic in terms of cases treated in Thailand. The three types of clinic included a central clinic in a large town, a peripheral clinic in a small market centre staffed by a single microscopist and a periodic mobile clinic which is staffed by a microscopist and an assistant who travel by motorcycle to five villages in the area on a weekly schedule.

Their results indicated that compared with the 'no clinic' option, the central clinic treated 4926 cases at a cost of 20 *baht* per case. With the addition of the peripheral clinic, an additional 547 cases were treated at a cost of 49.81 *baht* per case. The third option considered, that of the addition of mobile periodic clinics, managed to treat an additional 531 cases for 104 *baht* per case. One of the conclusions they came to was that increasing access to malaria clinics in highly malarious areas like the one under study was much more cost-effective than providing services in low-prevalence areas.

A final word of caution: sensitivity analysis

By now you will have noticed that every economic analysis includes many assumptions, some of which are based on relatively good data while others are mainly the judgement of the economist. Others depend on external factors such as the price of a drug or the prevalence of a disease. Some will change in different population settings and it is useful for the reader to be able to see how the results might change if the situation was closer to his or her own.

The way this possible variability in key values is handled is through *sensitivity analysis*. This involves systematically varying the value of a probability or a cost to identify which variable or cost has the greatest impact on the overall results of the analysis. This helps to identify where additional effort should be placed in getting more precise results. It is important for each analysis to identify which variables are most important to the overall result, and to perform sensitivity analysis on different values of that variable. All good studies will include a comprehensive sensitivity analysis.

Summary

So far you have learned quite a lot about ways to decide about the allocation and use of scarce resources. You should now have a good idea about the costs of interventions, the costs of illness and the main methods of economic evaluation – cost-effectiveness and cost–benefit analysis. In the following chapter you will be able to review and consolidate some of the key concepts that have been covered.

References

Anand S and Hanson K (1998) DALYs: efficiency versus equity. *World Development Journal* 26:307–10.

Bobadilla J-L, Cowley P, Musgrave P and Saxenian H (1994) Design, content and financing of an essential national package of health services. *Bulletin of WHO* 72:653–62.

Drummond MF, O'Brien B, Stoddart GL and Torrance GW (1997) *Methods for the economic evaluation of health care programmes* (2nd edn). Oxford: Oxford University Press.

Ettling MB, Thimasarn K, Shepard DS and Krachaiklin S (1991) Economic analysis of several types of malaria clinics in Thailand. *Bulletin of WHO* 69:467–76.

Foster S and Buvé A (1995) Benefits of HIV screening of blood transfusions in Zambia. *Lancet* 346:225–7.

Gilson L, Mkanje R, Grosskurth H, Mosha F, Picard J *et al.* (1997) Cost-effectiveness of improved treatment services for sexually transmitted diseases in preventing HIV-1 infection in Mwanza Region, Tanzania. *Lancet* 350:1805–9.

Murray CJL and Lopez AD (eds) (1996) *The global burden of disease: summary*. Geneva: World Health Organization.

World Bank (1993) *World Development Report*. Washington DC: World Bank.

20 Evaluation in perspective

Overview

You have learned how to calculate the costs and benefits of interventions and you have been given frameworks to use when comparing these costs and benefits. This final chapter will allow you to stand back and look at the limitations and advantages of economic evaluations and to analyse examples of evaluation in practice. It will help you to revise and expand on what you have learned so far about the basic types of economic evaluation.

Learning objectives

After studying this chapter, you should be able to:

- **display an awareness of the critical assumptions made in an economic evaluation**
- **discuss the limitations of an economic evaluation**
- **discuss areas of application of economic evaluations**

The critical issues in economic evaluations

Economic evaluation is being applied to an increasing range of health problems. The technique is important as it helps clinicians and managers in making choices about interventions. However, as you have seen, the results of economic evaluation are highly sensitive to a number of critical issues.

 Activity 20.1

Explain how the decisions taken at each step can critically affect the results of an analysis.

 Feedback

1 *The perspective or viewpoint assumed for evaluation.* For example, an intervention that seems to offer no advantage from the health services perspective may look significantly different from the societal viewpoint.

2 *The way costs are assessed.* For example, real cost may be higher than the budget

figures would suggest, if opportunity costs are considered. Sometimes accurate cost figures of a programme are difficult to obtain so that expenditure data or the fees charged to purchasers have to be used as a proxy measure of cost.

3 *Methods of measurement of consequences.* Outcome measures need to be valid and reliable. The outcomes observed need to be caused by the intervention and not by other concurrent interventions or a Hawthorne effect (i.e. that the awareness of participating in an experiment influences individual behaviour and thus results).

Economists are aware of these problems and over the last few years the scientific rigour of economic evaluation has improved. A number of scientific bodies have released guidelines to improve the state of the art of economic evaluation. You can keep yourself informed of recent trends by looking at the websites of institutions engaged in the dissemination of results of economic evaluation and health technology assessment.

In recent years, new types of analysis, based on prospective data collection, have been developed. Increasingly, economic evaluations are being designed alongside clinical trials. Where an economic evaluation is appropriate, a randomized controlled trial can be used as a vehicle to collect individualized data on cost and resource use in both the intervention and control group and to integrate these data with the outcome of interest. Where a trial is not appropriate, a non-randomized study design may be used, for example by assessing cost changes before and after the intervention. Any interpretation of results needs to be based on a careful evaluation of the roles of chance, bias and confounders.

Ten questions to ask of any study

As a decision maker in the health sector, you may find yourself in the position of receiving an economic evaluation on the basis of which you may be expected to take some action. The following questions were drawn up by Drummond and Stoddart in a 1985 article, and they have stood the test of time. These questions provide a framework for assessing the results of any evaluation study.

1 Was a well-defined question posed in answerable form?

   a) Did the study examine both costs and effects of the service(s) or programme(s)?
   b) Did the study involve a comparison of alternatives?
   c) Was a viewpoint for the analysis stated or was the study placed in a particular decision making context?

2 Was a comprehensive description of the competing alternatives given?

   a) Were any important alternatives omitted?
   b) Was (should) a 'do-nothing' alternative (have been) considered?

3 Was there evidence that the programmes' effectiveness had been established? Was this done through a randomized, controlled clinical trial? If not, how strong was the evidence of effectiveness?

4 Were all important and relevant costs and consequences for each alternative identified?

a) Was the range wide enough for the research question at hand?
b) Did it cover all relevant viewpoints (e.g. those of the community or society, patients and third-party payers)?
c) Were capital costs as well as operating costs included?

5 Were costs and consequences measured accurately in appropriate physical units (e.g. hours of nursing time, number of physician visits, days lost from work or years of life gained) prior to valuation?

a) Were any identified items omitted from measurement? If so, does this mean that they carried no weight in the subsequent analysis?
b) Were there any special circumstances (e.g. joint use of resources) that made measurement difficult? Were these circumstances handled appropriately?

6 Were costs and consequences valued credibly?

a) Were the sources of all values (e.g. market values, patient or client preferences and views, policy makers' views and health care professionals' judgements) clearly identified?
b) Were market values used for changes involving resources gained or used?
c) When market values were absent (e.g. when volunteers were used) or did not reflect actual values (c.g. clinic space was donated at a reduced rate) were adjustments made to approximate market values?
d) Was the valuation of consequences appropriate for the question posed (i.e. was the appropriate type, or types, of analysis – cost-effectiveness, cost–benefit or cost–utility – selected)?

7 Were costs and consequences adjusted for differential timing?

a) Were costs and consequences that occurred in the future 'discounted' to their present values?
b) Was any justification given for the discount rate used?

8 Was an incremental analysis of costs and consequences of alternatives per-formed? Were the additional (incremental) costs generated by the use of one alternative over another compared with the additional effects, benefits or util-ities generated?

9 Was a sensitivity analysis performed?

a) Was justification provided for the ranges of values (for key parameters) used in the sensitivity analysis?
b) Were the study results sensitive to changes in the values (within the assumed range)?

10 Did the presentation and discussion of the results of the study include all issues of concern to users?

a) Were the conclusions of the analysis based on some overall index or ratio of costs to consequences (e.g. cost-effectiveness ratio)? If so, was the index interpreted intelligently or in a mechanistic fashion?
b) Were the results compared with those of other studies that had investigated the same questions?
c) Did the study discuss the generalizability of the results to other settings and patient/clinic groups?

d) Did the study allude to, or take account of, other important factors in the choice or decision under consideration (e.g. distribution of costs and consequences or relevant ethical issues)?
e) Did the study discuss issues of implementation, such as the feasibility of adopting the 'preferred' programme, given existing financial or other constraints, and whether any freed resources could be used for other worthwhile programmes?

Limitations of economic evaluation

Though sensitivity analysis tries to deal with the uncertainty around the measurement of cost and consequences, economic evaluation has a number of limitations and constraints and it is important to be aware of these.

Activity 20.2

From what you have learned in this book, what limitations do you think there are in interpreting and using the results of economic evaluations?

Feedback

1 Economic evaluations are like a snapshot providing an analysis for a certain point in time. However, conditions in health services may change rapidly. The cost of inputs change and new technologies may become available.

2 Observation or follow-up time can be crucial because important effects may become visible only after some time.

3 You need to assess how generalizable a study's findings are. The context and the setting of the study play an important role and it may be difficult to apply results to a different country or region or to extend results to different institutions, as these have a different case mix and cost structure.

Areas of application of economic evaluation

Throughout this book you have read of individual economic evaluations, their methods and their findings. Here you will review briefly a major area of application of economic evaluation, that of pharmacoeconomics, and a notable use of economic evaluation, that of priority setting of health services.

Pharmacoeconomics

In industrialized countries pharmacoeconomics has developed as a field of application and the number of published studies has grown rapidly. Drug firms have a vested interest in demonstrating the economic and social benefits of their products, as it improves their market position. Increasingly, governments and purchasers are demanding proof of cost-effectiveness of a new drug over existing drugs before a new treatment is made available. Although there have been substantial methodological advances, there remain serious problems with the aspects of use (and abuse) and the quality of studies sponsored by the pharmaceutical industry (De Graeve and Nonneman 1996).

Health services need to examine carefully their clinical practices so that excessive costs and waste can be reduced without compromising patient care. Cost-effectiveness data can be used to assemble drug formularies or limited lists which recommend drugs with approved cost-effectiveness. Take for example anaesthesia: Watcha and White (1997) analysed drug costs for anaesthesia and found that though cost savings in an individual case may be small, the total savings may be impressive because of the large numbers of anaesthetics performed. Drug costs are highly visible costs which are easy for managers to scrutinize, if appropriate information on cost-effectiveness is made available.

The Oregon experience

Economic evaluation has been used to ration health services by influencing the design of an essential package of care in low and middle income countries. From high income countries there are only a few such examples. A scheme that attracted considerable interest and debate was the Oregon plan.

In 1989 the US state of Oregon launched an initiative to ration treatment under the Medicaid scheme, which mainly provides publicly-funded health services for the poor. The aim was, under a fixed budget, to provide the most efficient services to the largest number of people, rather than providing less efficient services to all. The approach developed a league table which ranks health care interventions in terms of their gains in health-related quality of life. The principles of this approach were discussed in Chapter 19. Since 1989 several lists have been developed allowing some flexibility for change and improvement of methodology. For example, in the version that was implemented in 1994, 565 treatments were listed and only these treatments were reimbursed by Medicaid. Notably, the public has been involved in this process and preferences and values of community committees were incorporated into the complex process of ranking of treatment outcomes (Ganiats and Kaplan 1996).

During public discussions the approach was criticized for a variety of methodological, ethical and political reasons:

1 Is it justified to use preferences of non-Medicaid recipients to prioritize services for the poor?
2 Are the methods used to attach utility weights reliable? Different methods yielded different weights.
3 As recipients of Medicaid are mainly the poor and among them women and children, does the rationing discriminate against those who are most vulnerable and need care most?
4 Do politicians have a mandate to ration health services, before other sectors of expenditure such as defence or space exploration come under similar close scrutiny?

Proponents of the scheme have argued that rationing occurs in all health care systems, though mostly invisible and implicit, whereas attempts such as the Oregon plan make rationing explicit and visible. They also emphasized that the plan had increased access to care for many recipients. As the debate demonstrated, economic evaluation for priority setting involves complex political and ethical issues and is not merely a technical exercise.

Reviewing economic evaluations

As you have seen, economic evaluation can be applied to a variety of different areas. Not all relate to health care interventions. Some evaluate the economic consequences of management activities in the health sector. The following extracts illustrate the broad range of economic evaluations that are carried out. They will give you practice in identifying the salient points when reading reports of economic evaluations.

 Activity 20.3

The following abstracts have been slightly modified for the purpose of this activity. While reading them, focus on the basic types of evaluation performed. Don't worry about the technical details of measurements or statistics. For each of the studies make brief notes in answer to the following questions:

1 What type of economic evaluation was conducted?
2 What was the intervention under investigation compared to and what is the unit of assessment of the economic evaluation?
3 What do the results of the evaluation suggest?

 A needle exchange programme: an economic evaluation of a local experience (Gold *et al.* 1997)

Objective

To determine whether providing a needle exchange programme to prevent HIV transmission among injection drug users would cost less than the health care consequences of not having such a programme.

Design

The study used an incidence–outcome model to estimate the number of cases of HIV infection that this programme would prevent over five years. The researchers assumed that the HIV incidence rate would be 2% with the programme and 4% without it, and that an estimated 275 injection drug users would use the service over this time.

Outcome measures

Estimated number of cases of HIV infection expected to be prevented with and without the programme over five years; estimated lifetime health care costs of treating an AIDS patient. The indirect costs of AIDS to society (e.g. lost productivity and informal care giving) were not included. Projected costs were adjusted (discounted) to reflect their present value. In a sensitivity analysis, three parameters were varied: the estimate of the HIV transmission rate if no needle exchange programme were provided, the number of injection drug users participating in the programme, and the discount rate.

Results

With very conservative estimates, it was predicted that the needle exchange programme will prevent 24 cases of HIV infection over five years, thereby providing cost savings of $1.3 million after the programme costs are taken into account. This translates into a ratio of cost savings to costs of 4:1. The sensitivity analysis confirmed that these findings are robust.

 ## Economic evaluation of chemotherapy for prostate cancer (Bloomfield *et al.* 1998)

Purpose

To evaluate the economic consequences of the use of chemotherapy in patients with symptomatic hormone-resistant prostate cancer (HRPC) in the context of a previously randomized trial.

Patients and methods

The trial randomized 161 patients to initial treatment with mitoxantrone and prednisone (M + P) or to prednisone alone (P) and showed better clinical outcomes in terms of palliation with M + P. There was no significant difference in survival. A detailed retrospective review was performed of resources used from randomization until death of 114 of 161 patients enrolled at the three largest centres: these included hospital admissions, outpatient visits, investigations, therapies (which included all chemotherapy and radiation), and palliative care. Cancer centre and community hospital costs were calculated. QOL was measured every three weeks on trial using the European Organization for Research and Treatment of Cancer (EORTC) QLQ-C30 questionnaire and the last known value was extended through to death or last follow-up.

Results

(Note that the cost findings are given in Canadian Dollars.) The mean total cost until death or last follow-up by intention-to-treat was M + P = CDN$27 300; P = CDN$29 000. The 95% confidence intervals on the observed cost difference ranged from a saving of $9200 for M + P (with palliative benefit) to an increased cost of $5800 for M + P. The major proportion of cost (M + P 53% v P 66%; $14 500 v $19 100) was for inpatient care. Initial M + P was consistently less expensive in whichever time period was used to compare costs. M + P was shown to be the preferred strategy with an upper 95% confidence interval for the incremental cost / QALY of $19 700.

 ## Intensive patient education and supervision for asthmatic patients (Kauppinen *et al.* 1998)

Purpose

Economic evaluation of intensive versus conventional education and supervision for the selfmanagement of mild asthmatic patients.

Patients and methods

Consecutive newly diagnosed asthmatic patients (n = 162) were randomized into an inter-vention group (IG) and a control group (CG) with 1 year of treatment and follow-up. Intensive education was given to 77 patients at visits every third month in the outpatient clinic. Eighty CG patients received conventional education and advice at the baseline visit only. All patients received similar inhaled anti-inflammatory treatment. At baseline and at 12 months standard clinical lung functions and health-related quality of life (HRQOL) were measured, the latter by the disease-specific St George's Respiratory Questionnaire and the generic 15D. Furthermore, the use of extra health care services, medication and sickness days was recorded.

Results

The IG experienced a significant improvement in all clinical and HRQOL outcome variables. The same applied to the CG except lung function which showed a significant difference only in terms of the measure of forced expiratory volume in one second (FEV1) (P < 0.05) in favour of the IG. There was a significant difference between the groups in extra costs. The mean cost (in Finmarks with UK sterling equivalents) was FIM2351 per patient (£294) in the CG and FIM2757 per patient (£345) in the IG, of which the interven-tion cost was FIM1978 per patient (£247). Also, a valuation of outcomes in monetary terms resulted in a negative net benefit (loss) of FIM406 per patient (£51).

 Evaluation of a hospital picture archiving and communication system (Bryan et al. 1999)

Objectives

To establish the net costs to the hospital and the broad range of benefits associated with a hospital-wide picture archiving and communication system (PACS) that comprised digital acquisition, storage and transmission of radiological images via a hospital-wide network to 150 workstations.

Methods

'Before and after' comparisons and time series analyses at Hammersmith Hospital (London, UK), and comparison with five other British hospitals where PACS was not being installed. The cost analysis considered implementation costs and changes in key elements of hospital running costs, including the impact of changes in the length of inpatient stays. A range of benefit measures were investigated, including image availability, avoidance of repeat imaging, avoidance of exposure to radiation, patient turn-round speed, time from examination to image availability in intensive care, avoidance of diagnostic 'errors' by casualty doctors, the additional diagnostic value of PACS-based images and clinician satisfaction.

Results

The annual equivalent capital cost of the PACS was £1.7 million (annual equivalent replacement cost: £0.8 million). Overall, the PACS substantially increased running costs. No convincing evidence of a PACS-induced change in length of inpatient stay was found. PACS was associated with some improvements in the performance of the radiology department: improved image availability (97.7% versus 86.9%), lower repeat imaging rate (7.3% versus 9.9%) and 20% lower total radiation doses for examinations of the lateral lumbar spine. No improvements were identified in the quality of the radiology reporting service. Benefits outside radiology included shorter time from examination to image availability for routine uses in intensive care (19 versus 37 minutes), and a lower rate of diagnostic 'errors' in casualty (0.65% versus 1.51%). High levels of satisfaction with PACS were found amongst both providers and clinical users.

Conclusions

PACS was almost universally preferred by users and brought many operational and clinical benefits. However, these advantages came at a significant capital and net running cost.

An economic evaluation comparing two schedules of antenatal visits (Henderson *et al.* 2000)

Objectives

To conduct an economic evaluation comparing a traditional antenatal visiting schedule (traditional care) with a reduced schedule of visits (new style care) for women at low risk of complications.

Method

Economic evaluation using the results of a randomised controlled trial, the Antenatal Care Project. This took place between 1993 and 1994 in antenatal clinics in South East London and involved 2794 women at low risk of complications.

Result

The estimated baseline costs to the UK National Health Service (NHS) for the traditional schedule were £544 per woman, of which £251 occurred antenatally, with a range of £327–1203 per woman. The estimated baseline costs to the NHS for the reduced visit schedule was £563 per woman, of which £225 occurred antenatally, with a range of £274–1741 per woman. Savings from new style care that arose antenatally were offset by the greater numbers of babies in this group who required special or intensive care. Sensitivity analyses based on possible variations in unit costs and resource use and modelled postnatal stay showed considerable variation and substantial overlap in costs.

Conclusions

Patterns of antenatal care involving fewer routine visits for women at low risk of complications are unlikely to result in savings to the Health Service. In addition, women who had the reduced schedule of care reported greater dissatisfaction with their care and poorer psychosocial outcomes which argues against reducing numbers of antenatal visits.

 Feedback

Check your notes against the feedback below to see how well you understood these abstracts.

Needle exchange programme

1 Epidemiological model to assess programme cost-effectiveness, cost savings/cost ratio.

2 The alternative is not implementing an exchange programme.

3 The authors conclude that needle exchange programmes are an efficient use of financial resources.

Note that this is an incidence–outcome model, which is not based on real observations of HIV incidence among programme participants. Rather it is based on assumptions of HIV incidence and cost estimates for both groups. As a model it is a simplified representation of reality and cannot take account of all factors affecting outcomes and cost, but sensitivity analysis allows testing a wide range of reasonable assumptions.

Chemotherapy for prostate cancer

1 A cost–utility analysis as part of a randomized clinical trial.

2 Prednisone (P) alone or a combination of prednisone and mitoxantrone (P + M) incremental cost–utility ratio expressed in CDN$ per QALY gained.

3 The intervention improves outcomes in terms of quality of life and has the potential to reduce costs in other areas.

Intensive health education for asthmatic patients

1 A cost–utility and cost–benefit study as part of a randomized controlled trial.

2 Intensive vs. conventional education and supervision for the self-management of mild asthmatic patients. Net benefit.

3 Despite a small difference in medical outcomes there was no difference in quality of life but a large difference in costs. In the first year follow-up the intensive education programme did not prove to be cost-effective regardless of what effectiveness measure was used (cost–utility or cost–benefit ratio).

The authors argued that a longer follow-up may be needed before definitive conclusions can be drawn. Note that a cost–benefit analysis is rarely performed in health care evaluation, due to the problems arising from the conversion of consequences into monetary values.

Hospital picture archiving and communication system

1 A cost-effectiveness analysis comparing before and after in one hospital and also comparison with control hospitals.

2 A hospital-wide picture archiving and communication system. Change in patients' length of stay and several other process measures such as image availability.

3 The new system cost more than the existing systems but it resulted in some benefits.

Two schedules of antenatal visits

1 A cost-effectiveness study as part of a randomized trial.

2 A reduced schedule of antenatal clinic visits.

3 The reduced schedule led to lower antenatal costs but women were less satisfied and there were poorer psychosocial outcomes (intangible cost). Overall costs were higher with the reduced schedule as a result of greater use of special and intensive care for the babies of women who had fewer antenatal visits.

Summary

In this chapter you have stepped back from the tools and techniques of economic evaluations and looked at their uses and limitations. The results of economic evaluations are particularly sensitive to the perspective of the evaluators and the ways in which costs and outcomes are measured. Increasingly evaluations are performed alongside randomized trials. A growing area of application is pharmaco-economics and some countries have introduced mandatory economic evaluation of new drugs prescribed on the health services. In this chapter you have also read about the issues arising from the use of economic evaluation in priority setting of health services, taking the Oregon plan as an example.

References

Bloomfield DJ, Krahn MD, Neogi T *et al.* (1998) Economic evaluation of chemotherapy with mitoxantrone plus prednisone for symptomatic hormone-resistant prostate cancer: based on a Canadian randomized trial with palliative end points. *Clinical Oncology* 16:2272–9.

Bryan S, Weatherburn G, Buxton M, Watkins J, Keen J and Muris N (1999) Evaluation of a hospital picture archiving and communication system. *Journal of Health Services Research & Policy* 4:204–9.

De Graeve D and Nonneman W (1996). Pharmacoeconomic studies: pitfalls and problems. *International Journal of Technology Assessment In Health Care* 12:22–30.

Drummond M and Stoddart G (1985) Economic analysis and clinical trials. *Controlled Clinical Trials* 5:115–28.

Ganiats TG and Kaplan RM (1996) Priority setting: the Oregan example, in Schwartz FW, Glennerster H and Saltman RB (eds) *Fixing health budgets: experience from Europe and North America*. New York: Wiley & Sons.

Gold M, Gafni A, Nelligan P and Millson P (1997) Needle exchange programs: an economic evaluation of a local experience. *Canadian Medical Association Journal* 157:275–7.

Henderson J, Roberts T, Sikorski J, Wilson J and Clement S (2000) An economic evaluation comparing two schedules of antenatal visits. *Journal of Health Services Research & Policy* 5:69–75.

Kauppinen R, Sintonen H and Tukiainen H (1998) One-year economic evaluation of intensive vs conventional patient education and supervision for self-management of new asthmatic patients. *Respiratory Medicine* 92:300–7.

Watcha MF and White PF (1997) Economics of anaesthetic practice. *Anesthesiology* 86:1170–96.

Glossary

Actuarial (experience) rating Premium based on an individual's risk of illness.

Adverse selection When a party enters into an agreement in which they can use their own private information to the disadvantage of another party.

Agent A person who acts on behalf of another (the principal).

Allocative (Pareto, social) efficiency A situation in which it is not possible to improve the welfare of one person in an economy without making someone else worse off.

Annual cost The cost of an intervention, calculated on a yearly basis, including all the annually payable capital costs as well as the yearly recurrent costs.

Annualized costs The annual share of the initial cost of capital equipment or investments, spread over the life of the project – usually modified to take account of depreciation.

Asymmetry of information A market situation where all participants do not have access to the same level of information.

Average cost Total cost divided by quantity.

Barriers to entry Factors which prevent a firm from entering a market.

Benefit–cost ratio (BCR) A way of presenting the results of a cost–benefit analysis, this is simply the benefits divided by the costs.

Burden of disease A measure of the physical, emotional, social and financial impact that a particular disease has on the health and functioning of the population.

Capital cost The value of capital resources which have useful lives greater than one year.

Capitation payments A prospective means of paying health care staff based on the number of people they provide care for.

Ceteris paribus The assumption that all other variables remain unchanged.

Commodities (or production outputs) are the results of combining resources in the production process. They are either goods or services.

Community financing Collective action of local communities to finance health services through pooling out-of-pocket payments and ensuring services are accountable to the community.

Community rating Insurance premium based on pooled risk of a defined group of people.

Complements Goods used along with an identified good.

Consumer efficiency A situation where consumers cannot increase their satisfaction by reallocating their budget.

Consumer surplus The difference between what a consumer pays for a good and the maximum they would be willing to pay for it.

Co-payments (user fees) Direct payments made by users of health services as a contribution to their cost (e.g. prescription charges).

Cost The value of resources usually expressed in monetary terms.

Cost–benefit analysis An economic evaluation technique in which outcomes are expressed in monetary terms.

Cost-effectiveness analysis Economic evaluations with outcomes measured in health units.

Cost-effectiveness league tables A ranking of interventions according to cost per unit of health outcomes.

Cost–utility analysis Economic evaluations where the outcomes are measured in health units which capture not just the quantitative but also the qualitative aspects of the outcome, such as quality of life.

Cross-elasticity of demand The percentage change in quantity demanded of a commodity divided by the percentage change in the price of another related commodity.

Deadweight loss The loss in allocative efficiency resulting from the loss of consumer surplus is greater than the gain in producer surplus.

Demand The relationship between the price of a good and the quantity demanded.

Demand curve A graph showing the relationship between the quantity demanded of a good and its price when all other variables are unchanged.

Diagnosis related group (DRG) Classification system that assigns patients to categories on the basis of the likely cost of their episode of hospital care. Used as basis for determining level of prospective payment by purchaser.

Diminishing returns to scale As the quantity of one factor (input) increases, *ceteris paribus* output increases but by ever-diminishing quantities.

Direct cost Resources used in the design, implementation, receipt and continuation of a health care intervention.

Disability Adjusted Life Years (DALYs) A measure of health based not only on the length of a person's life but also their level of ability (or disability).

Discount rate The rate at which future costs and outcomes are discounted to account for time preference.

Discounting A method for adjusting the value of costs and outcomes which occur in different time periods into a common time period, usually the present.

Diseconomies of scale Technological conditions under which long-run average cost increases as output increases.

Economic evaluation The systematic assessment and interpretation of the value of a health care intervention. It is done by systematically examining the relationship between their costs and outcomes.

Economic model Representation of the real world, which omits all variables that are not relevant to the specific issue the model was designed to address.

Economies of scale Technological conditions under which long-run average cost decreases as output increases.

End-state equity A situation where there is an equal distribution of income (or utility, or health etc.).

Exchange efficiency Is achieved when the price at which a good or service is exchanged is equal to both the marginal social cost and the marginal social benefit of that good or service.

Expected utility The benefit or satisfaction that an individual anticipates getting from consuming a particular good or service.

Externality Cost or benefit arising from an individual's production or consumption decision which indirectly affects the well-being of others.

Fee-for-service (FFS) A payment system where a provider receives a payment for each service provided.

Financial (budgetary) cost The accounting cost of a good or service usually representing the original (historical) amount paid – distinct from the opportunity cost.

Financial intermediary An agency collecting money to pay providers on behalf of patients.

Fixed cost A cost of production that does not vary with the level of output.

Formal labour Employment with taxable income.

Health care intervention A programme, activity or technology designed to reduce a health problem. Interventions include prevention, control, screening, diagnostic tests and treatment.

Health maintenance organization (HMO) Organization that provides comprehensive health care for a fixed, periodic per capita payment.

Health production function The relationship between consumption of health inputs and subsequent health status.

Horizontal equity The equal treatment of individual's or groups in the same circumstances.

Human capital approach An approach that uses wages to measure the value of productivity lost through illness.

Income elasticity of demand The percentage change in quantity demanded of a commodity divided by the percentage change in population income.

Incremental cost-effectiveness ratio (ICER) The ratio of the difference in costs between two alternatives to the difference in effectiveness between the same two alternatives.

Indirect cost The value of resources expended by patients and their carers to enable individuals to receive an intervention.

Inferior goods Goods for which demand decreases as income increases.

Intangible cost The cost of pain and suffering.

Intermediate health outcome A short-term measure of outcome known to be associated with a long-term outcome.

Law of diminishing marginal utility A hypothesis that states that as consumption of a good increases so the marginal utility decreases.

Marginal analysis The study of the consequences of small changes in a variable.

Marginal cost The change in the total cost if one additional unit of output is produced.

Marginal utility The change in total utility derived from a one unit increase in consumption.

Market Any situation where people who demand a good or service can come into contact with the suppliers of that good.

Market equilibrium A situation where the price in a given market is such that the quantity demanded is equal to the quantity supplied.

Market failure The failure of an unregulated market to achieve an efficient allocation of resources.

Monopoly power Ability of a monopoly to raise price by restricting output.

Moral hazard A situation in which one of the parties to an agreement has an incentive, after the agreement is made, to act in a manner that brings additional benefits to themselves at the expense of the other party.

Natural monopoly A situation where one firm can meet market demand at a lower average cost than two or more firms could meet that demand.

Net benefit The benefits of an intervention minus its costs.

Normal goods Goods for which demand increases as income increases.

Normative economics Economic statements that prescribe how things should be.

Operational (technical, productive) efficiency Using only the minimum necessary resources to finance, purchase and deliver a particular activity or set of activities (i.e. avoiding waste).

Opportunity (economic) cost The value of the next best alternative forgone as a result of the decision made.

Outcomes Change in the result of the system processes (in the health services context, the change in health status as a result of care).

Out-of-pocket (direct) payment Payment made by a patient directly to a provider.

Overhead cost Costs that are not incurred directly from providing patient care but are necessary to support the organization overall (e.g. personnel funtions).

Over the counter (OTC) drugs Non-prescription drugs purchased from pharmacists and retailers.

Payroll deduction Contribution raised as part of people's wages.

Perfect competition A market in which there are many suppliers each selling an identical product and many buyers who are completely informed about the price of each supplier's product, and there are no restrictions on entry into the market.

Positive economics Economic statements that describe how things are.

Preferred provider organization (PPO) Private insurance that restricts choice to approved providers.

Price discrimination Offering the same product at different prices to different people.

Price elastic When the quantity demanded is relatively responsive to price changes; when price elasticity of demand is greater than 1.

Price elasticity of demand The relative responsiveness of the quantity demanded of a good to a change in its price. It is the percentage change in quantity demanded divided by the associated percentage change in price.

Price elasticity of supply The percentage change in quantity supplied of a commodity divided by the percentage change in the commodity's price.

Price inelastic When quantity demanded is relatively unresponsive to price changes; when price elasticity of demand is less than 1.

Price taker A supplier that cannot influence the price of the good or service they supply.

Principal A person on whose behalf an agent acts.

Process equity A situation where people have the same opportunities even if the outcomes are unequal.

Process measures Measures of the activities carried out by health care providers such as admission rates and length of hospital stay.

Production function The functional relationship that indicates how inputs are transformed into outputs in the most efficient way.

Production possibilities frontier (PPF) A graph that illustrates the different combinations of outputs that are achievable with a limited set of resources.

Progressive tax A tax that takes an increasing proportion of income as income rises.

Proportional tax A tax that takes a constant proportion of income regardless of income level.

Public good A good or service that can be consumed simultaneously by everyone and from which no one can be excluded.

Quality Adjusted Life Years (QALYs) A year of life adjusted for its quality or its value. A year in perfect health is considered equal to 1.0 QALY.

Quantity supplied The amount of a good that producers plan to supply at a given price during an identified period.

Recurrent cost The value of recurrent resources with useful lives of less than one year that have to be purchased at least once a year.

Redistribution A government intervention to transfer income and wealth between groups of the population.

Regressive tax A tax that takes a decreasing proportion of income as income rises.

Regulation Government intervention enforcing rules and standards.

Resources Every item within the economy that can be used to produce and distribute goods and services; classified as labour, capital and land.

Returns to scale The proportional increase in output that occurs when all inputs are increased by the same percentage.

Risk aversion The unwillingness of an individual to take on an identified risk.

Scale efficiency A situation where the provider is producing at an output level such that average cost is minimized.

Social cost Private cost plus external cost.

Subsidy A payment made by the government to a producer or producers where the level of payment depends on the exact level of output.

Substitutes Goods that can be used in place of other goods.

Supplier-induced demand Increased demand as a result of a provider (e.g. a doctor) exploiting an asymmetry of information.

Supply curve A graph showing the relationship between the quantity supplied of a good and its price when all other variables are unchanged.

Time frame The period of time from the intervention to assessing the outcome.

Time preference People's preference for consumption (or use of resources) now rather than later because they value present consumption more than the same consumption in the future.

Total (economic) cost The sum of all the costs of an intervention or health problem.

Transaction costs The costs of engaging in trade, i.e. the costs arising from finding someone with whom to do business, of reaching an agreement and of ensuring the terms of the agreement are fulfilled.

Universal coverage Extension of health services to the whole population.

Unofficial payments Spending in excess of official fees, also called 'under the table' or 'envelope' payments.

Utility Happiness or satisfaction a person gains from consuming a commodity.

Variable cost A cost of production that varies directly with the level of output.

Vertical equity The principle that individuals who are unequal should be treated differently according to their level of need.

Welfare (or social welfare) Happiness or satisfaction a population gains from consuming a commodity.

Willingness to pay (WTP) A method of measuring the value an individual places on reducing the risk of developing a health problem or gaining an improvement in health.

Index